American Sweethearts

COLUMBIA PICTURES presents

Kiss and Tell

starring

SHIRLEY TEMPLE
(as Corliss Archer)

American Sweethearts

Teenage Girls in Twentieth-Century Popular Culture

Ilana Nash

Indiana University Press • Bloomington and Indianapolis

This book is a publication of

Indiana University Press
601 North Morton Street
Bloomington, IN 47404-3797 USA

http://iupress.indiana.edu

Telephone orders   800-842-6796
Fax orders   812-855-7931
Orders by e-mail   iuporder@indiana.edu

The paper used in this publication meets the minimum
requirements of American National Standard for
Information Sciences—Permanence of Paper for Printed
Library Materials, ANSI Z39.48-1984.

Manufactured in
the United States of America

Library of Congress Cataloging-in-Publication Data

Nash, Ilana.
American sweethearts : teenage girls in twentieth-
century popular culture / Ilana Nash.
    p. cm.
Includes bibliographical references and index.
    ISBN 0–253-34659–2 (alk. paper)—
    ISBN 0–253-21802–0 (pbk. : alk. paper)
    1. American fiction—20th century—History and
criticism. 2. Girls in literature. 3. Young adult fiction,
American—History and criticism. 4. Teenage girls—
Books and reading—United States. 5. Drew,
Nancy (Fictitious character). 6. Teenage girls in
popular culture. 7. Teenage girls in motion pictures.
8. Teenage girls in literature. I. Title.
    PS374.G55N37 2006
    813'.50935252—dc22   2005009297

1 2 3 4 5 11 10 09 08 07 06

Contents

Acknowledgments

Many people and institutions have contributed to the successful completion of this book. While the project was in its initial stages, the American Culture Studies Program at Bowling Green State University provided me with travel funds to facilitate research, a fellowship, and a supportive and encouraging atmosphere in which to work. The final stages of the book's research would not have been possible without a generous Arts & Science Faculty Teaching and Research Award from Western Michigan University. The staffs at the Popular Culture Library at Bowling Green State University, the UCLA Film and Television Archive, the Museum of Television and Radio in New York, and the Manuscripts and Archives Division of the New York Public Library offered valuable and knowledgeable assistance in my research. Special thanks go to Randi Hokett and Haden Guest at the USC Warner Bros. Archive, who spent considerable time helping me locate and reproduce numerous documents and images from the Nancy Drew film series. Carol Lee Bowers, reference manager at the American Heritage Center at the University of Wyoming, went far beyond the call of her duties in facilitating my trip to the archive and in sharing insight, candor, and camaraderie during my brief stay.

Over the last several years I have been lucky to find a community of scholars in the growing fields of youth culture, girls' studies, and popular culture who have assisted this project immeasurably by generously sharing their own work, critiquing mine, and exchanging ideas and support with me. Beginning as colleagues and becoming true friends, these people deserve more gratitude than I can adequately express, as well as the affection that I hope I express to them often enough: Joe Austin, Miriam Forman-Brunell, Kristen Hatch, Timothy Shary, Gwen Tarbox, Steve Waksman, and Marilyn Yaquinto. Joe Austin in particular gave countless hours to the early development of this project, sharing ideas, sources, and laughter over several years. His unswerving support, and his continued efforts to offer advice and help, make him the best mentor I have ever known. Well-earned thanks also go to the many colleagues who have helped me locate facts and sources, and have been willing to think with me about the complex and often hidden history of girls: Mary Celeste Kearney, Kristen Kidder, Leslie Paris, Lynn Sacco, Kelly Schrum, and the members of the Girls Studies Scholars discussion list. Kathleen Chamberlain, Michael Colacurcio, Kris Fresonke, Deidre Johnson, James Keeline, and Jeff Smith have offered a strong network of good will and good advice over the years, as both colleagues and friends.

Here at Western Michigan University I've found the most welcoming group of colleagues one could ask for. Many thanks to my department chair, Arnie Johnston, for his understanding support of my research goals; to Nic Witschi, for reading a long chapter when he had little time; and to Jon Adams, Heather Addison, Beth Amidon, Beth Bradburn, Margaret Dupuis, Steve Feffer, Todd Kuchta, Lisa Minnick, Chris Nagle, Gwen Raaberg, Judi Rypma, Eve Salisbury, Jana Schulman, Grace Tiffany, Allen Webb, and the many others who have supported my work and shared their friendship with me.

Finally, my mother, Nomi Kluger-Nash, and my grandmother, Theodora Jacobs (1913–2001), deserve special mention, for they are indirectly responsible for my undertaking this project. When I was still too young to read, my grandmother often took me to the famed Silent Movie Theater in Los Angeles, just blocks from her house, and whispered the titles to me while I sat mesmerized by the dramatic images. Sometimes we went to the L.A. County Museum of Art when they had a retrospective of classic films. My mother, too, made certain I grew up familiar with the actors, films, and songs of the 1930s and 1940s; throughout my life this is a joy we've always shared. I owe both these women an enormous debt for teaching me to love and understand the popular culture of the early twentieth century. And, more importantly, for helping me to learn what female agency really means.

American Sweethearts

Introduction

"How dare those people keep
treating us like stupid teenage
girls?"
    "We *are* stupid teenage girls."

—dialogue from *Dick* (1999)

 In the middle of *Gidget Goes Hawaiian*,
a popular 1961 teen film, a musical se-
quence encapsulates one fragment of
America's interpretation of female ad-
olescence. A young man performs a dance routine at a nightclub, playing
the role of a popular entertainer. The choreography comments upon the
pitfalls of his fame; after a few minutes alone on stage, the young man
is approached by a female dancer, costumed as a teen schoolgirl, who
brandishes an autograph book. He attempts to elude the importunate fan
but then appears to surrender: he dances with her in his arms, lifts her
up, and puts her . . . in a garbage can. Within moments his peace is shat-
tered again by another girl, identical in costume to the first. Both female
dancers continue to plague him; one erupts out of a different garbage
can, and the exasperated young man shoves the lid down on her. The
girls finally perch on a bench that topples backward, tossing them off the
stage and out of sight, whereupon the young man poses triumphantly
alone in center stage, freed at last from the girls' predations.

Out of context, this scene might suggest that the films' producers had
a low opinion of teenage girls, who are represented here rather like
bugs—interchangeable pests who multiply rapidly, dwell amidst garbage,

and must be exterminated. In context, however, the sequence becomes confusing, for the film's central heroine is a beloved teenage girl named Gidget, the subject of a popular mass-media narrative cycle in the late 1950s and 1960s. Charming, sweetly sexy, gifted, and irresistibly popular with her peers, Gidget enjoys an exalted position that depends on her purity; the film's plot revolves around a false rumor that Gidget has "gone all the way," a gross libel that is finally corrected at film's end, when Gidget emerges victorious and glorious.

How could two such apparently contradictory images of female adolescence, the exalted and the abject, co-exist in one film? More puzzling, how could the many young girls in the audience have watched filmic representations of themselves—girl fans—being treated like garbage without, apparently, batting an eyelash? The answer lies in the fact that these apparent contradictions would not have seemed contradictory to contemporary audiences. By 1961, consumers of popular fiction, plays, films, radio, and television had become accustomed to portrayals of adolescent femininity that routinely engaged such paradoxes. From the moment of their earliest proliferation in the 1930s, representations of teenage girls as heroines of mass-culture comic entertainments rapidly coalesced into a limited range of interpretive options: either the girl was a quasi-angelic creature, praised for her bubbly charm, her obedience to authority, and her chastity, or else she was an exasperating agent of chaos who challenged the boundaries and hierarchies of a patriarchally organized society (one that protects the social, economic, sexual, and political privileges of mature males). In both these roles the teenage girl unfailingly appears either more or less than human, never simply a whole person with her own three-dimensional subjectivity. Instead she becomes a "type" and often, indeed, a stereotype—an iconic abstraction representing dominant culture's desires or nightmares. Cultural critic bell hooks summarizes the functions of stereotypes, arguing that they "are created to serve as substitutions, standing in for what is real. They are there not to tell it like it is but to invite and encourage pretense. They are fantasy, a projection onto the Other that makes them less threatening. Stereotypes abound when there is distance."[1] The steadily employed stereotypes of adolescent femininity in the United States would suggest a great deal of distance between teen girls and the producers of popular culture, whose fictions persistently view girlhood as radically Other to an unnamed but implicit "self": adult men, teen girls' polar opposites in age, sex, and cultural alliances.

I began this project because I wanted to know why American culture has for so long collectively imagined the adolescent girl as a non-person constructed as a foil for adult men, the persons whose needs and desires a patriarchal society caters to, and who predominantly controlled the production and circulation of popular culture during the twentieth century. Girls' representations in comic narratives reflect a patriarchal culture's concerns regarding changes in American society during the twentieth century. American news media, political rhetoric, entertainment industries, advertising, and other modes of public address have historically viewed the world through the eyeglasses of the mature male, a perspective that casts non-males and non-adults as Other. Consequently, both women and youth figured in mainstream culture throughout the twentieth century as objects of intense pleasure, curiosity, and anxiety.

A vast discursive field surrounding the teenager emerged in twentieth-century mass culture, which frequently described youth in language that was quasi-anthropological in its discussion of teens' puzzling fads, slang, and "tribal" peer culture. Discussions of female teens, however, were also overlaid with older expressions of misogyny, which often situated women within a binary that many have called the "madonna/whore" dichotomy—a polarization of women's options between approved chastity and obedience, and a seductive sexuality that is simultaneously shunned and avidly consumed. Youth scholars Joe Austin and Michael Nevin Willard have similarly noted "the bifurcated social identity of youth as a vicious, threatening sign of social decay and 'our best hope for the future,'" an age-based version of the madonna/whore dichotomy.[2] Because women and youth share the status of Other, their representations in culture have tended to bounce repetitively between fantasies of the impossibly good and the impossibly bad.

Standing at the crossroads between childhood and womanhood, the teen girl faces Janus-like in both directions, a liminal figure who combines two identities that incite pleasure and anxiety in the adult male. She has therefore been consistently put "back in her place" by mass-media narratives that burden her with the worst of both worlds: her femininity makes her more sexually objectified than teen boys in the same narratives, while her youth makes her more ignorant and diminished than grown women. Through this double enforcement of oppressive representation, discourses surrounding teenage girls reaffirm the "rightful" primacy of adult males in the organization of American culture. Purporting to define the average girl, teen-centered texts also tacitly define the average man by suggesting that these opposed identities drew their boundaries in contradistinction to each other.

One of the foundational arguments in cultural studies of marginalized populations holds that the discursive field surrounding a fetishized yet reviled Other provides fantasies of difference that constitute the imagined identity of the oppressor's culture. The project of representation, then, reveals as much about a text's creators as about its topic. Edward Said has noted, in an argument similar to hooks's description of "distance" in stereotypes, that the West's construction of the Orient relies upon "exteriority," a cultural and critical remove that authorizes a commentator to assess foreign cultures in light of, and for the purposes of, his own: the Orientalist "makes the Orient speak, describes the Orient, renders its mysteries plain for and to the West. He is never concerned with the Orient except as the first cause of what he says. . . . The principal product of this exteriority is of course representation."[3] If we replaced "Orient" with "teenage girl," we would have here an accurate description of the female adolescent's rendering in popular culture. In texts centrally concerned with explaining teenage girls as a cultural category, the producers' position exterior to adolescent femininity authorizes them to classify and interpret their subject in accord with self-serving ideologies. They are not concerned with the teenage girl except as the first cause of what they say. In a 1945 installment of *The March of Time*, a newsreel produced by Time-Life and screened in cinemas around the country, the announcer begins by noting, "Of all the phenomena of wartime life in the United States, one of the most fascinating and mysterious, and one of the most completely irrelevant, has been the emergence of the teenage girl as an American institution in her own right."[4] These words encode the paradox of desire and disgust underlying the view of youth that circulated in the news and entertainment industries. *The March of Time* frames girls as a puzzling "them" who oppose an imagined, superior "us." The exterior voice that calls girls "fascinating, mysterious, and completely irrelevant" thus implicitly defines grown men as unremarkable, comprehensible, and relevant—in other words, people who are normal and important.

As the "principal product" of this mentality, representation is the first place to look to learn how American culture has envisioned its identity in opposition to caricatured Others. While a great deal of work has mapped our culture's caricatures of numerous marginalized or oppressed populations, to date only a few scholars have attempted to systematically analyze and historicize girls' representations. Indeed, girlhood in general long remained a severely under-studied field in many academic disciplines, even among scholars in the social sciences who studied youth—a category often discussed and defined as though it were exclusively masculine. When I speak of our dismissive attitude about girlhood, I describe a stance that has influenced conceptions of female adolescence in academe as well as in the wider culture. However, while the academy still has not widely embraced the significance of youth studies or girls' studies, several scholars in numerous fields have begun to address this girl-shaped gap in the study of American culture. Analyses of youth in film and popular culture now focus more consciously on girlhood than those of an earlier generation,[5] while several historians have begun exploring girls' labor history, consumer culture, sexuality, peer culture, and more.[6]

American Sweethearts joins this growing conversation by analyzing the position of "the teenage girl" as a fixture in popular American narratives: this book tells a story about storytelling, about the formation and dissemination of one segment of our cultural mythology. Who has told this story, and to whom? Whose needs has it served, and how has it persisted and changed across many years? By anatomizing girls' portrayals in mainstream media—both in narrative forms and in popular periodicals—I trace those portrayals to the development of female youth over the twentieth century as an increasingly potent and visible social category. Famed columnist Walter Winchell used to address his broadcast audience as "Mr. and Mrs. America, and all the ships at sea." Mr. and Mrs. America are the imagined center of this book: what they knew about teen girls, when they knew it, and how they knew it. I went in search of averageness, of the "common knowledge" that Americans came to share about teenage girls. Therefore, I focus not on all of popular culture, but rather only on the branch of it that reached the greatest number of Americans most frequently: the "main stream" of public conversation, which circulates through the professional news and entertainment industries.

The body of texts chosen for analysis here are comic "narrative cycles," a collection of stories about a single character across several media. This use of the word "cycle" differs from that often used by film scholars to describe a group of unrelated films with similar themes and styles. I use "narrative cycle" rather than "franchise" to distinguish the texts I study from their modern-day counterparts. Today, entertainment conglomerates often introduce new characters with the intention of exploiting their brand simultaneously in several different markets—not only narrative forms but also clothing, games, and other merchandise. Characters at the center of a modern-day franchise need not prove their popularity with audiences before finding themselves disseminated in numerous, disparate commercial forms. But in the early to mid-twentieth century, cultural producers would usually extend a character into different media only after it achieved success in its first iteration; a character's continuation from a single text to a body of interrelated texts thus suggests a degree of preexisting popularity among consumers.[7] Thus, the Junior Miss cycle begins as a series of magazine stories (1939) successful enough to warrant collection in book form (1941) and translation into a stage play (1941), which is successful enough to warrant a radio series (1942), which leads to a film (1945). In turn, the collective success of these texts justifies the intermittent extension of the radio series up to 1954, and the further creation of a *Junior Miss* television musical in 1957.[8] The existence and extension of a narrative cycle in this period, suggesting a genuine level of popular success, highlights consistent patterns in public tastes. When consumers repeatedly embrace a single character across multiple media, over a considerable span of time, they signify an unusually potent appeal in that character. In short, this book analyzes narrative cycles because their intense and widespread success can tell us something about American consumers' preferences for a certain vision of girlhood.

Moreover, the cycles—through the sheer weight of their numerous individual texts—clarify and illuminate the ingredients of teen-girl portrayals that affect nearly *all* narratives about teen girls, not just cyclic ones. Readers familiar with the history of teen-centered narratives will recognize that *American Sweethearts* omits many more texts than it includes, but such omissions are necessary, given that part of this project's aim is to examine representational patterns through close, sustained analyses of individual texts; such analysis would not be possible in a comprehensive survey of the scores of teen-centered books, films, plays, and television programs produced during the twentieth century. But while numerous and varied in their details, the clear majority of those narratives are remarkably similar in their structure, tone, characterization, and even plot. The narrative cycles I study here were chosen because they demonstrate the full array of tools in the ideological toolkit that built all teen-girl texts, cyclic and non-cyclic. In *American Sweethearts* I attempt to provide a rubric for identifying and interpreting patterns of representation that one can easily find in dozens of other comic texts from the same period.

The representational patterns explored here influenced not only other narratives of the mid-twentieth century, but even the popular culture we consume today in the early twenty-first. Constructions of girlhood have broadened considerably over the last forty years or so, but certain ingredients in girls' images today remain true to the stereotypes codified in earlier periods, particularly in such issues as teen girls' fetishized sexual liminality, their romanticized relationships with their fathers and father figures, and the codes of incompetence and diminishment that continue to apply even in stories that purport to extol girls' strength or skill. For example, girls in teen comedies today have a tendency to slip and fall on their rear ends at critical moments—as in *The Lizzie McGuire Movie* (2003) and *Confessions of a Teenage Drama Queen* (2004)—just as Gidget did on television forty years ago. The cycles examined herein had such far-reaching influence that the images they concocted have become de-fining components of adolescent femininity in the American popular imaginary.

Narrative cycles were familiar to audiences before the interwar pe-riod, for entertainment executives have long recognized the adaptation of a popular story from one medium to another as an efficient means of maximizing profits and minimizing the risks of launching new material. Even in the nineteenth century several popular novels inspired theatrical plays, such as the successful "tom shows" that derived from Stowe's novel *Uncle Tom's Cabin*. In the twentieth century, Hollywood relied often upon successful literary and theatrical texts as source material for films. In the 1930s and 1940s, when narrative entertainment thrived in the medium of radio, popular characters from theater and fiction resurfaced in radio serials,[9] and when commercial television developed after World War II, much of its early narrative content derived, in turn, from preexisting radio series.[10] Narrative cycles about teens spread quickly and widely between the 1930s and the 1960s, across all available media. Those fic-tional narratives are the primary form of popular culture under investi-gation here, with secondary attention to popular mainstream magazines —such as *Life, Look, Newsweek, Ladies' Home Journal,* and *Reader's Digest*— which helped to disseminate the received wisdom about adolescent fe-males to Mr. and Mrs. America.

Teen-centered cycles are usually comedies, and that provides another distinction for the texts studied here. Although plenty of dramas included adolescent characters in the earlier twentieth century, it was uncommon before the late 1950s for such texts to focus mainly or exclusively on adolescent protagonists. When they did so, they tended to emphasize the kinds of psychological issues, hard decisions, and emotional anguish that appeared in adult dramas as well. In other words, dramas about teenagers tended to be versions of the *bildungsroman,* the literary genre in which young people find the path to their adult identities through a "coming of age" conflict. By contrast, comedies of the period show scant interest in defining teen protagonists as travelers on a path to adulthood; rather than incorporating adolescence into the narrative of maturity, comedies treat the teen years as a time of opposition to adults and adult values, a time of subcultural Otherness. This approach results in a keener focus on the figure of the teenager, and on the definition of "teenageness," than we usually find in dramatic stories of the same era.

If we consider, for example, three of the most popular novel-to-film dramatic cycles about girls in the 1940s—*National Velvet* (1944), *A Tree Grows in Brooklyn* (1945), and *I Remember Mama* (1948)—we see fairly quickly that they focus far more on the question of how youngsters become adults and find their place in their world, with attendant emphases on crisis and challenge, than on the question "what is a teenager?" which centrally, if implicitly, informs teen comedies. Each of these three dramas has a chronologically and/or geographically remote setting (all are set at the turn of the twentieth century, and *National Velvet* takes place in Britain), while teen comedies tend to be set in an idealized version of the here-and-now, strongly defining the teenager as a contemporary phenomenon. Even when teens appear in dramas set in the current moment, those characters usually function in the service of a theme other than adolescence. In the case of *Since You Went Away* (1944), David O. Selznick's sentimental drama of a homefront family coping with the absence of their husband and father, the privations and demands of wartime existence drive the film; while two teenage daughters figure prominently in the family and in the narrative, their definition as specifically adolescent does not dominate the story's themes. Nor are these girls the main protagonists of the film; that honor goes to their mother, for dramas of this period also tend to subordinate teen characters within well-developed ensemble casts of adults. When Peggy Ann Garner starred in two feature films in 1945, she received top billing as the title character in the comedy *Junior Miss*, but only seventh billing in the drama *A Tree Grows in Brooklyn*. While her character in the latter case had clearly been the central protagonist in Betty Smith's popular novel, she became secondary to the story of her parents in the film version. Dramas, in sum, do not offer the same opportunities that comedies do for studying specific American myths of adolescence; only in comedies do we consistently see teenagers themselves as central figures, and the issues of adolescent culture and behavior as primary topics of investigation. Indeed, the tone and purpose of the mid-century teen comedy is fundamentally taxonomical: it categorizes and elaborately explains the teenager as a discrete Other, so alien as to need interpretation. Just as the Orientalist provides an image of the East that "renders its mysteries plain for and to the West," as Said put it, so the producers of teen-centered comedies attempt to define so-called average teens, rendering their mysteries plain for and to adults.

By focusing only on the most widely disseminated narratives of adolescence, I necessarily restrict myself to an analysis of white characters. The most obvious reason for this apparent discrimination is that non-white girls almost never appear as protagonists in any mainstream entertainment in this period, let alone anything as popular as a narrative cycle.[11] That omission bespeaks the ideologies at stake in celebrations of whiteness. Because teen girls appear as types rather than people, they are subject to a form of idealization. Central to all the texts studied here is an assumption that the (white) teenage girl embodies an ideal of innocence, loveliness, and purity; even texts that portray her as a maddening hellion draw upon the unspoken assumption that she should, and can, be otherwise. This assumption echoes the celebration of white womanhood in much of Western culture, an association with purity that has historically not applied to women of color. As Richard Dyer puts it, whiteness has for centuries been "the colour of virtue," especially for women, in myriad Western art forms.[12] Whiteness signifies the compulsory ingredients of a good woman's construction: domestic protection, angelic innocence, and superior spirituality. Many film scholars have traced the subtle and not-so-subtle associations between women's whiteness and their purity in classic Hollywood cinema.[13] This partly explains why teen girls are so often drawn as types instead of persons: they operate like allegorical figures, signifying ideal abstractions more than the interiority of a three-dimensionally rendered human. Small wonder, then, that American images of teen girlhood have historically been all but barren of racial Otherness.

The ideals projected onto whiteness intensify in the portrayal of white female *youth* in particular, because, as Austin and Willard said, adults have so often required the young to represent "our best hope for the future." In his autobiography, Mickey Rooney—star of the Andy Hardy films of the 1930s and 1940s, and hence the king of the Hollywood teenagers—explains the importance of these ideals to the success of his films, which celebrated a fantastically harmonious middle-class family and a mythic image of small-town normalcy: "Parents became Andy Hardy fans, just as much as their kids did. They liked to think that they could have kids like Andy Hardy and that they might, someday, be the kind of parents Andy Hardy had. . . . In our heart of hearts, we know it's unrealistic to expect something like that for ourselves. . . . The Andy Hardy movies didn't tell it 'like it is.' They told it the way *we'd like it to be*, describing an ideal that needs constant reinvention."[14] Interestingly, Rooney's description of idealizations uses the same phrase bell hooks uses in describing stereotypes; neither type of fantasy can "tell it like it is," for both avoid the factual present in order to dazzle us with visions of an intriguing place somewhere between the present and the future—a sort of conditional tense of the imagination where idealizations express eager hope, and stereotypes express negative, yet obsessive, anticipation. Teenagers attract both types of images because of their liminal age; on the verge of becoming full-time adults, at the moment they still hold that position only part-time, displaying enough malleability to keep their ultimate destinies somewhat uncertain and hence an object of fascination.

Rooney's insightful remarks bespeak the anxieties behind wish fulfillment, for to need the "constant reinvention" of certain stories is tacitly to admit the real-life instability of the ideals those stories convey, ideals of an imagined averageness that offers comfort by reminding us that, no matter how disparate otherwise, we share common identities as family members. The members of the Aldrich family, who form one of the most popular teen cycles of the 1940s, live in a fictional town called Centerville, suggesting that sugary visions of "normalcy" are indeed the center of American experience, not unusual or idealized at all. The Aldrich cycle claims its characters to be Everyfamily, living in a town just like your own. Consumers of popular narratives have used the teen-centered comedy—populated by white, middle-class Christians—to pretend that such pretty parables are within everyone's reach. Writing in 1991, Rooney could cite the African American cast of television's *The Cosby Show* as a latter-day example of the perfect family with perfect teenagers,[15] but in earlier decades only white protagonists could signify Everyfamily in allegories of averageness and thereby evoke the fantasy that drew millions of hungry consumers to teen-centered tales.

The heroines of these texts are consistent in their race, class, and religion, but vary a bit in age. In his study of contemporary youth films, Timothy Shary descries the boundaries of adolescence as beginning at twelve and ending at college age.[16] I tend to follow the same model, except that in the early 1950s, when specifically high-school-aged girls become scarce in mainstream entertainment, I necessarily consider some characters of approximately nineteen or twenty who fill the same narrative positions that younger teens fill before and after that period. Regardless of their actual age, I never describe these characters as young women because, simply, they are not drawn as women. These texts burden their heroines with behavioral traits that strongly signify immaturity; my terminology thus follows the tone of representation. Furthermore, legal majority in this period was not reached until the age of twenty-one, and there is no contradiction in referring to a minor as a girl. For the most part, however, the stereotype under discussion here focuses specifically on "teenageness," which applies most often to characters of high-school age.

The audiences for such characters have tended to be either adults or youths roughly between the ages of nine and fourteen. Known today as "tweens," these youngsters have historically consumed popular texts about high-school-aged characters more than actual high school students have. For example, the Nancy Drew series of books initially centered on a sixteen-year-old heroine but was marketed by the publisher to readers between ten and fifteen. When the fifteen-year-old character Gidget appeared on television, she was promoted with merchandise like board games, paper dolls, and comic books, suggesting that her target audience was younger than she. Historian Kelly Schrum's data about movie preferences among one group of teens of the late 1930s and early 1940s demonstrate that the Andy Hardy series was more popular with girls fourteen and younger than with older teens, for after the freshman year of high school, girls' interests shifted toward adult movie stars; she further notes that the Hardy series ranked as a higher favorite with white girls than with white boys, or with African Americans of either sex.[17] Such data are rare; unfortunately there is no systematic way to determine the races, classes, or ages of film viewers of this period. The largest segment of consumers for teen-girl narratives probably resembled the protagonists—white, middle-class girls—but, as we will see in chapter 1, Nancy Drew's readership sometimes included girls of various ethnicities, colors, and classes, and the same may have been true of other teen-girl texts.

Questions of audience and reception, however, are not my focus here; I am concerned rather with the narratives' content and the producers who created them, in order to glean the composition of a particular American mythology of female adolescence. In his study of American frontier myths, Richard Slotkin notes that "by focusing on the producers [of popular culture] we can study more closely the dynamics of myth-production in the particular cultural site that has acquired the power to address us *as if* it spoke for an 'American' national culture."[18] The myths of the American West that Slotkin studies more overtly address national identity issues than teen comedies do, since the frontier has so potently symbolized America for centuries. But stories about teenage girls, less obviously, also speak to national identities and images—not of exploration and wilderness-taming, but of domesticity and the practice of democratic ideals in the father-centered family unit that symbolizes the American nation. These associations became particularly strong during World War II, when state authorities used images of home and family as propaganda tools to synecdochally represent the essence of the American polity.

Narrative cycles did not appear in a cultural vacuum, but were intimately related to several social and cultural events during these decades—particularly to the growth of the public visibility, freedom, and perceived influence of youth and women. Teenagers in general, and girls in particular, have been consistently imagined as a potential threat to the security of established social practices and standards; the terms in which this threat is rendered for public consumption have changed over time to reflect the particular concerns of a given period. It hardly needs to be said that teenagers have never "taken over" society in any real sense, yet adults' concern that they might do so, in various ways, has fueled much of the public commentary about youth over time. A sustained reading of teen-centered texts, both in the news media and in narrative forms, reveals a deep and persistent fear of teens' potential to disrupt the patriarchal status quo. Every chapter herein provides connections to the events in each period that reignited these anxieties, to demonstrate how girls' representations reflect and respond to concerns about female adolescence as a disruptive social force.

If the primary aim of this project is to anatomize popular culture's role in creating stereotypes of teen girlhood, a related goal is to explore the texts' support of patriarchal gender ideologies. Although popular culture creates nothing *ex nihilo*, instead engaging and amplifying ideas already in circulation, it nonetheless is a powerful ideological tool in teaching socially acceptable assumptions and beliefs. This book implicitly contends that popular culture has been a primary means of reinscribing the social, sexual, and intellectual subjugation of young girls, an argument with antecedents in numerous studies of media, cultural theory, and youth. Media critic Meenakshi Gigi Durham, for example, analyzes girl culture through the lens of Louis Althusser's theory of interpellation and "Ideological State Apparatuses." Althusser, whose arguments have buttressed many investigations of marginalized people's roles in culture, held that individuals form their identities in conjunction with their culture's dominant ideologies, which they absorb through institutions like the media. By virtue of this absorption process, individuals are "interpellated" into those ideologies, becoming complicit in their own subjugation. This complicity allows the governing order to reproduce itself with the full assistance of the governed, without requiring the use of direct state force. Durham draws upon this theory to analyze teen magazines, noting that such publications train their girl readers to accept the traditional dictates of heterosexuality: in particular, that girls must please boys with submissive and erotic styles of self-display. Such lessons "uphold patriarchal articulations of girls' sexuality and reaffirm cultural hegemonies," and they "play a strong symbolic role in constituting [girls'] subjectivities and identities."[19] Culture produced for girls, then, potentially teaches its consumers that their subordination to patriarchy is normal, proper, and even desirable. In questioning narrative culture's circulation of hegemonic sexual ideologies, *American Sweethearts* asks, like Durham, what girls learn from the cultural products that are marketed to them as "their own."

This learning involves lessons about age as well as gender. Mickey Rooney calls our attention to the strongly prescriptive effect of popular images on the young: "Through the years, I keep meeting people who tell me, 'Andy Hardy? Hey, he taught me how to be a teenager.' From remarks like this, I conclude that many American teenagers and would-be teenagers went along with the celluloid ideal fashioned by Metro's writers."[20] Teen-centered movies offered an informal education to such youngsters, from which they could mentally take notes on how to perform their own impending adolescence. Although the Andy Hardy films featured young actresses as Andy's girlfriends, boyhood is the series' central topic, and we can assume that Andy's lessons in "how to be a teenager" applied more to boys than to girls. A principal argument of *American Sweethearts* is that girl-centered texts have offered their young female consumers implicit lessons in self-subordination to paternal(istic) authority—for that authority is ultimately what these entertainments were designed to celebrate and protect.

It may seem odd to assert that comic fictions about teenage girls function primarily for the good of middle-aged men, since girls and women were often the main consumers of such texts, but it is important to remember the distinctions between individuals and ideologies. Some of the narratives studied here may not have directly reached many men (although, as we shall see, some did), but they uniformly support the ideologies that uphold patriarchy, and thus benefit a social arrangement that ultimately favors mature men. They can be read, in one sense, as instructional texts teaching young girls how to accept and properly perform the roles their society expects them to play. As such, these tales participate in a long history in American media of training women to judge themselves critically through the eyes of an assumed, unspecified masculine critic. Even today we see the cosmetics and fashion industries, especially, selling ideals of beauty that assume a discerning male end-user whose apparently exacting standards must be appeased. But in the interwar and postwar periods, before the improvements made by second-wave feminism, public discourse more overtly burdened women with male-serving expectations, often delivered in a decidedly harsh tone.

In just one compelling example, a magazine article from 1945 seems, at first glance, to advise boys of girls' irritating behaviors:

> Females are fun. But full of foibles. It's all a guy can do to keep his head, his balance and his temper. You think you have a girl figured out, when she launches something you hadn't thought of. A woman can dazzle you, puncture your poise and plans and stretch your good humor till it snaps. . . . A guy can take this if he's nicked with love. If not, it's a tough spot. 'Cause she's put her hex sign on you. And man, you're in her hands![21]

The rest of the article presents an alliterative list of women's flaws—including "possessive," "perverse," and "positively perplexing"—with lengthy descriptions of each. But the apparently masculine "you" addressed here is actually a teenage girl. "Female Foibles" was the January installment of a monthly magazine column called "The Sub-Deb" (a term for a teenage girl younger than those officially called "debutantes"). The *Ladies' Home Journal* launched the Sub-Deb column in 1928, providing a page for girls at a time before teens had magazines of their own. The column ran for several decades and was always written by women; the instance quoted here was by Elizabeth Woodward, who held that post for many years. Remarkably, an article written by a woman, for girls, and published in an exclusively women's magazine assumes a masculine voice to essentialize and excoriate female behavior.

This complaint about young women would already be obvious to any male predisposed against "female foibles." The people who need Woodward's instructive advice are, rather, those least likely to know how unpleasant girls can be: girls themselves. The masculine voice of address and the illusory implication of a male reader induct girls into the temporary adoption of a masculine persona; the column is designed to make girls identify with men, to pity them, and at last, to become so ashamed of their own "foibles" that they repent and labor to make themselves more user-friendly to boys. What form would this labor take? A text-box at the bottom of the same page answers that question, finally addressing girls as girls: "KEEP ON BEING A DUNDERCLUMP! Be shy and awkward, be fluttery-handed and fuzzy-tongued, and you'll cut quickly any chances of dating any boy. . . . It's better to be bright about boys. And you can be, with the Sub-Deb booklets under your belt." Readers could order a (free) catalog of (not free) booklets containing lessons in how best to serve boys' moods and desires. But of course, no one published this kind of advice for boys in men's magazines; the labor of neurotic self-correction was assumed to be women's work, and popular culture often functioned as a factory whistle reminding girls and women—in a "fun" way—to get busy. The teen-girl comic narratives analyzed in this book function much like the "Female Foibles" article, offering a father-centered worldview to daughters and implicitly teaching them to judge themselves from an adult, masculine perspective. By so doing, these texts interpellate girl consumers into patriarchal ideologies, cooperating in a larger public project of taming young women's "disruptive" effects on social order.

But female youth were not the only consumers of girl-focused narratives, not the only people exposed to the cycles' gender ideologies. Adults, too, learned the signifiers of adolescent girlhood from popular culture, which could affect how they imagined and interacted with young girls. Two of the cycles studied here, Junior Miss and the variously titled Corliss Archer texts, had successful runs as Broadway plays. The New York theater was primarily an adult milieu, for plays ran until late at night and were more likely to contain mature themes and language than the carefully censored products of the film industry (comparisons of screenplays with the stage plays they derive from often reveal that Hollywood routinely excised words like "hell," "damn," and "bitch," which were acceptable in Broadway productions). Children and teens did attend some Broadway plays, but usually at matinée performances; the 1938 teen-centered comedy What a Life, in addition to its resounding success with adult audiences, was popular with groups of youngsters from local schools, clubs, and orphanages. But the high turn-out of youth groups was due partly to the producers' unusually aggressive marketing campaigns targeting those specific institutions;[22] adults were the dominant consumers of Broadway productions, and adults were the first to embrace teen comedies.

Similarly, girl-centered films often drew audiences of mixed ages and sexes, and if the parents who took their youngsters to the movies might have been mothers as often as fathers, the films' patriarchal operations remain intact: as Carolyn Heilbrun reminds us, mothers have often functioned as "female mentor[s] from the patriarchy" whose job it is to teach their daughters the strict lessons of approved femininity.[23] Indeed, the longevity and popularity of the Sub-Deb column in the *Ladies' Home Journal* suggests that mothers—by far the dominant portion of the magazine's intended (and probably actual) readership—were strong enforcers of patriarchal standards, willing participants in myths about male authority and the need to protect it. The most egregiously diminished and marginalized of all teen-girl heroines of the 1940s, Corliss Archer, debuted in a series of popular short stories in another women's magazine, *Good Housekeeping.*

Men, too, encountered popular entertainments with teen-girl protagonists, either because they attended plays and films with their families or simply because popular texts are often visible on culture's general radar screens: during these years, *Time* and *Newsweek*—magazines clearly marketed to an adult and largely male readership—sometimes carried advertisements for girl-centered movies and news items about their stars. Such material employed the codes of the teen-girl stereotypes, presenting the girl as diminished, inconsequential, or sexually available. One 1959 issue of *Newsweek* carried a brief article about teen actress Sandra Dee, titled "I Giggle." A photograph showed Dee wearing short shorts, over the caption "Sophisticated baby." In the text, Dee praised her recently completed film *A Summer Place*, noting that the role had given her the chance to play a wide range of emotions: "I'm in love. I get pregnant. I get hysterical. I giggle." The editors thus titled their article about a real person with a phrase meant to describe a film role and, moreover, they chose the most banal of Dee's phrases as the one with which to identify her. These decisions define Dee herself as a "giggling" creature and thus signal what the *March of Time* newsreel would have called her "irrelevance." Meanwhile, the appearance of her slender thighs and the sobriquet "sophisticated baby" complete the picture of an adorably frivolous and sexy girl, an *hors d'oeuvre* for the adult male palate.

It is not necessary for one to be either a literal patriarch (an authoritative father) or a cultural patriarch (an adult male in an influential profession) to uphold the ideologies of patriarchy. Stratifications that assume the superior authority of adult men have been the dominant paradigm in American cultural history; in such circumstances, when patriarchy becomes so familiar as to seem like "common sense," anyone—regardless of age or sex—can have an investment in accepting this social structure as true and good (or at least as inevitable) and can thus support the notion that the supremacy of adult males is natural and necessary for the maintenance of "normal" life. Throughout this book, I occasionally describe audiences as "supporters of patriarchy." When I do so I have no specific demographic in mind, nor do I mean to pinpoint, once and for all, any individual's beliefs about social organization and the positions of dominant and marginalized groups. Such pinpointing cannot be possible, for individual subjects activate different parts of their identities at different moments. The man who tries to rear his daughter to be an intelligent and dignified citizen when he is at home may, in a movie theater, howl with laughter at the sight of a teenage girl's sexualized humiliation. The teen girl who writes angry letters to the press, protesting its dismissal of her cohort as "silly," may avidly consume movies and radio programs about unquestionably silly teenage girls. To call audiences "supporters of patriarchy" is only to describe the subject position delineated for them by the texts they willingly consume; as they read, watch, or listen, consumers are asked to adopt patriarchal perspectives as the necessary eyeglasses through which to view the narrative in question. In those moments, if they consent to wear these glasses, such consumers indeed support patriarchy, even if that support may be unconscious or partially contradicted in other segments of their lives.

This study begins in 1930 because that is roughly the moment at which mass culture began to take systematic notice of teenagers as a distinct category; general consciousness of teen identity manifested very sparsely before the 1930s. After the 1904 publication of psychologist G. Stanley Hall's ambitious *Adolescence: Its Psychology and Its Relations to Anthropology, Sociology, Sex, Crime, Religion, and Education*, discussions of adolescence became increasingly common in the rarified discourses of institutions like those Hall names, but the professional journals of these institutions were hardly common reading for the general populace (though the experts who published in them might occasionally contribute an article to a general periodical, where conversations about undifferentiated "children" of all ages were not uncommon). Cultural producers in some industries recognized adolescence before others did; Peter Stoneley has suggested that authors and distributors of girls' literature had a notion of specific social roles attaching to female adolescence as early as the late nineteenth century, and Kelly Schrum notes the interactions between girls and the fashion industry in the 1920s.[24] But these discrete signs of a dawning sensibility of adolescence did not coalesce in American mass culture until later; in the adult-oriented entertainment industries, only a handful of popular narratives before 1930 focused on adolescence *per se*, as opposed to the numerous texts which did not systematically differentiate categories within youth.[25] By the 1920s we see a widespread interest in college-aged youth; the generationally distinct cultural practices of "flappers" and "sheiks" (about nineteen years old) sparked an intense public scrutiny that did not often extend to their younger siblings.[26] Nonetheless, the general 1920s focus on youth influenced a gradually expanding awareness of teens which began to blossom in the 1930s and became a full-blown cultural obsession over the following decades. More particularly, 1930 marked the debut of Nancy Drew, the first cycle heroine I analyze. Although other teenage serial heroines for children existed earlier, Nancy Drew had an unprecedented impact; she was the most popular and the most influential literary heroine for girls at the historical moment when adolescence came to public consciousness.

American Sweethearts ends with 1965 because that is when the teenage girl "ended," too; I locate the *Gidget* television series, which debuted in 1965, as the last moment in which the original tropes of adolescent girlhood consistently cohered. In the late 1960s and beyond, changes in women's and girls' roles in American culture caused images of girls to splinter into numerous kinds of representations, all of which borrow some ingredients from the stereotypes codified in this study, but which do not always display them in such a unified manner. For example, the combined influence of feminism and the growing culture of physical fitness after the 1970s has given us more teen-girl characters who display a certain "kick-ass" physicality, like Buffy the Vampire Slayer—who nonetheless manages to perpetuate some of the stereotypes of adolescent femininity defined in this study. The teen girl "ended" in another way, too, after 1965: she was displaced as the lightning rod for popular desires and fears by her older sisters, college activists and hippies. College-aged people dominated the discursive position of youth in popular consciousness throughout the years of the counterculture. By the 1970s, images of teenagers existed alongside equally common images of young women, so that "female youth" meant something broader and less coherent than it had in earlier periods. By then, the discourse of adolescence was firmly established and popular entertainments no longer had to "explain" the teen girl to baffled adults. Her representations after 1965, then, along with being diluted by images of older girls, became rather stale. Nearly all the mass-culture representations of teenage girls since the 1960s have drawn, to varying degrees, upon a hoary stockpile of assumptions and signifiers developed during the period studied here. The following section offers an overview of the central themes in girls' construction, which inform all the materials explored in subsequent chapters.

The Sexiness of Emptiness: Teen Girl as Woman and Child

Long traditions in Western culture construct both children and women as exotic and erotic Others. The discourses surrounding these populations often function by establishing a precondition of emptiness in the Other—a lack of the qualities by which the dominant culture defines itself. That emptiness renders the subject of discussion less of a full person than are members of the dominant population. Because teenage girls combine womanhood and childhood, they have been culturally imagined as a position of double "lack," which facilitates their portrayals as diminished, fetishized, and frequently sexualized. James Kincaid, using examples from Victorian culture, notes that modern society's dread of the pedophile, a monstrous figure, displaces our anxieties about our own, "acceptable" erotic fetishization and consumption of children. That consumption operates through a discourse of innocence that sees childhood as a phase of absence or lack—a lack of knowledge, sin, or other formulations of experience. The biblical usage of the word "know" to mean sexual intercourse suggests this chain of associations; to have experience or knowledge is to be less pure, less innocent. Thus the successful consumption of children as objects of love (or lust) depends upon assumptions of the child's blank innocence: "This hollowing out of children by way of purifying them of any stains (or any substance) also makes them radically different, other. In this empty state, they present themselves as candidates for being filled with, among other things, desire. The asexual child is not . . . any the less erotic but rather the more."[27]

Such assertions may have the ring of blasphemy, for it seems that few want to recognize or interrogate the slipperiness of our dearly held distinctions between acceptable and unacceptable forms of child fetishization. Beauty pageants in which little girls strut in full make-up and womanly costumes are embraced as a wholesome, fun activity by plenty of parents who, nonetheless, would be horrified if any "sick" person had an erotic response to the child whom those parents have, paradoxically, worked hard to eroticize. Healthy adults are imagined to look at the sexualized child without experiencing any sexual response, and perhaps without even interpreting the child's appearance through a sexual framework. Such operations are possible only by focusing on the child's innocence: we can tolerate a six-year-old's looking sexy as long as *she* doesn't know she looks sexy—that is, as long as her performance of womanly seduction is clearly an act of simple mimicry, and not an expression of personal knowledge. Her assumed ignorance and innocence allow viewers to enjoy the visually pleasurable sexual spectacle she presents without feeling besmirched by any stain of impropriety.

Shirley Temple perhaps embodied this paradox most clearly in American popular culture. Bret Wood has noted that Temple's earliest films, a series of shorts titled *Baby Burlesks*, placed their toddler actors in suggestive scenarios, speaking lines with crude *double entendres*. Yet few filmgoers looked askance at these productions: "it was [Temple's] very youth—her irrepressible innocence—that exempted her films from criticism; not even the moral watchdogs of the industry . . . dared look upon so sweet a child as a sexual icon (lest they be branded lascivious)."[28] When British novelist Graham Greene notoriously dared to do what "moral watchdogs" did not, publishing an essay that called Temple "a fancy little piece" with "a well-developed little rump," and noting how often her fans, curiously, seemed to be middle-aged men, he and the magazine for which he wrote not only were branded lascivious, they ignited a transatlantic scandal and were successfully sued for libel by Temple's film studio.[29] But the supposedly unthinkable thought that Temple aroused a non-paternal yearning in men was actually integral to many moments in her films, most of which show men, far more than women, cuddling and adoring the little moppet. Jeanine Basinger notes the frequency of such intimate scenes in Temple's *oeuvre* and wonders "how many incestuous nightmares were fed by her warbling to Papa, 'In every dream I caress you.'"[30] These overtones are apparent even without direct physical affection; Wood notes that *Curly Top* (1935), for example, "is loaded with scenes in which the seven-year-old becomes a visual fetish for a wealthy, single male."[31] In one scene this man sings a love song to the famous paintings on his walls, in which he fantasizes that little Temple has replaced the central figures. A later shot conspicuously foregrounds Temple's curvaceous bottom, barely covered by a bathing suit, rocking back and forth on an inflatable beach toy. In her real life, too, Temple encountered men for whom the sexual turn-on of innocence was hardly unthinkable; her autobiography recounts a private meeting she had at age twelve with film producer Arthur Freed, during which he suddenly announced, "I have something made just for you," and exposed his erect penis to her.[32] It is not merely the girl herself, but the fact of her youth, that allows consumers of her image to feel desire. Her emptiness, her "hollowed out" innocence, invites a symbolic penetration the way fresh snow invites footprints.

The allure of grown women, too, has often been represented through suggestions of emptiness or absence—not of experience, but of consciousness. In his history of *fin-de-siècle* art, Bram Dijkstra notes a trend to represent women in a state of "inanition" (either sleep or death). Paintings of dead or sleeping women paradoxically allowed an ethereal depiction of "the transcendent spiritual value of passive feminine sacrifice," while also inviting an erotic response, "a necrophiliac preoccupation with the erotic potential of woman when in a state of virtually guaranteed passivity."[33] A fully present woman—awake, conscious, mature, rational—challenges male dominance, while an "absent" woman facilitates it. The artistic trend toward images of inanimate women extended to similar images of young girls, for "[t]he very purity of the child seemed to preclude the threat of a sexual challenge."[34] Thus visual artists combined femininity and childhood into a single figure, and presented her as an open invitation to a probing male gaze disguised as a "spiritual" love of women's and children's (constructed) passivity and purity, masking a deeper desire to dominate without interference or revolt.

The erotic gaze could also be disguised as scholarly inquiry when expressed through discourses of science rather than art. Ludmilla Jordanova has located a version of this emptying and Othering process in the rhetorics of nineteenth-century medicine, which constructed woman as a mysterious creature of nature whose depths it was the challenge of science to plumb. This construction employed a dichotomy between disciplined logic (what men possess as the embodiments of culture, knowledge, and reason), and the undisciplined, irrational, "natural" state that supposedly defined women's minds. Because women were thus imagined as an absence rather than a presence, lacking the rationality that allowed men to enjoy the privileges of full personhood in post-Enlightenment societies, scientists and other authorities could assert power over a woman by making her an object of their studies. Such attentions often had undertones of sexual consumption. Jordanova analyzes a German painting of a medical scene, in which

> a beautiful young woman, who had been drowned, [was] being dissected by an anatomist . . . who was interested in the physical basis of female attractiveness. A group of men stand around the table on which a female corpse is lying. She has long hair and well-defined breasts. One of the men . . . is holding up a sheet of skin, the part which covers her breast, as if it were a thin article of clothing, so delicate and fine is its texture. The corpse is being undressed scientifically, the

constituent parts of the body are being displayed for scrutiny and analysis. The powerful sexual image is integral to the whole pictorial effect.[35]

She underscores the sexual exploitation inherent in this scene by noting that "science itself [is] a sexual activity in its relationship to nature," since both scientific study and sexual intercourse involve "penetration," a synonym for insight. When it comes to men's study of women, the boundaries between representation and exploitation have historically been slippery.

Popular culture in the United States has consistently fetishized and "studied" teenage girls much as though they, too, were beautiful autopsy subjects on a laboratory slab. Combining the categories of children and women, teen girls are celebrated for their double emptiness—the child's lack of experience, and the woman's lack of agency or rationality. Consequently, teen girls have traditionally appeared in the media as irrational, ignorant, mildly crazy, and often balanced precariously on a fine line between sexual innocence and experience. The effect is one of radical Otherness: the constant refrain of cultural commentary about girls in the mid-twentieth century puzzled over their strange slang, their allegiance to peer groups, their immoderate consumerism, their obsessions with popular culture, their fashion eccentricities, and their incomprehensibly mad reaction to teenybopper idols (like the unfortunate autograph seekers portrayed in *Gidget Goes Hawaiian*). Journalists, educators, doctors, and a host of other influential adults who made public remarks about female adolescence described these traits in rhetoric borrowed from social sciences like anthropology, which fostered a hierarchy between rational, civilized observer and natural, primitive Other. This narrative tone, common to most of the teen-girl comic cycles, explains and exploits the girl's oddities as a source of humor, holding her up for scrutiny and naming her various parts to exercise the power of reason over the threat posed by uncontrollable "nature."

Indeed, teenage girls' link to nature is especially keen because adolescent femininity combines the womanly attribute of the womb (with its attendant curse of hysteria) with the common constructions of childhood as a more "natural" or primitive state than adulthood. As natural beings, children are supposedly possessed of both an innocence that makes them precious and a dangerous proclivity to slip "back" into primitive (prerational) behavior, which requires that they be closely monitored.[36] In the case of teenage girls, the paradox of cherub and she-beast maps neatly onto preexisting paradoxes of good and evil that apply to grown women;

femininity marks the teenage girl in ways that parallel and reinforce how she is marked by youth. Already imagined as a condition that inclines its possessors toward instability and "mysteriousness," womanhood is all the more unstable at the moment when it arrives in that sudden, disorienting rush of hormones upon which the medical discourse of adolescence depends. Mischievous and uncontrollable agents of nature, hormones visibly inscribe changes upon the body: the swelling of breasts and hips inducts the female irrevocably into the condition of "to-be-looked-at-ness," in film theorist Laura Mulvey's famous phrase.

The liminality of the adolescent girl makes her simultaneously disturbing and attractive to patriarchy. Poised between innocence and experience, her combination of a womanly body and a childlike mind offers male authorities the best of both worlds: a female both pure and ripe, young enough to leave unchallenged the dominance of mature men, but old enough to be "hot." This logic continues to operate today in such films as the Oscar-winning *American Beauty* (1999), and more generally in the innumerable texts that employ some version of the "jail-bait" motif, such as Britney Spears's early music videos. In the narratives analyzed herein, the most frequent articulation of the voyeuristic appeal of female adolescence is the recurrence of what I call "the chrysalis moment," the carefully manipulated scenario in which an adolescent female is shown crossing a threshold of sexual maturity, like a caterpillar's transition to butterfly. Actresses best known for playing children or barely pubescent girls during the 1930s and 1940s—like Deanna Durbin, Jane Withers, Bonita Granville, and Shirley Temple—would regularly undergo a Hollywood initiation when cast in their first romantic leading roles. Such films often made their newly mature actresses the centers of intensely voyeuristic publicity campaigns that touted their "first kiss," thus turning these sexual initiations into public events and making such voyeurism appear a normal, expected element of a teen girl's public portrayal.

Such rituals occurred even when factually untrue. Shirley Temple's "first screen kiss" in 1942's *Miss Anne Rooney* inspired a barrage of half-prurient publicity, even though the kiss she received was, deceptively, a mere peck on the corner of her mouth. Ironically, Temple had performed much sexier kisses, full on the lips, as a three-year-old in the *Baby Burlesks* shorts. But now that Temple was old enough to operate within the discourse of romance and dating, publicists' desire to manipulate her into the cute predictability of the chrysalis moment led them to wholly discount her earlier kisses. Significantly, too, we should note that no such publicity campaigns attended the first onscreen kisses of *male* adolescent actors, whose sexual maturation was taken more for granted, not deemed sufficiently noteworthy to warrant spotlights. Chrysalis moments have remained a staple of girl-centered entertainment, often in make-over scenarios in films like *She's All That* (1999) and *The Princess Diaries* (2001), in which supposedly unattractive girls undergo comically laborious transformations into paragons of loveliness. American producers and consumers still scrutinize rituals of girls' transformations into womanhood, turning these performances into necessary components of mature female attractiveness: half the fun is in the detailed voyeurism of watching the intimate process of change, turning the adolescent girl into an even more intensely fetishized object than adult women who have less permeable boundaries. The teen female body, even more than the mature female body, is constructed as a public spectacle.

The publicity surrounding actresses' chrysalis moments bespeaks not merely men's desire, but also their anxiety; one might see in these carefully orchestrated scenarios an effort to control and contain teen-girl sexuality by ritualizing it, subjecting it to the interpretation and narration of patriarchal ideology. The same onset of sexuality that intrigues patriarchs can also worry them because it signals the girl's entrance into public circulation, at which point her fascinating body can be used for potentially mutinous purposes: who else might find it fascinating, and what might they do to destroy its luscious purity? Worse, what might the *girl* do with it, once she learns how to wield the power it grants her? A girl who consciously deploys her sexuality can create chaos that threatens her own father as well as her societal Father: the threat of pregnancy can destroy the nuclear family, while the threat of promiscuity can demoralize innocent men and even destroy the very fabric of society—at least, so said the pervasive rhetoric about female sexuality that recurred throughout the twentieth-century discourse of juvenile delinquency. The problem of how to exploit a teen girl's sexual appeal without losing control of it (how to catch a tiger by her piece of tail) is a problem that informs nearly every narrative about teenage girls in mid-twentieth-century popular culture.

A frequent method of simultaneously exploiting and containing the girl's sexual appeal is to juxtapose it with the concerns of a father or father figure. Teen-girl narratives are overwhelmingly told from the perspective of girls' parents, often specifically their fathers. Time and again we find a dyad established between a lively, sexually appealing but fundamentally innocent young girl and a loving but anxious daddy who sweats when confronted with the implications of her budding sexuality.[37]

The portrayal of an adolescent girl's chrysalis moment sometimes involves casting her father as an assistant to her maturation process: it may be the father who buys his daughter her first pair of high heels, as in the film *Junior Miss* (1945), or who attempts to assist her entrance into the sexual marketplace by procuring—with comic misadventure—a boyfriend for her (as in *Father Was a Fullback*, 1949). Additionally, a girl's inappropriate deployment of her sexuality can get her father into serious trouble, as in *Kiss and Tell* (1945), when Corliss Archer's careless public kissing leads her father into a bloody fist-fight to defend her reputation.

Fathers in this genre must often struggle to contain their foolish daughters' obsessions with love and romance within approved channels. Such portrayals of father/daughter relationships served partly to suggest that the potentially disruptive phase of adolescence was not as bad as it appeared, because it was really subject to patriarchal authority after all. This reassuring message addressed concerns about the perceived erosion of paternal authority in American society during the twentieth century.[38] The girl's frequent pairing with her father as the texts' central characters signals the broader fact of girls' significance to patriarchy writ large: her sexual maturation vexes her father because it also vexes the societal "Father." This dynamic manifests in narrative portrayals of romantic relationships between younger women and older men (an extremely common element of popular narratives), and sometimes the relationship is literalized as a father/daughter sexual couple, as in the case of Nabokov's *Lolita*, in which narrator Humbert Humbert cannot resist the charms of his "nymphet" stepdaughter.

Even without a direct romance between young girls and father figures, a lustful desire to fill up the "empty" young girl is one of the oldest, most enduring assumptions to inform the American entertainment industries. Marianne Sinclair surveys the parade of "nymphets" that began to pass through Hollywood generations before *Lolita* was published, noting that even "[s]ilent movie heroines had to project in purely visual terms a combination of sexual innocence and desirability, and the easiest way to do this was . . . to stress [their] extreme youth."[39] Even texts not explicitly about sex or romance will frequently code their heroines through erotic signifiers, as do the series of Nancy Drew films discussed in chapter 2.

In the narratives studied here, an emphasis upon the quality most associated with youth—emptiness—allows the successful representation of adolescent feminine sexuality, exploiting it while keeping it subordinate to patriarchal interpretation and control. If a woman's conscious deployment of sexual power makes her a potential threat, the key to successfully representing a girl's erotic appeal is to render her *un*conscious of it, or not in control of it—to "hollow out" her subjectivity, her will, or her competence. This emptiness or lack can take many forms. Often, it manifests as an absence of corruption or of selfish will, as in the angelic ingénues of the 1930s and 1950s. Girls' diminishment sometimes appears as a lack of stature, either literally in the figure of a very small girl (as with Gidget, whose name conflates "girl midget"), or else symbolically in the portrayal of a girl as subordinate to other characters, particularly males, and often fathers. Sometimes this lack of stature affects the girl's narrative position, as in the case of the 1947 film *The Bachelor and the Bobby Soxer*, which ostensibly focuses on its teenage heroine, and yet renders that heroine as a non-person relative to others in the cast: she has less interiority than they and functions solely to help them define their rational selves in opposition to her insane Otherness.

But the commonest form of emptiness in these representations is a lack of intellect; girls are often "empty-headed," or at least so immature as to be noticeably ignorant. This quality is usually represented as simultaneously exasperating, humorous, and romantically desirable, for it allows boys and men to appear smarter, and thus makes the girl the approved object of males' attention. Empty-headedness can also be desirable when combined with the innocence and other-directedness of the ingénue, whose lack of intellectual acumen heightens her possession of an instinctive form of knowledge coded as better, within limits, than formal education. In the Tammy cycle (1948–1967) we thus have Tammy Tyree, a sheltered Southern maiden whose folksy wisdom charms and assists sophisticates who have lost their way. Tammy's lack of knowledge encodes sexual innocence as well as a lack of book-learning; in the 1963 film *Tammy and the Doctor*, the bayou belle charms a Los Angeles surgeon who tells Tammy how sincerely he appreciates the "wisdom in that uncluttered mind of [hers]." Suggesting that a lack of clutter in one's mind reflects a lack of sin in one's body, Tammy replies by quoting an elderly friend who has described Tammy's mind as "a virgin page, waitin' to be writ on." Significantly, this formulation of Tammy's mind as a "virgin" does not originate *from* that mind; too innocent to articulate her own innocence, she must quote an older and more experienced acquaintance. Proving that all this sparkling virginity incites arousal, the doctor falls in love with Tammy, and the final shot of the film shows them locked in a passionate kiss. Paradoxically, the ultimate purpose of fetishized purity is to ignite a desire to destroy it.

The narratives discussed in *American Sweethearts* all demonstrate some version of this pattern, celebrating girls most enthusiastically in proportion to their emptiness or diminishment. Whether that blankness manifests as intellectual stupidity, sexual objectification, non-human idealization, smallness of stature, or narrative displacement in favor of male characters, heroines of teen-centered tales are no match for their domestic and institutional Fathers, the literal and figurative patriarchs of American culture. The girl's lack of integrity, intellect, or strong will has been the central ingredient necessary for her representation in mass culture, particularly in narratives consumed partly or wholly by adults. As we shall see in chapter 1, however, this image has co-existed with other representational options in entertainment marketed exclusively to children. The personhood absent in mainstream representations of girls was in greater evidence in for-girls culture, and nowhere more strikingly so than in the most popular series of girls' books in American history—the Nancy Drew Mysteries—which suggests that girls themselves, and producers who wrote for them, were capable of envisioning alternative definitions of girlhood. Chapter 1 discusses the history, content, and significance of this literary character, and establishes the concept of "personhood" that informs this entire study: by locating a representation of a dignified and autonomous identity as a crucial factor in the popularity of Nancy Drew, we can compare her with the images of girlhood in texts produced for a general audience and a general cultural gaze. The shift from a girls-only audience to a general audience prompts a shift in portrayals of teen girlhood, suggesting that girl consumers and male or adult consumers had different needs and desires at stake in the social construction of adolescent femininity.

Chapter 2 dramatizes the first example of that shift by analyzing the series of Nancy Drew films created by Warner Bros. (1938–1939). This film series radically alters the fictional series, inscribing its heroine with marks of diminishment that damage the integrity of the fictional character, and by implication the dignity of adolescent girlhood. Chapters 1 and 2 contrast the methodologies, attitudes, and assumptions of the different producers of the books and films, noting that the socio-cultural demands of the Depression, and the "crisis of masculinity" that accompanied it, influenced the reshaping of this teen heroine for a mass medium.

Chapter 3 treats the explosion of teen-consciousness that occurred during the 1940s, when the social category called "teenager" became widely disseminated and firmly cemented in American public consciousness. The most consistent ingredients of the teen girl's portrayals in the news media during this decade were her status as a consumer and her potentially dangerous sexuality. Chapter 3 links these social developments to the representations of girlhood in two major narrative cycles of the 1940s: Junior Miss, a collection of texts about a thirteen-year-old named Judy Graves, and the cycle centering on a fifteen-year-old named Corliss Archer. Chapter 4 addresses the whiplash effect in girls' portrayals during the 1950s and 1960s: from an extended period of near-total disappearance during the early 1950s, the tropes surrounding the teenage girl returned suddenly and forcefully at the end of the decade and continued through the middle of the next, most influentially in the figures of Gidget and Patty Lane, heroine of the popular *Patty Duke Show.* Like the others, this chapter charts the rising and falling fortunes of teen girls in popular narratives as responses to the various discourses surrounding youth and gender during those years, and to contemporary events like the emergence of the baby-boomer consumer market. In each instance, historical tensions between the powers of men and of young girls drive the tensions of the narratives' plots. Masquerading as simple entertainment, fun "for the whole family," these texts actually dramatize hotly contested power struggles between ages and sexes in American cultural history and, in so doing, naturalize girls' subordination to patriarchs so that this form of oppression takes on the appearance of something sweet, cute, and "wholesome." *American Sweethearts* attempts to demystify these myths by interrogating America's traditional attitudes toward its daughters. Once we can locate and define an oppressive pattern of representation, we can better recognize its implications and work to combat its influence on our culture's perceptions of, and reactions to, young girls.

1

Radical Notions

Nancy Drew and Her Readers, 1930–1949

What do women want, Dr. Freud?
Let me tell you about Nancy Drew.

—Frances Fitzgerald, 1980

 The Nancy Drew Mysteries, written
under the pseudonym "Carolyn Keene,"
are the longest-lived and most endur-
ingly popular series of books for girls
in America. Debuting in 1930, the character of Nancy Drew has continued to the present day, undergoing numerous revisions and renovations
to maintain her appeal to modern sensibilities. In 2004 the series' publisher, Simon & Schuster, unveiled its latest makeover for Nancy in the
new Nancy Drew, Girl Detective series. Meanwhile, the original core
series has long been considered a classic element of American girlhood.
Many readers and critics have praised Nancy Drew as a proto-feminist
role model whose independence, authority, and intelligence offered an
empowering vision of adolescent girlhood. But the series contains many
contradictions and paradoxes; even as it champions its heroine's strength
and ingenuity, it also reinforces patriarchal privilege and oppressive social
politics. Similar paradoxes have been explored by scholars like Janice
Radway and Nan Enstad, who have demonstrated that "trashy" genre
literature (romance novels and dime novels, respectively) can provide its
female readership with a crucial "place to dream," in Enstad's phrase—

a location for imagining an effective subjectivity—despite circumstances that hinder such a condition in readers' real lives, and also despite the books' support of hegemonic ideologies.[1] Similarly, the Nancy Drew series serves two masters at once, relying on conservative ideologies of race, class, and even gender while simultaneously promoting a somewhat progressive vision of girls' agency.

It is the latter quality that most attracted girl readers, and Nancy Drew's enormous popularity, particularly in the first two decades of the series (the 1930s and 1940s), helps us to understand the disparities between popular culture produced for child and adult audiences. Among the many characters examined in this study, only Nancy was intended solely for children, and specifically for girls (although her readership has always included some boys, as well). To begin with an examination of Nancy Drew is to learn what young girls chose for themselves when they had the opportunity to choose, and there is ample evidence that reading Nancy Drew did, indeed, constitute a passionate choice for millions of girls. Nancy demonstrates a condition I will explain herein as "personhood" for an audience frequently denied that condition in their real lives. Once we see how this series balanced "what [young] women want" with what their parent culture wanted, we can use that knowledge in subsequent chapters to assess how entertainment more explicitly aimed at adults constructed young heroines as inadequately authorized to claim the rights of personhood.

The Stratemeyer Syndicate and the Girls' Fiction Market

Edward Stratemeyer (1862–1930), Nancy Drew's first creator, revolutionized children's fiction at the turn of the twentieth century. Beginning as a writer of dime novels and serial fiction in children's and adults' periodicals, Stratemeyer soon ran his own "factory" of children's book production: in 1905 he established the Stratemeyer Literary Syndicate, which hired freelance ghostwriters to complete books based on his plot outlines. The books were then published under Stratemeyer's various pseudonyms. Using this mass-production method, Stratemeyer produced over a hundred different series during his lifetime, some of which achieved such success that they became household names: the Bobbsey Twins, Tom Swift, the Hardy Boys, and Nancy Drew. From the 1910s through the 1930s, the "golden age" of series books, those produced by Edward Stratemeyer and his Syndicate dominated the market.[2] A handful of series, such as the Bobbsey Twins, were written for and about very small children, but the bulk of the Syndicate's output focused on adolescents and the older children who today are called "tweens." The most consistent element of these series was their fanciful portrayal of youthful agency and freedom. Stratemeyer's teen heroes and heroines pursue adventure without the hindrance of parental restraint; they win every competition they enter; they travel in tightly knit peer groups, making teen camaraderie the books' central focus; and they usually enjoy sufficient wealth to maintain a comfortable standard of living. Adolescents are powerful, righteous, and happy in Stratemeyer's world; no wonder his series struck such a responsive chord with young people.

Portrayals of empowered youngsters in children's books contrast with portrayals of youth in books for adults. Lucy Rollins, in her comparison of Stratemeyer's books to Booth Tarkington's classic *Seventeen*, "the best-selling book in the entire country in 1916," notes that Tarkington presents "an amused and tolerant adult point of view" on adolescence, which has the effect of mocking the novel's long-suffering teenage protagonist. This comparison reveals "quite a discrepancy between how adults wanted to see teens and how teens wanted to see themselves."[3] For most of the twentieth century, adult literary critics often dismissed series books as unrealistic and sensational, qualities which partly manifest in the books' portrayal of teenagers with fantastical levels of competence and privilege. The lack of realism adults considered a flaw was thus the very component that made these books so successful with their intended audience; in such tales, young readers could see the teen years as a time of potent possibility.

Nancy Drew is by far the most potent of all Stratemeyer's female protagonists, and part of her initial success stemmed from her departure from established norms in girls' books, even those produced earlier by the Syndicate. Edward Stratemeyer initially showed little affinity for, or interest in, writing girls' stories; although he well knew that some of his boys' series had female fans, he did not develop a series specifically for girls until long after he had established his reputation as a boys' writer. When he did, the results were often uninspired: one of the Syndicate's earliest girls' offerings, the Dorothy Dale series (1908–1924), centered on a rather insipid heroine more reminiscent of Victorian than modern girlhood. That conflict was not unique to Stratemeyer; the production of girls' books, at large, underwent some fluctuations in the early twentieth century. The sentimental tradition of the late nineteenth century still had a residual influence on girls' fiction, although such recent social changes as the movement for women's suffrage and the rise of women in public roles made increasingly unsatisfying the domestic, passive heroines of older literature for girls. Between 1900 and 1930, a proliferation of new series tried to bridge Victorian and modern sensibilities about girlhood. Adventuresome heroines who used modern technologies to get out of the parlor and into the public sphere populated such series as the Motor Girls, the Airplane Girls, the Automobile Girls, and numerous series about Girl Scouts, among others.[4] But the heroines of most of these series did not so much depart from earlier representations as expand upon them; the girls remained traditional in many respects, including their sometimes passive roles in comparison with boys. While these hiking, driving, and flying heroines covered many miles geographically, they advanced only a few feet ideologically.

The first popular series to expand significantly upon this limited formula was a Stratemeyer property, and thus Nancy Drew's direct foremother. The Ruth Fielding series, although forgotten today, was among the most popular series for girls in the 1910s and 1920s.[5] Early volumes portrayed Ruth in accord with typical nineteenth-century sentimental heroines (orphan and schoolgirl), but as the series progressed, Ruth evolved into a career woman in the fledgling film industry, producing and starring in her own films as well as traveling the globe and solving mysteries. The last of several ghostwriters to contribute to this series was one Mildred Wirt, a young journalism student in Iowa. Pleased with her work, Stratemeyer paid her the compliment of asking her to inaugurate a new series he was just developing—the Nancy Drew Mysteries.[6]

Nancy Drew: History, Reception, and Themes

In 1927 Edward Stratemeyer had launched the Hardy Boys Mysteries, the first children's series to focus solely on mystery. Satisfied with the series' moderate success, Stratemeyer determined that the genre was sufficiently popular to warrant his creation of a complementary girls' series. Mildred Wirt proved an inspired choice as Nancy Drew's initial ghost: an athletic and professionally ambitious woman still in her early twenties, Wirt disdained the "boring and namby pamby" books for girls that had proliferated in her own childhood. She determined to make Nancy Drew appeal to modern sensibilities: "the times were exactly right for a new kind of heroine," she later recalled.[7]

The heroine Wirt developed in the initial volumes was an assertive young woman who didn't hesitate to oppose or contradict adults. Wirt often said, in later years, that Stratemeyer was "bitterly disappointed" with her early manuscripts because he felt she had overstepped the bounds of propriety; he found Nancy too "flip" and aggressive for a girl her age.[8] Stratemeyer accepted Wirt's manuscripts nonetheless. The Nancy Drew breeder set (the first few volumes of a new series, released simultaneously to stimulate reader interest) was published in April of 1930 and found an enthusiastic audience. Ironically, Stratemeyer did not witness the fruition of what would be his greatest triumph; he died of pneumonia less than two weeks later. His daughters, Harriet Stratemeyer Adams (1892–1982) and Edna Stratemeyer (1895–1974), soon took over the operations of the Syndicate and continued to employ Wirt as Nancy Drew's primary ghostwriter while they provided her with outlines and edited her manuscripts.

Wirt wrote twenty-three of the first thirty volumes of the Nancy Drew series. Although different ghosts wrote the other seven (non-consecutive) volumes, the template Wirt created of a self-possessed and autonomous heroine was sufficiently secure to ensure that Nancy's portrayal stayed consistent in volumes ghosted by others. By 1943 Edna Stratemeyer Squier, who had plotted many of the early Drews, had married and retired from the Syndicate. Wirt stopped writing for the Syndicate in the early 1950s, and Harriet S. Adams assumed complete control of Nancy Drew shortly thereafter, writing the subsequent volumes until her death in 1982. Tensions had complicated the relationship between Adams and Wirt for some years prior to Wirt's departure; Adams considered Wirt's Nancy Drew to be "too bossy, too positive," and she thus introduced a tamer and less autonomous heroine. As Wirt later recalled, "My Nancy was not Mrs. Adams' Nancy. Mrs. Adams was an entirely different person—she was more cultured and refined. I was a rough and tumble newspaper person who had to earn a living and was out in the world. My Nancy was making her way in life and trying to compete and have fun along the way. We just had two different Nancys."[9]

Under Adams's authorship Nancy Drew remained an active and impossibly accomplished heroine. But she became more group-oriented and less autonomous, more deferential to adults (particularly men in uniforms), and less assertive or defiant. Indeed, Adams's vision of appropriate femininity echoed the adherence to conformity and docile female behavior celebrated in 1950s mass culture. Adams's alterations appeared not only in the new volumes she wrote, but also in revisions of Wirt's texts undertaken in 1959, when the Syndicate launched a lengthy project of overhauling old volumes of its most famous series to update them for a new generation of readers. These "cut downs," as the Syndicate staff termed them, sometimes merely shortened the original novels and sometimes completely replaced them with new plots while keeping the original titles intact. By 1977, the last of Mildred Wirt's original texts had been replaced by revisions.[10] Clearly, there have been many different Nancy Drews over the decades. In this study I focus solely on "classic Nancy," the heroine as she first appeared in 1930 and as she stayed for twenty years, plotted by the Stratemeyer sisters and largely ghostwritten by Wirt. This is the Nancy who set the course for the series' entire trajectory, and with whom readers first fell in love. Subsequent references to the series' author will name her as Carolyn Keene, a composite identity.

Despite Nancy's popularity among children, she received a chillier response from some adults. Formulaic series books grew out of the lowbrow dime-novel genre, and thus did not qualify as "good literature" in the eyes of children's educators and librarians. Nancy Drew debuted during a period when professional educators had been waging an active campaign against the dangers of "trashy" children's books for many years. This trend, part of the larger movement of Progressive social reform, arguably began with Anthony Comstock's renowned blood-and-thunder tract *Traps for the Young* (1883). It intensified exponentially in the 1910s and 1920s, not coincidentally the same period in which the fields of children's literature and educational theory became increasingly professionalized. Children's librarians and schoolteachers routinely published essays lambasting series books as sensationalist, two-dimensional twaddle that damaged children's intellectual development.[11]

Stratemeyer's books were targets of reformers' zeal for many years, but he sidestepped the dangers of such campaigns through shrewd marketing tactics. He persuaded his publishers to reduce the standard price of a series book to a mere fifty cents, enabling children to buy books out of their allowances.[12] By appealing directly to the hearts and wallets of young customers, Stratemeyer circumvented the need for adults' involvement in children's reading. The intellectual niceties over which educators fretted were immaterial to children; as Stratemeyer boasted in 1927, "Any writer who has the young for an audience can snap his fingers at all the other critics. To the average boy a book is either dandy or punk."[13] The general consensus found Stratemeyer's books dandy, and his loyal readership rewarded him with stellar sales; by the time of his death, Stratemeyer had a personal fortune exceeding half a million dollars, in addition to the millions he had generated for his publishers.[14]

The fervency of public debates about children's series books had somewhat dissipated by the 1930s, but the topic did not vanish. In 1935, a teacher of library science complained that series books offer shallow, predictable characters that "have no living equivalent," and employ such a limited and repetitive vocabulary that they demand no intellectual engagement from young readers. "Overdoses of this type of reading," she asserted, "result in mental laziness which will, if not taken in hand, prevent the reader from ever finishing a book which requires any effort whatsoever."[15] Similar articles continued to pepper the journals of educators, librarians, parents, and publishers for many years. These condemnations were hardly uniform, however; the inscriptions of many a 1930s-era Nancy Drew book prove that adults—parents, aunts, grandparents—frequently gave children these books as gifts.[16] Public libraries, however, did not widely stock Nancy Drew until the 1960s or later. As one bookstore employee said of the Drew series in 1975, "They are discouraged by librarians and teachers but the 10-year-olds still buy them like hotcakes."[17] Edward Stratemeyer's marketing tactics continued, long after his death, to let children afford the books they loved without relying on adult assistance.

The concept of what children can afford becomes more complicated when we consider that Nancy Drew debuted in the first year of the Depression, when even fifty cents could represent a fortune to some children. Historian John Modell has noted that adolescents' recreation and leisure commodities, which had proliferated during the affluent 1920s, were often the first things to go when families had to trim their budgets. In more financially secure homes, however, children's recreational funds might have stayed intact: "Families that suffered no direct economic deprivation seem, on the whole, to have maintained their prior consumption habits."[18] Series books' relative affordability to a middle-class child remained a crucial factor in their sales. Nancy Drew books also circulated informally; children often traded and borrowed each other's series books, so that a girl's exposure to Nancy Drew could surpass the volumes she personally owned.

By 1932 Nancy had achieved an exceptional level of success. *Publishers Weekly* noted, with some surprise, that her sales controverted the truism that boys' books routinely outsold girls'; the Drew titles were "the topnotch sellers of the many bestseller juvenile series," including the most popular boys' books.[19] Two years later *Fortune* magazine surveyed the lucrative industry of series-book production, highlighting the work of the Stratemeyer Syndicate. Here, too, mention is made of Nancy Drew's outperforming even Bomba the Jungle Boy, another Syndicate property and the best-selling of all boys' series: "In the six weeks of the last Christmas season Macy's sold 6,000 of the ten titles of Nancy Drew compared with 3,750 for the runner-up, Bomba, which had fifteen titles to choose from. . . . [H]eroine Nancy Drew outsells them all, male and female."[20] The Christmas of 1933 was one of the harder Christmases of the Depression, too early as yet for Roosevelt's relief efforts to have made a widespread impact. For Nancy Drew to sell 6,000 units in one store during a period of general privation is an impressive feat, made more impressive still by Nancy's single-handed disruption of the dominance of boys' books, and by her accomplishment of these acts in a climate of some cultural disapproval.

What gave this series such unprecedented appeal? The basic Nancy Drew formula fits the pattern established in several previous Syndicate series. Nancy lives in the fictional Midwestern town of River Heights with a housekeeper named Hannah and her father, Carson Drew, a handsome widower and former district attorney who has gone into private practice. Like all of Stratemeyer's protagonists, the Drews are well-to-do but not ostentatiously rich, and Carson supplies his daughter with any items she needs or wants—including a roadster which older readers often remember as the greatest symbol of Nancy's freedom. Her car not only allows her mobility, it frees her from the chafing ritual of begging her father for permission to use his car. When villains disable Nancy's vehicle, or when Carson simply feels like pampering her, he buys her a newer model.

As her automobile gives her freedom on the road, so her family structure gives her freedom at home. Although he wholly supports her financially, Carson Drew treats Nancy more like a peer than a daughter. He trusts her judgment and lets her do as she pleases, warning her only to "be careful" when she sets off to trail a violent criminal. Nancy benefits, too, from the absence of a mother. As Walt Disney would later do, Edward Stratemeyer made many of his protagonists semi-orphans. While the Syndicate's series for little children usually include both parents, in the adolescent series mothers are often either dead or extremely marginal to the action. Teenagers, in order to effect the kind of perfect agency which Stratemeyer excelled at portraying, needed freedom of movement. Mothers were seen as a restraining force whose apron strings bound the child to home and hearth, while fathers in Stratemeyer series are all prominent professionals, and as such, they bridge their children's journey from the confines of the home into worldly accomplishments.

In the case of Nancy Drew the absence of a mother also loosens gender-related constraints. Carolyn Heilbrun has observed that mothers often function as teachers of patriarchal imperatives to young girls; it is the mother who tells her daughter "to cool it, be nice, let the boys win, don't say what you mean. Mothers have long been . . . those who prepare their daughters to take their proper place in the patriarchy," which explains why adventurous literary heroines are often motherless. "The lack of a mother bestows possibility on a young girl."[21] Mrs. Drew's death during her daughter's childhood frees Nancy to grow up as the lady of the house, the mother of her own identity, and the apple of her father's eye. Proud of his daughter's maturity and acumen, Carson Drew consults her for advice on his law cases and asks her to assist clients who have mysteries that need solving. But helpless crime victims find Nancy even without her father's referrals, for her success ensures that her name appears frequently in the local newspapers. She has unlimited time to help these people, since (without explanation) she does not attend school at the age of sixteen, nor is she employed. Magically, she bears no responsibilities beyond those she considers fun: solving mysteries.

In addition to these heady combinations of mature responsibility and total freedom, Nancy enjoys an array of skills that blur the boundaries between genders. She can throw a hard punch, fix anything from flat tires to stalled outboard motors, and handle a gun like a man, but she also flawlessly performs such traditionally feminine pursuits as nursing, ballet dancing, sewing, playing the piano, and taming naughty children with the demeanor of a cheerful governess. She dresses in fashionable "frocks," remaining impeccably elegant even while fighting off burly thugs twice her age. Not above using feminine charms to gain her ends (she's capable of eyelash-batting and even *faux* fainting when necessary), she nonetheless eschews the type of silliness that preoccupies other girls, who are often drawn as stereotypically emotional, giggly, and prone to gossip.

In her social life, too, Nancy enjoys traditionally feminine prerogatives while evading their limitations. Early volumes establish her as properly heterosexual by sending her on the occasional date with one handsome boy or another, but those dates do not impede the action-driven plots; their descriptions are markedly brief, compared to those of her sleuthing activities. In the series' seventh volume, *The Clue in the Diary* (1932), the Stratemeyer sisters introduced a permanent boyfriend for Nancy: Ned Nickerson, a handsome college football player. But like Nancy's earlier beaux, Ned plays only a minor role in the series. In typical girls' books, heroines with boyfriends often devote considerable thought to their romantic relationships, but in the Drew series it is Ned, not Nancy, who thinks most often about these issues. When Ned attempts to whisper sweet nothings to her in the moonlight, Nancy wriggles away to pursue clues. Like Carson Drew, Ned Nickerson is an unrealistic presence; rather than resenting his girlfriend's widespread fame and her all-consuming hobby, he willingly follows her lead and never complains: "You tell me what to do and I'll obey orders with no questions asked."[22] Ned functions as something of an accoutrement for Nancy— one of the many perquisites an attractive girl enjoys—to highlight the ideal perfection of her life, while attesting to her properly "normal" sexuality. Similarly, Nancy's two best friends serve as foil characters who heighten her atypical femininity, paradoxically, by making her seem more average. Bess Marvin and George Fayne, female cousins, represent polar oppositions: Bess is frilly, plump, and squeamish, while George is a blunt and athletic tomboy, proud of her masculine name. Nancy nestles comfortably between these caricatures as a golden mean, and thus models a highly idealized femininity that magically disguises itself as average.

One of the most pervasive weapons in the arsenal of misogyny over the centuries has been the accusation of women's changeability: in discourses ranging from art to medicine, women's bodies and minds have historically been defined as unstable, permeable, and susceptible to influence, thus lacking firm integrity. Nancy Drew avoids these stereotypical liabilities because of her exceptional self-containment. Her body, thoughts, and feelings retain their original shape at all times, so that she exhibits perfect integrity both without and within. This static portrayal sometimes makes Nancy appear more robotic than human. Throughout the series she is often knocked out cold, poisoned, thrown down stairs, drugged, toppled by falling trees, and even struck by lightning, but always manages a full recovery almost immediately. Her risible lack of realistic biology has prompted one writer to marvel sarcastically that Nancy never sustains brain damage, despite being "bludgeoned into unconsciousness . . . enough to reduce her to a lifetime of hanging around Stillman's Gym looking for odd jobs."[23] As with her brain, so with her mind and heart: Nancy avoids vulnerabilities of thought and emotion, displaying no insecurities, no jealousy or petulance, infrequent jubilation, and no grief (on a few occasions she finds herself on the verge of tears, but she never openly sobs). In contradiction of the old stereotype of women as gossips, Nancy keeps her own counsel and tightly locks the gates to the information she possesses; even her closest friends are rarely privy to her thoughts as she gathers clues and forms hypotheses. Emotionally, biologically, and intellectually, Nancy skirts the charges of leaky instability that patriarchal cultures have long leveled against women.

Keene's portrayals of Bess and George further heighten Nancy's perfection in this regard, for both exhibit some facet of the old associations between women, hyperemotionalism, and bodily excess or instability. George, although described as "athletic," has none of Nancy's grace; she is forever spraining or bruising some part of herself, revealing a body far more vulnerable than Nancy's. Often called "blunt," George rushes to express her strong, and often ill-considered, opinions. Bess, an overweight sensualist, loves the pleasures offered by food, physical comfort, and (chaste) flirtations with handsome boys. These proclivities limit her physical endurance and her willingness to take risks, making her a hindrance to the disciplined demands of sleuthing, and her tendencies toward sentimentality and fear often override her logic. This triumvirate of characters flatters Nancy by comparison and suggests that the ideal girl is she with no vulnerabilities, no appetites, no overt feelings, and perfect self-discipline.

Nancy's relative inhumanity led some girls to prefer series with more believable heroines, like the popular Judy Bolton mysteries (1932–1967). But while Nancy Drew had many competitors, none achieved anything like her success, suggesting that her lack of realism might actually have helped her sales more than hindered them. Nancy is drawn so sketchily that a great deal of room is left for readers' identification with her, an important ingredient of the relationship between Nancy and her fans. Rather than portraying the specificity of a realistic girl, Keene constructs Nancy through a series of hints, like the hasty yet suggestive lines of a caricaturist. What emerges is a heroine just specific enough to be recognizable, but not so specific as to discourage a girl from projecting herself into the character: as Kathleen Chamberlain puts it, "What young readers see in Nancy is not themselves as they are, but as they *would* be. . . . Nancy is to readers a mannequin that they can dress in their own fantasies."[24] Completely outside a normal girl's life, she offers readers the potent fantasy of living adventurously without the familiar hindrances of societal conventions or the limitations inherent in girlish weaknesses of body or mind. Given that this series thrived during the same years that saw increasing advancements in women's roles, it is no wonder that many have attributed the series' success to its supposed illustration of feminism.

Nancy Drew as Feminist Icon

Since the popularization of second-wave feminism in the late 1960s and 1970s, the most consistent theme of Nancy Drew commentary, both journalistic and scholarly, has been the celebration of her as a role model for nascent feminists; *Ms.* magazine hailed "Good Old Nancy Drew" in 1974, as did countless other periodicals.[25] But such an interpretation obscures the highly conservative elements of Nancy Drew's character, which are wholly or partly antithetical to feminism, and which have been just as popular among readers as the more progressive elements. Furthermore, generalizations about Nancy's feminism misrepresent that philosophy through a faulty comparison, and also misdirect our attention from the more salient message of this series, which is not feminism *per se* but rather integrity and personhood, a concept I will explain further on.

The popular definition of feminism purveyed most often in American culture is the belief that women can be competent and independent. Nancy Drew conforms perfectly to this vague description, which is why so many women have credited Nancy with inspiring their ambitions.[26] When the Syndicate's publishers threw a fiftieth anniversary party for Nancy Drew in 1980, the event drew many prominent women who reminisced about the feminist-friendly messages Nancy had imparted to them. Ruth Bader Ginsburg, then dean at Columbia Law School and later a Supreme Court justice, recalled fondly that Nancy "was adventuresome, daring and her boyfriend was a much more passive type than she was."[27] In 1996 one middle-aged member of a Nancy Drew fan club told the *Los Angeles Times* that "[r]eading Nancy Drew gave a lot of women my age hope. . . . [It] opened the door for us to be doctors, to be lawyers, to be professional people."[28] Authors Carole Kismaric and Marvin Heiferman note in their history of Nancy Drew that she has "always imparted a radical idea to girls—that it's okay to take action, be smart, compete, talk back, fight, succeed. That message has kept Nancy popular among girls for decades. For despite all the talk about equality . . . girls still have to walk on eggshells when it comes to asserting themselves."[29]

Kismaric and Heiferman's claim that Nancy imparts a "radical idea" to readers deserves interrogation, for it reveals a selective memory: Nancy "talked back" and "fought" far more before 1950 than after. Even in the earliest volumes, conservative positions on age, gender, class, and race counteract the radical autonomy Nancy displays. Indeed, for every reader who champions Nancy's debut as "A Moment in Feminist History,"[30] another's praise rests on retrograde gender values. Noted author Susan Brownmiller told journalists that she had "drooled over Nancy Drew in her pre-feminist stage. 'She was a winner,' Brownmiller remembers. 'I mean her friend George dressed like a boy and Bess was fat, so you didn't want to be her. Nancy had the car, Nancy had the boyfriend.'"[31] This revealing comment scolds the failed femininities of Nancy's friends, suggesting that the appeal of identifying with Nancy rested upon such stereotypically gendered signifiers as her consumerism, her slenderness and fashion sense, and her successful heterosexuality.

A different kind of retrograde femininity informs the remarks of another adult fan who disparages the alterations made to Nancy's character in the 1990s spin-off series: "They have changed Nancy Drew in a frightening way, taking away her manners, her roadster, her white gloves."[32] This reader values Nancy not because she fought patriarchy, but rather because she *supported* it as a proper young lady with gracious etiquette and prim sartorial habits. In fact, the entire environment of the Nancy Drew series conforms to a model of conservative, upper-class femininity, in which refined ladies attend flower shows and take luncheon at charming old inns. As Bobbie Ann Mason has observed, the series' settings "are all feminine, domestic, aristocratic, slightly Gothic—quaint reminders of a traditional, Victorian, idealized world."[33] These settings complicate one's ability to read the series as progressive or modern; it presents a largely backward-looking milieu, more appropriate to Phyllis Schlafly than to Gloria Steinem. But perhaps the most potent suggestion of Nancy's inherent conservatism appears in the remarks of Representative Joseph Minish of New Jersey, who praised Nancy Drew (a product of his home state) in his address to the U.S. House of Representatives in 1980, the series' golden anniversary year: "Nancy Drew has not succumbed to the increasing social pressures of a teenage world, a world in which traditional morality is unpopular and old fashioned. . . . Harriet Adams has given us an unflinching character of solid moral fiber."[34] The "traditional morality" so enthusiastically celebrated here is one of the social codes that feminists have often resisted because of its repressive effects on women's life choices. Nancy Drew's rigidly Victorian sexuality hinders our interpreting her as a truly feminist role model, despite her competence and achievements.

Although some commentators have noted the paradox of Nancy's feminist qualities and her concessions to conservative morality, few have seen the biggest fallacy in calling the Nancy Drew Mysteries a feminist series: Nancy is the *only* female who embodies multiple admirable traits.

Not only Bess and George, but all women in the series, lack the qualities that distinguish Nancy. The often female beneficiaries of Nancy's good works embody the familiar stereotypes of women as helpless, passive, and easily frightened. Although Keene does not overtly censure these victims, she implies that their passivity and timidity make them weak. Alternatively, they may have some other glaring flaw, as in the case of Mrs. Chatham in *The Quest of the Missing Map* (1942), who arouses scorn by being a careless mother to her bratty child. Other females may be similarly bad mothers, materialistic social climbers, or scatterbrained simpletons who impede Nancy's sleuthing. Female criminals are the only women who exhibit shrewdness or initiative, but the uses to which they put these traits naturally disqualify them for authorial approval. Nor are these women particularly competent; they are often drawn as the less-clever accomplices of male masterminds.[35] This series has nothing kind to say about women at large, for they embody incompleteness or one-sidedness—all are "too" something, or "not enough" something—in order to heighten Nancy's extremely unrealistic balancing of multiple subject positions. Neither women as a sex nor any style of femininity (other than Nancy's impossible one) is championed.

Feminism, in one of its most basic tenets, recognizes gender inequities as a systemic problem that affects women collectively; but the Nancy Drew series does not see its heroine as part of a collective. Instead it emphasizes her splendid exceptionalism, celebrating her in part by opposing to her the flaws and failures that tarnish other female characters.[36] Thus, a few commentators—usually academics—have been canny enough to observe that Nancy Drew is hardly a feminist role model. As one said of her, "A liberated woman? Absolutely! But the Nancy Drew series is no feminist handbook. Nancy could [not] care less about the general status of women; she is apart from the society she moves in."[37] Although Adams and Wirt (born in 1892 and 1905, respectively) both balanced full-time careers with marriage and motherhood decades before such combinations were common for middle- or upper-class white women, both of them refused to identify themselves as feminists. Both, however, consciously strove to impart some inspiration to their young readers that would encourage girls toward increased personal and social agency. Nancy reflects her creators' beliefs that women could be *agents*—an idea compatible, but not synonymous, with modern feminism.

The Desire to Inspire

Harriet Adams, educated at elite Wellesley College and later the wife of an investment banker from a prominent old Dutch family, led the life of a high-society matron while running the Stratemeyer Syndicate. Her work for various women's clubs, charities, Christian groups, and local Republican committees expressed her belief in a sort of "civic motherhood"—a model of female citizenship predicated on *noblesse oblige*, in which women influence the public sphere by uplifting the less fortunate and performing acts of philanthropy. Adams frequently told interviewers that she used the Wellesley College motto to inform the character of Nancy Drew: "Non ministrari, sed ministrare" ("Not to be ministered unto, but to minister").[38] This vision of the ideal woman as a sort of Lady Bountiful replicates old-guard attitudes about women's roles as nurturers; though Adams supported notions of women's public achievement, she perceived the issue more in accord with the ideas of the first-wave feminists of the turn of the century, whose vision of proper womanhood remained conservatively focused on the white privileged classes, and often on maternally inflected definitions of female agency. After 1970, interviewers frequently asked Adams if she had deliberately fashioned Nancy as a feminist icon. Adams acknowledged that Nancy appears liberated, but disavowed any intentional support in her series for "women's lib," as second-wave feminism was often called then: "I approve of it up to a point, but I think they go too far," she told the *New York Times* in 1977.[39] In 1980 she elaborated further: "I'm all for women so long as they are old-fashioned in their family lives, which means having children and bringing them up strictly. I think many feminists overdo it, though I do think women have a place in this world and that mentally, they are equal to men."[40]

Mildred Wirt had a less gentrified childhood than Adams and began early to prepare herself for a writing career. She published her first story at the age of thirteen and later became the first student to earn a master's degree in journalism at the University of Iowa. In addition to her many years of writing children's books (her own, as well as the Syndicate's), she maintained her career as a journalist until her death at the age of ninety-six. Wirt displayed an early ambition in her leisure activities as well, enjoying competitive sports throughout most of her life. Recalling her youth, Wirt once said that "girls were discouraged from all sorts of athletics, and I fought that tooth and toenail right from the start, because I felt that girls should be able to do the same things that boys did."[41] But despite her progressive views on women's professional and athletic opportunities, Wirt denied crafting Nancy as any kind of political comment, saying that she simply wanted to give girls a genuinely adventurous heroine. Commenting in 1998 on feminists, Wirt sniffed that "they confuse freedom with license," perhaps referring to their pursuit of sexual and reproductive freedoms for women. When asked how she felt about the many feminists who had adopted her as an early inspiration, Wirt said mildly, "They can adopt me if they like. I don't adopt them."[42] Nonetheless, Wirt endowed Nancy with traits many have found compatible with feminist philosophies. Wirt once said of Nancy, "Although I never consciously used her to launch a campaign for women's equality [she] always inspir[ed] courage, determination, and a driving desire for accomplishment."[43] Her words prove that "inspiring" girls was part of her mission, and Adams's public recital of the Wellesley College motto proves the same about her; while her vision of a "ministering" angel was more Victorian than modern, it allowed a construction of Nancy that showed a young girl having a positive effect on the world instead of passively sitting at home.

This conscious commitment to inspiring readers could have a tremendous effect on the portrayal of a heroine, as the following comparison suggests. In 1934 the Syndicate launched the Dana Girls Mysteries (1934–1978), deliberately crafted to exploit the success of Nancy Drew (like Nancy, the Dana sisters are teenage sleuths, and they were published under the pseudonym "Carolyn Keene" to ensure that young customers saw the connection). Yet despite moderate success, the Dana Girls never inspired readers' passion the way Nancy did, perhaps because their authors never found the characters particularly interesting, let alone potential inspirations for young readers. Harriet Adams assigned the Dana Girls breeder set to Leslie McFarlane, the regular ghostwriter for the Hardy Boys series. In his autobiography, McFarlane later recounted his distaste for the new assignment: "I felt almighty foolish about becoming Carolyn Keene, but my wife promised she wouldn't tell anyone. So I spent a couple of months banging away at the Dana sisters. Perhaps the expression is indelicate. Nobody ever banged the Dana girls—at least, not for the record."[44] Embarrassed by having to adopt a female persona, McFarlane makes the Dana sisters the butt of a sexual joke to assuage the threat to his masculine pride. Since sexual humor obviously could not appear in children's books, McFarlane's contempt manifests in the finished product as simple boredom; he wrote the Dana sisters as flat, dull characters. Adams quickly reassigned the series to Mildred Wirt, but the Danas' flaccid personae were already established, and Wirt, too, took little interest in them; "I never felt the same kinship with the Danas that I did with Nancy," she later recalled, asserting that the pleasure of writing Nancy came partly from knowing that she had a blank canvas to work on, without any trace marks left by previous artists.[45]

The kinship Wirt felt for Nancy added a crucial emphasis to her desire to "inspire" girls; she thus produced a heroine who addressed a gap in girls' experience. Harriet Adams understood that gap as well. Despite their different educations and class positions, both women saw Nancy as a means to effect their agendas with young readers; whether believing that "girls should be able to do the same things that boys" do, as Wirt said, or only that "women have a place in the world," as Adams said, both women wanted Nancy Drew to model an active and efficacious mode of living. The ultimate reason Nancy Drew made such a cultural impact is not that she was a feminist, but that she was a full person, a condition her readers could not attain so easily.

Personhood

When women celebrate Nancy's "independence," they are referring to her agency and the concomitant qualities of full personhood which underlie, but do not solely define, feminism as a philosophy or political movement. Personhood is a condition that allows an individual the freedom to draw the shape and boundaries of her own self-definitions, and, more importantly, to demand that those definitions receive respect from others. A woman's personhood can exist fully only in a society that supports it; in her own mind, she might see *herself* as a competent and self-determining agent, but unless her society shares that view, she will not enjoy real freedom in shaping her life. Legal theorist Drucilla Cornell states that women continue to suffer inequality because society's governing institutions do not imagine women's having an anterior personhood equal to men's. As she argues, "Each of us is a unique person . . . whose integrity and freedom must be recognized by the law and by other basic institutions. We all have equal intrinsic value and should be recognized as capable of generating our own evaluations of our life plans. Equal intrinsic value is . . . an aspect of the politically conceived free person."[46] She grounds her argument in a discussion of Kant's statement that human freedom "can be expressed in the following formula: no one can compel me to be happy in accordance with his conception of the welfare of others, for each may seek his happiness in whatever way he sees fit."[47]

Because Cornell theorizes the preconditions for just treatment under the law, her arguments clearly apply more to women than to girls, for legal minority already comprises a certain exclusion from equality in the civic sphere. Minors, of course, do not have the same freedoms of self-determination that adults have. Nonetheless, Cornell's arguments can inform our readings of girlhood in cultural texts, for her thesis expands upon an idea long familiar to feminists, as expressed in the popular slogan "Feminism is the radical notion that women are people." The field of youth studies might similarly be said to rest on the radical notion that children are people. Cornell's assertion that one's "integrity and freedom must be recognized by the law and by other basic institutions" has never applied to children in our culture, where institutions like schools, churches, youth groups, and even the family do not construct the child as "free" or as having the right to "seek his happiness in whatever way he sees fit," in Kant's words. As noted earlier, the impressive sales of Stratemeyer's books, in which all teen heroes are superhumans, suggests children's marginal status: the prisoners were dreaming of freedom. In Nancy Drew, readers found "a young person who suffers none of the humiliation our society hands youth."[48]

As Nancy's authoritative power contradicts our expectations of youth, so it does our gendered expectations. Kant's statement about the right to seek happiness imagines the political subject as male. For a female child, the problem of subjectivity is compounded when adult "wisdom" asks her to adopt essentialist notions of gender roles, a demand routinely made in girls' fiction. Edward Stratemeyer's success proved that children of both sexes like to read about powerful fantasy figures, but those figures tended to populate his boys' series more than his pre–Nancy Drew girls' series. He was not alone; in children's literature generally, books for and about boys teemed with potent agency while books for and about girls seldom did. Sally McNall notes a recurring theme of pragmatism in interwar children's books, whereby young protagonists struggle to accept the realities and requirements of their impending adulthoods. For heroines of girls' novels, such pragmatism often shaped plots about girls' awkward transition from childish, self-centered tomboys to graceful, other-directed women. In the 1936 novel *Roller Skates*, the young heroine approaches this hurdle with some hesitancy. Her older brother instructs her in the ways of patriarchy: "You've reached the point where the poet says childhood and womanhood meet. Lots of things can happen to you. . . . You can stay a fighting, disagreeable hoyden, or you can grow in understanding, in lovely ways, in a gentle giving-in that won't hurt you."[49] This brother's notion of what hurts and what doesn't fails to consider girls who might not wish to "give in" to anyone.

Roller Skates is hardly unique; such moral lessons abound in girls' fiction from the early to mid-twentieth century. In just one example, L. M. Montgomery's classic Anne of Green Gables series (1908–1939) portrays in its early volumes an impish, brainy, and athletic heroine who does just as she pleases, much to adults' chagrin. By the time she matures, however, much of her adventuresome (and somewhat subversive) auton-omy has faded, gradually replaced by stasis and mawkishness in her roles as a wife and mother. In countless similar novels, young heroines learn that leaving childhood means reorienting themselves toward the care and nurture of others, abandoning their dreams of self-fulfilling adventure. While boys' books encouraged them to go out in the world and make a name for themselves, girls' books told them to go back into the home and give up their name for someone else's. Bearing that in mind, let's return to the Kantian concept of freedom: "No one can compel me to be happy in accordance with his conception of the welfare of others, for each may seek his happiness in whatever way he sees fit." It's a pity no one required that girls' authors read Kant before sitting down to their typewriters.

Nancy does not suffer the same fate as typical heroines; her boyfriend Ned may drop hints about marriage, but Keene keeps him on a short tether, never allowing his fantasies of domestic bliss to stick to Nancy. Indeed, Nancy dodges all projections, domestic and otherwise. At no point is her behavior successfully constrained by others' definitions of her sex or her age. A frequent device pits Nancy against an unpleasant adult who makes the grave error of mistaking her for a normal girl— with all the assumptions of triviality and expectations of deference that adults project onto that identity. When such conflicts occur the experi-enced Drew reader knows, with immense pleasure, what will happen next: Nancy will draw herself up to the full height of her dignity and reveal, coolly and articulately, that her interlocutor has grossly under-estimated her. The following exchange, from *Nancy's Mysterious Letter* (1932), is characteristic. Old Mr. Dixon, the kindly neighborhood mail-man, has had his mail pouch stolen from him while on duty. Wishing to help, Nancy accompanies him to the office of the postmaster, who angrily berates the elderly man.

"Mr. Cutter," [Nancy] said to the postmaster. . . . "I don't see that your scolding and shouting help matters in the least. I came here to help. I have a brief description of a suspect, but we are wasting time now."

Cutter's eyes nearly popped out of his head.

"Of all the impudence in the world!" he roared. "You dare to tell me how to run my office and how to maintain discipline? Who are you, I'd like to know. Miss Wise Lady from Know-it-all, hey?" . . .

Nancy was fully capable of taking her own part. She was not in the least ruffled by the postmaster's rudeness. Waiting until he had finished, she merely asked:

"Are you interested in the description of the thief?"[50]

When the disagreeable man finally learns her identity, he is properly awed: "You mean—THE Nancy Drew?" Cutter asks, and changes his demeanor accordingly. Scenes like these provide great satisfaction for Nancy's young readers, who are not likely ever to effect such comeuppance against male officials who belittle them. Keene allows no one to underestimate Nancy Drew; projections ricochet off her the way bullets ricochet off Wonder Woman's magic bracelets.

Is this an honest depiction of life, a realistic example of what treatment girls can expect as they grow into their teens? Surely not, and that is one reason why educators and librarians have faulted the series. But it also explains readers' love for the character. As someone who enjoys the authority to control the definitions of her identity and to have her self-formulated plans respected, Nancy is the kind of free subject imagined by Cornell. She thus offers her readers a vicarious experience denied to them in their real lives. Mildred Wirt used a different formulation of this idea in explaining the staggering fame of her protagonist: "Nancy was popular, and remains so, primarily because she personifies the dream image which exists within most teen-agers."[51] Nancy invites her readers, "pretend to be me," and there is substantial evidence that many girls have accepted the invitation, locating and strengthening a dream-image of themselves through Nancy's adventures.

Some of that evidence appears in the magazine and newspaper articles about Nancy Drew that proliferated after the 1960s. Writing for *Glamour* in 1979, Sally Helgeson ponders the questions "Who Was Your Girlhood Heroine? . . . Have You Let Her Down?" Helgeson recalls patterning herself after Nancy Drew "with fervor" while in elementary school, keeping a journal that catalogued Nancy's extraordinary skills and attempting to develop them in herself. "I shared the secrets of my Nancy diary with a friend who informed me that she thought it was dumb. . . . I knew right then that something had been lost between us forever. She was content with the real world. I was not." Other girls echoed Helgeson's passion: "I've met a number of women . . . who modeled themselves on Nancy Drew. [One] confessed to me that at the age of twelve she used to lead whole slumber parties out onto the street at midnight with the hope of performing rescue missions—although who might be in need of rescue was never defined."[52] Such girlhood memories speak directly to the issue of agency. Girls, in most popular narratives, need rescuing; Nancy's readers wanted to rescue. Whereas many critics have been satisfied to call Nancy Drew "wish fulfillment," this trivializing phrase fails to record the high stakes of those wishes. These are no run-of-the-mill daydreams; they constitute nothing less than one's ability to imagine herself as a competent and important presence in the world. Helgeson's question about "letting down" our girlhood heroines suggests that a woman must strive to keep faith with her dreaming twelve-year-old self, in spite of the many blows the "real world" will level against her as she matures. Reading about a heroine like Nancy Drew isn't merely a pleasant pastime; it can be a training ground where girls develop the self-images that might sustain them for the rest of their lives.

This training ground—a sort of safe haven for trying on different dreams and identities—brings us to another aspect of Cornell's theory, the imaginary domain. Because women's inequality is so tied to culture's oppressive definitions of what "female" means, a woman's imagination can help her to visualize herself as she *might* be without those projections: "The imaginary domain gives to the individual person, and to her only, the right to claim who she is . . . through her own representation of her sexuate being. Such a right necessarily makes her the morally and legally recognized source of narration and resymbolization of what the meaning of her sexual difference is for her."[53] One must be able to imagine herself as free of sex-related oppression before any such freedom can actually be gained. Cultural critic bell hooks, whom Cornell quotes, makes a similar case in her reminiscence of her own abusive childhood and the imaginative measures necessary to recover from it: "[t]he ritual of inventing a character who could not only speak through me but also for me, was an important location of recovery for me." Cornell describes hooks's invented character as "an ideal representative for [hooks], the imaginary healer, the therapist who could see and hear herself differently." Because hooks's imaginary alter ego existed outside the sphere of real life, she "could come to embody the self not ensnared in the matrix of abuse."[54] The Nancy Drew series offers precisely this kind of imaginary domain. By projecting themselves into Nancy, many girls have partially healed the wounds received in the "matrix of abuse," the cycle of patronizing belittlement, projection, and dismissal in which adult- and male-centered culture ensnares its daughters. I should clarify that I do not mean to equate the abuse suffered by working-class African American girls, which bell hooks was, and middle-class white girls, which most of Nancy's readers are. But, unfortunately, there are several abusive matrices; female childhood is a damning enough condition even for those with privileged color and class affiliations.

Cornell describes the imaginary domain through a spatial metaphor of interiority: "the boundaries of individuation [are] the person's to 'draw.' The 'space' in which those boundaries are personalized and represented is the sanctuary of the imaginary domain."[55] Space and boundaries; bounded space. Too many have literalized Virginia Woolf's famous cry for "a room of one's own," says Cornell, who notes that the room is more psychic than literal. It is both, actually; Nancy Drew "draws" her own "boundaries of individuation," and the mysteries symbolize these boundaries not just in Nancy's character itself, but in the books' frequent use of small, confined spaces. The series is riddled with secret holes and hidden gaps like those under loose floorboards, in cupboards with false backs, or behind bricks that slip out of a wall. Such spaces are never meaningless; Keene imbues them with special numinosity, for they invariably contain "the key," the treasured clue upon whose revelation the solution of the mystery depends. The books' very titles use images of interiority to stimulate readers' interest: *The Hidden Staircase, The Clue in the Diary, The Clue of the Broken Locket, The Message in the Hollow Oak, The Mystery of the Brass-Bound Trunk, The Clue in the Jewel Box, The Clue in the Crumbling Wall, The Clue in the Old Album.*

Tellingly, the Stratemeyer Syndicate linked such images of precious interiority specifically with girlhood. Several of these titles evoke a traditionally feminine aesthetic of sentiment (diaries, lockets, jewel boxes, photo albums). By contrast, the titles for Nancy Drew's male counterparts, the Hardy Boys, evoke exteriors more than interiors: *The House on the Cliff, The Secret of the Old Mill, The Shore Road Mystery, The Mystery of Cabin Island, The Great Airport Mystery, Footprints under the Window.*[56] We can partly attribute that disparity to cultural stereotypes that associate men with the great outdoors, and women with domestic privacy. Interiority also, of course, symbolizes female sexuality more than male. Bobbie Ann Mason makes this point when citing the following exchange between Nancy and her friends as they investigate an attic wall:

"I can feel something with my fingers!" Nancy said in an excited voice. "A little bump in the wood!"

"Probably it's a knothole," George contributed skeptically.

"It's a tiny knob!" corrected Nancy. "Girls, I've found a secret compartment!"[57]

"With hilarious clarity," Mason jokes, "I see here the girls' mysteries as a celebration of masturbation!"[58]

Adams and Wirt might be surprised by that suggestion, but it does express a symbolic truth. If we think of the series' numerous secret compartments as symbols, not of vulvas but of the imaginary domain, we can see how such scenes might indeed catalyze a valuable "self-loving." In at least one documented case, a Nancy Drew reader's attraction to bounded space is linked explicitly with her need for a "location of recovery," in hooks's phrase. Betsy Caprio, examining Nancy Drew through the lens of analytical psychology, relates the story of an adult fan named Sue, who read the series initially in the 1940s: "I remember how the titles just got better and better. They were about lockets and albums and trunks and jewel boxes—all places where some secret could be hidden away. . . . Something in me really longs for whatever it was I found in Nancy Drew." Using Sue's memory of the books' titles and the bounded spaces they conjured, Caprio emphasizes the importance of what she calls "set-apart space . . . that youthful part of us concerned with autonomy." Nancy Drew gave Sue a sense of autonomous personhood that she lost when conforming to the culturally dictated script for women: "When I first read the Nancy Drew stories I tried to be just like her and, by high school, I really did begin to feel like my own person, like I knew who 'Sue' was. Then I got married." Like many women who suffered from "the problem with no name," as Betty Friedan famously put it, Sue followed the traditional expectations of wives and mothers and gradually lost her identity in tedious domestic routines: "[One night] I must have sobbed for two hours, and one of my thoughts was, 'whatever became of Sue?' I'd lost her. She's still not back." Caprio interprets Sue's longing for Nancy Drew as a means to regain her "psychological virginity," her autonomous selfhood.[59] Writing within different disciplines, Caprio and Cornell both gesture to the same idea: the most felicitous human condition is surety in one's sense of self and the ability to protect one's integrity and dignity within an inviolable sanctuary.

The phrase "psychological virginity" suggests a link between autonomous selfhood and a premarital identity. The literal virgin is she whose embodied boundaries have not yet been breached; the psychological virgin is she whose psychic boundaries—whose personhood—*cannot* be breached. Both literal and psychological virginity depend upon the sanctity of the interior space and require its vigilant protection. In subsequent chapters I will return to the idea of the virgin as an icon, for the texts examined in this study reveal a disturbing paradox: in American popular culture, the image of "the virgin" has had as much appeal for adult patriarchs as it has for young daughters, but for precisely opposite reasons. When girls crave Nancy Drew and other figures of solo, powerful females, it is psychological virginity that offers the most pleasures. When adult men produce and consume images of teenage girls, it is often girls' *physical* virginity that fascinates them, and the literal boundary—the hymen—becomes a fetish object. Throughout the twentieth century and into the twenty-first, the ubiquitous subtext of mass-culture narratives about teen girls is a desire to "get inside." By contrast, the most powerful appeal Nancy Drew offered girls was her insistence on keeping people out—resisting projections, thwarting assaults, and asserting rights that others must honor.

In its ideal form, and as it is sometimes practiced, the post-virginal state of marriage need not violate a woman's sense of autonomous personhood. But more than one adult Nancy Drew fan has found the imperatives of women's gender roles a fatal foe to her dignity. At a national Nancy Drew conference in Iowa in 1993, one participant, like Sue, placed Nancy and marriage at opposite ends of the personhood spectrum: "Around 1980, I was involved in a terrible marriage. On one winter night before I got out of my marriage, I went to my parents' house and I got all my Nancy Drew books. I reread every single one and it helped me feel *like a person* again, not like the crazed woman I had become."[60] Her poignant comments, like Sue's, demonstrate that Nancy Drew can function for readers as "the imaginary healer, the therapist who could hear and see [the girl] differently," as Cornell says. Instinctively drawn to Drew, these damaged women found in her stories the means to "feel like a person again." By imaginatively occupying the Drewian subject position, some women can address the damage done by a patriarchal culture that denies females the rights of full personhood.

Particularly for Nancy Drew's original audience, during the 1930s and 1940s, the notion that a girl could enjoy the benefits of the "free person" was a radical notion indeed. Why, then, did it not excite more critical comment? Why was the series' lack of literary merit its sole controversial aspect? The following section examines in detail the type of personhood Nancy Drew models, to suggest that she subordinates herself to hegemonic ideologies even while seeming to subvert them. Nancy may know how to "talk back [and] fight," but Keene's decisions about who deserves back-talk, and when, reveal that the personhood Nancy models so beautifully is anything but simple or unflawed. As with all its other characteristic paradoxes, the series employs impossible juxtapositions that allow Nancy to operate simultaneously as a freedom-fighter and as a dutiful daughter to oppressive regimes.

The Great White Hope

While many have found Nancy Drew a role model for girls' empowerment, no one concerned with issues of social justice or progressive policies can praise the series very far. Its messages about gender are hopelessly mixed, while those regarding class and race are more consistently negative. Characters in the Nancy Drew series generally fall into one of four categories: Nancy and her inner circle, crime victims whom Nancy helps, villains whom she conquers, and incidental characters. Without fail, minorities and the working class never appear in Nancy's inner circle, nor do they usually rank even as the virtuous victims.[61] When they appear at all, it is either as villains or as incidental characters, usually menial laborers. Keene uses dialogue to signal Otherness: non-whites and white ethnics usually speak in broad dialects, while Anglo villains reveal a contemptible lower-class status through their poor grammar. Keene sees the American-born middle and upper class of European descent as the only social category worthy of unalloyed admiration. Within that category, women receive authorial approval only to the extent that they personify the conservative codes of femininity prescribed in discourses of whiteness and wealth.

The series' fundamentally retrograde social politics camouflage its more progressive elements, allowing Nancy's image of powerful personhood to pass unchecked. At the same time, however, the radical notion of girls' personhood also becomes less radical when we realize how heavily it depends upon her negative interactions with the oppressed. These reviled characters in fact help to constitute Nancy's freedoms: she achieves her status as a full person partly through scenes that juxtapose her with characters who are less than persons. The ego strength Nancy models for readers, then, necessarily carries a toxic link to bigotry. While class consciousness pervades the Nancy Drew mysteries somewhat more intensely than other Syndicate series, a preference for whiteness and privilege is, in general, one of the family traits that identify Stratemeyer products. Before analyzing the operations of race and class hierarchies in specific Nancy Drew texts, it is worth considering the Syndicate's general legacy in these matters and the impact their decisions could have on young readers.

Edward Stratemeyer was quite democratic in his lampooning of ethnic Others; he sometimes used German figures with heavy accents as objects of ridicule, despite (or possibly because of) his own father's emigration from Germany. Like many in his day, Stratemeyer believed that being American meant scrubbing away any traits that derived from a different culture. Nonetheless, the steady stream of immigrants into the New York area, where Stratemeyer lived and worked, did not fail to catch his entrepreneurial eye. In 1927 he spoke of how to tap into this potential new market of readers: "The American juvenile author of the next generation is going to have a difficult problem confronting him, due to our mixed population, and, whereas the heroes in the past have been American . . . the juvenile literature of the future will be called on to present heroes of many more nationalities, all, of course, more or less Americanised."[62] Ironically, the most pertinent members of the next generation—Stratemeyer's own daughters—did not share his (minimally) multicultural vision. Under their leadership, not only did the Syndicate's protagonists remain American-born Anglos, but so did even the secondary characters. At least Edward Stratemeyer, when plotting the original Hardy Boys novels, had included two white ethnics—a Jew and an Italian, with heavy accents—as part of the Hardys' social circle. Those two characters shrank in significance over the years, and the new series that Adams and her staff developed followed suit.[63]

In her comments to the press, Harriet Adams sometimes revealed a thorough ignorance of race both as a site of social and political unrest and as an indicator of cultural differences. Consider this excerpt from a 1977 article: "Perfectly ingenuous and seemingly unaware of the differences between her life and theirs, [Adams] tells a story of walking from her house to a woman's club and watching black domestic workers on their way home. 'They had worked all day, but they weren't tired,' she says. 'They were singing as they went home. It inspired me to write a poem called, "And they crooned in the afternoon."'"[64] Not surprisingly, the Syndicate received criticism of the racial stereotypes in its books in the years after World War II, as the civil rights movement gradually swelled. Adams often cited these complaints as a strong motivation behind her decision to revise her major series, but her public comments about the process were more grudging than gracious: "Children of the 1930s grew up with dialect [in their books]. In the older days, there weren't so many rules and organizations and committees that wouldn't allow things. . . . Now you can't do it."[65] She implies that children who grew up with dialect were none the worse for it, and that latter-day "organizations and committees" persecute harmless authors. By 1979 Adams was speaking more bluntly: "In the '40s we had all the ethnic groups after us. . . . We got letters from German groups and French groups and Chinese groups who didn't want their dialects in the stories. Oh, I was in despair at one point. I said that the only villain we can have now is a good old American."[66] Adams did admit, however, that she found the "colored dialect . . . hard" for modern readers to comprehend, though she criticized its syntactical oddity rather than its cruelty. When she spoke of her revisions, she often emphasized her removal of such language: "We went back and cleaned up much of the dialect, and now everyone speaks standard English."[67] But the removal of dialect, as it turned out, did little to solve the problem, for after Adams had jettisoned that language and erased the non-white villains, no people of color remained except for a small handful of incidental characters. The result of Adams's efforts was less a "cleaning up" than an ethnic cleansing.

While Adams did not recognize that an absence of diversity posed just as many problems as negative portrayals, some of her readers were more perceptive; the few available comments we have from readers outside the white middle class reveal a sharp awareness of their exclusions in this series. These readers do not, however, have uniform reactions. An Italian American participant at the 1993 Nancy Drew conference explained that the series' overwhelming biases of class and ethnicity forced her to abandon it altogether: "When I was a kid reading Nancy Drew I think I only went through about three of them before I gave up because Nancy Drew was everything I *couldn't* be, *not* everything I *could* be. She [represented] the kind of WASP ideal, the kind of kid who had a father with lots of money instead of a father who had never gone to college, whose mother—although she had died—was clearly not my mother, who had a foreign accent. So . . . I'm not here to celebrate Nancy Drew."[68]

At the opposite pole is an African American acquaintance who once told me she'd avidly read the series as a girl, but had to perform some mental gymnastics to identify with the heroine: "I just pretended Nancy was black." Given the books' constant descriptions of Nancy's fair coloring and her all-white milieu, this pretending must have required a good deal of effort. Caprio quotes another African American woman, Edith, recalling her pleasure in reading the Nancy Drew books she borrowed from the white girl whose family employed Edith's grandmother as a domestic worker: "It may seem funny that a black girl like me would use WASPy Nancy Drew as a role model, but she was *the only exciting young female I had ever come across.* . . . I remember how we both raised an eyebrow over the parts that put down blacks, and I was glad to hear that these were cleaned up later. I really believed I could be like Nancy . . . and today I'm a social worker at a university near my old home."[69] In Edith's case, gender identification overrode racial identification; the paucity of "exciting young females" in children's culture allowed her to bracket the racism in the Nancy Drew series while enjoying the experience of projecting herself into a powerful heroine.

A more conflicted account comes from Mary, a Mexican American member of an Internet discussion list for adult fans of girls' series books. During a debate in 2004 about the relevance of racism in the early Nancy Drew volumes, some of the list's white members considered the issue negligible because they personally had not noticed the racial slurs when they were children. They therefore believed that children of color would also not notice them, forgetting to consider that the people likeliest to notice a slur are those whom it targets. Mary corrected their assumption, revealing a divided consciousness: while she adored the elegant, somewhat Victorian tone of the Nancy Drew series, even as a child she recognized its inherent racial exclusions:

> My family, of Spanish/Mexican ancestry . . . were as American as the day is long but I knew that while I saw myself as an equal of Nancy, Bess and George, they would see me as "exotic and colorful" at best, "devious" at worst. I was neither. I was Mary, and I liked sunny yellow bedrooms, red and blue roadsters, charming tearooms, and pretty frocks. . . . Alas, I knew that even *if* that world [could] exist, I would have to constantly explain myself and would probably not be able to count these girls [as] friends.
>
> I saw myself as one of the girls. They were created to see me as other. I noticed.[70]

Readers' processes of identification with fictional characters are extremely difficult to theorize, for they vary so often from one individual to the next; what some find alienating others can ignore, while still others, like Mary, must balance an unresolved conflict between the two. But regardless of how many readers could overlook the racism, it is there, permeating the series at a level far deeper than the use of dialect, and it performs a function not yet adequately noted by other commentators.

The very sense of personhood that Nancy exhibits, and that powerfully attracted girls like Edith, is inextricably bound with ideologies of white supremacy and classist elitism.

The first volume in the series, *The Secret of the Old Clock*, contains a particularly egregious example. While sleuthing in someone's home, Nancy is interrupted by thieves who lock her in a closet and depart; she is later freed by the property's "colored caretaker," a drunkard named Jeff Tucker. Noting that the thieves would not have prevailed had Tucker attended soberly to his duties, Nancy scolds him for his laxity, and he offers this explanation:

> "Well, Miss, it was dis heah way: I was out in dah yard a-chorin' around last night and a-thinkin' how I wished I was some place wheah I wasn't—just any place, I didn't mind wheah. I was just all fed up bein' a caih-taker. . . . It ain't such an excitin' life, Miss, and while I's done sowed all mah wild oats, I still sows a little rye now and den."
>
> "Yes, Jeff—I can smell that on your breath right now."[71]

Nancy's arch reply proves that, though less than half Tucker's age, she has the authority to mock him, inviting readers' allegiance with her condescending humor. The lengthy scene between Nancy and Jeff, which continues to humiliate and insult him for over a dozen pages, has no equal in subsequent volumes; while racial minorities are consistently insulted throughout the series, *The Secret of the Old Clock* is the only book to use an African American as a stock figure of ridicule in a protracted scene of "humor." But as the first volume in the series, *Old Clock* was also the most widely read and the one purchased in the greatest numbers, for readers often choose to begin a series at the beginning. The single most widely read Nancy Drew book, before the 1959 revisions, was thus one that presents a minstrel-show vision of African Americans.

In other volumes African Americans most often appear as servants, but in one mystery they operate as the villains when Nancy suspects a "freckle-faced colored man" of being part of a criminal gang. As she ponders this issue, her boyfriend, Ned, comes up behind her:

> "Oh, you startled me!" Nancy laughed, whirling around. "I half expected to see a colored man leering at me."
>
> "Well, that's complimentary, I must say," the youth returned with a grin. "I'm pretty sunburned but I didn't know I looked as dark as that."
>
> Nancy told him about the missing tools and her theory that they had been taken by a colored person. . . .
>
> "Why, I met a darky on the street yesterday!" Ned exclaimed.[72]

Ned finds it supremely insulting to be mistaken for "darkies" who "leer"—a suggestive word that implies a sexual layer of aggression in the Other, making him a palpable threat not only to law and order, but also to the "bounded space" of white women's sexuality. Bobbie Ann Mason notes Keene's frequent rendering of villains as "symbolic rapists who want to violate the treasure, men who haven't the proper credentials . . . to claim it."[73]

The series also defames Gypsies, Jews, and other white ethnics, particularly working-class ones. In *Nancy's Mysterious Letter* (1932) Nancy, pursuing the theft of a bag of mail, seeks information at a neighboring house from a servant, "a brawny woman redolent of yellow soap." Learning that the woman speaks only Polish, Nancy—the very soul of diplomacy when addressing middle-class whites—barks pidgin English at this immigrant laborer: "'No, no, no!' Nancy cried. 'Please try to understand. Mailman—letters—somebody steal them. . . . Bad man steal!'"[74] Even when they are white and speak English, the servant class is often drawn as lazy, dishonest, or simple-minded. One apparent exception is the charming young Coya, a boy from India who flees from a violent guardian to take shelter at the Drew home, where he can work in exchange for room and board. Housekeeper Hannah initially protests:

> "If you think I'll take a brown-skinned boy to raise, you have another think coming! There's enough work in this house without adding to it."
> "That's exactly the point," said Nancy. . . . "I thought Coya could help you. He could mow the lawn and take care of the garden."

Coya eagerly accepts his new role: "'Coya scrub floors, too,' added the boy with a winning smile. . . . 'Wash windows very clean.'" Nancy decides to lodge the boy in "the room over the garage," and later, Bess supports Coya's request to accompany the girls on a picnic: "He would come in handy to lift the heavy hampers." Eventually we learn that Coya is no ordinary brown-skinned servant; he is a lost rajah, kidnapped in infancy by the evil guardian posing as his father. The discovery of the boy's royal blood justifies Keene's positive portrayal of his character, yet his Indian origin nonetheless stigmatizes him. When the series features Europeans of royal or noble blood, they are never positioned as servants or made to sleep above a garage, even temporarily. Dark-skinned royalty—especially from a country where "the natives have no idea about sanitation"—do not merit the narrative respect granted their white counterparts.[75]

Class issues surface in the series even more regularly than those of race. In River Heights the white and rich are unfailingly good, as long as they were born rich (*nouveaux riches* are loud and boorish). The unfortunates who seek Nancy's aid are frequently identified as "fine" people from "good stock" who have suffered an unjust reversal of fortune; as soon as Nancy rights the wrongs that have diminished them, they will return to their rightful privilege. Deborah Siegel reads this repeated plot as a comment on the Depression, noting that the series provided wish fulfillment with its implicit promise that prosperity was just around the corner. But she errs when describing Nancy as "a kind of Robin Hood for the 1930s."[76] Robin Hood took from the rich and gave to the poor; Nancy pledges her allegiance entirely to the moneyed classes, an "endangered aristocratic tradition [which] Nancy supports."[77] Genuinely poor people tend to disgust her or arouse her suspicions.

To segregate Nancy further from the working class, Keene refuses to let her earn money. This is a sharp gender-related difference from Nancy's immediate forebears, the Hardy Boys, who amass hefty savings accounts through their detective work. Nancy adamantly refuses remuneration except in the form of personal gifts. These souvenirs sometimes have high value (jewelry, antiques, *objets d'art*) but Nancy treasures them for their sentimental, not financial, value; she is too genteel a lady to sully her altruism with paid labor. Indeed, the series explicitly insists on Nancy's amateur status as proof of her social credentials. When Nancy is invited to join an exclusive group of schoolgirls on an ocean voyage, one mother objects to Nancy's inclusion on the grounds of her sleuthing activities:

> "I'll not have my daughter Nestrelda associating with any girl who goes around prying into people's affairs. . . . It was a mistake on the part of the headmistress to include a—a detective with the others." . . .
>
> "I suppose you are saying these things because you have heard I happen to have solved a few mysteries. I am not a professional detective in any sense of the word."[78]

After the woman leaves, Nancy's friends reassure her that no one has "higher social qualifications" than she. The Hardy Boys, however, are never upbraided—even wrong-headedly—for their *paid* sleuthing; no one accuses them of having lost their "social qualifications" either through their activities or through the rewards they reap. To Keene's mind, proper femininity means upper-class leisure.[79]

Another and far subtler use of race and class to establish Nancy's identity is the series' use of whiteness as the implicit source of all that is good. Richard Dyer, in his study of whiteness in visual texts, delineates the role of light in producing "the glow of white women," a class- and race-specific image of femininity that manifests when "idealised white women are bathed in and permeated by light." He contrasts this ethereal glow with "shine," which occurs when light bounces off the subject instead of permeating her: shine "is the mirror effect of sweat, itself connoting physicality, the emissions of the body and unladylike labour. . . . Dark skin too, when it does not absorb the light, may bounce it back. Non-white and sometimes working-class white women are liable to shine rather than glow in photographs and films." He establishes the historical connections between light, blondness, and spirituality, noting how the properties of light (and fair coloring) have meshed, in traditional Western iconography, with the "enlightenment" privileged in Christian discourse. Religious art thus portrays sanctified white people "enlightened" by the glow of haloes: " '[They] become light sources themselves, actively irradiating energy. Having become enlightened, they hand on the message.' . . . The secularisation and feminine specification of this seems to have been effected through the figure of the woman as angel, enlightened and enlightening."[80] These descriptions apply to Nancy Drew, who "hand[s] on the message" of enlightenment. Not only does her blue-eyed, blonde-haired prettiness make her appear angelic, her behavior epitomizes the traditional functions of angels: protecting, avenging, and ministering. Nancy's previously noted lack of tactile corporeality and strong emotion exemplifies her angelic status as well; her relative ethereality contrasts with less-favored characters whose bodies and feelings are more concrete, more human, and less controlled.

But Nancy's angelic "enlightenment" also carries the more common meaning of that term: she has a modern, highly evolved intellect. Keene pointedly delineates Nancy as free of superstition, a negative trait inherent in characters like manual laborers, foreigners, minorities, and addlebrained women. Because they are mysteries, many of the series' plots include supposedly supernatural elements, such as curses or ghosts. But, as Deidre Johnson notes, every novel that introduces the supernatural "demystifies [it] by tracing the phenomena to human agents."[81] By the end, Nancy has "handed on" her enlightened, rational worldview to those she helps.

Perhaps Nancy's strongest link to the softened "glow" of idealized white womanhood emerges through her deployment of a muted and diffuse sexual attractiveness. Johnson has noted how commonly early Syndicate girls' books "speak out against excess," privileging a conservative feminine appearance: "the experienced reader can usually identify a book's antagonist by her attire: she is 'an expensively dressed girl—almost flashily dressed' or 'rather overdressed' or 'dressed up like a little Christmas tree.'"[82] Nancy embodies the class-specific notion of good taste that privileges "glow" over the "shine" of flashy self-presentation. The Mrs. Chatham mentioned earlier, scolded for being a bad mother, is also scolded for her attire; Keene describes her as "a stout woman dressed in a flashy red and white silk dress." When Nancy attends a college ball with her boyfriend, in that same volume, we see the contrast to Mrs. Chatham in Nancy's wardrobe: "Nancy's new white dress made on simple lines accentuated her attractiveness."[83] Eschewing frippery and bright colors, Nancy Drew exemplifies the properly conservative white woman.

In one of the deepest paradoxes of the series, Nancy's unrealistic perfection in all tasks clearly differentiates her from average girls, yet in her overt display of feminine charms, Keene keeps Nancy life-sized: attractive but not beautiful, stylish but not ostentatious. Her "flashy" superhuman skills can shine only because they serve the public good. But to shine in her personal appearance is too selfish, too vain a goal. Nancy's personhood depends simultaneously on excess in her other-directedness and the total absence of excess in her self-directedness. Another form of this strict modesty surfaces at the end of nearly every volume in the series, when people laud Nancy's work and she blushingly deflects their praise, insisting that she doesn't deserve it. She may not quite hide her light under a bushel, but she doesn't let it shine, either; it only glows. Keene's emphasis on Nancy's sartorial and behavioral reserve carries firm lessons about approved femininity, the kind that reflect a race- and class-specific ideal of good breeding.

Through the complex chains of associations linking upper-class whiteness, superhuman perfection, and flawless femininity, Nancy models some disturbing attitudes along with her comforting fantasy of full personhood. Parasitically, the image of Nancy thrives on the blood it drains from surrounding foil characters. The structure of these novels is, then, literally black and white: a binary between Nancy and her Others. Where Nancy deflects or resists projections, these Others exist solely to receive her projections: spotting their low-class ways or their non-white skin, Nancy reaches absurdly hasty conclusions about their guilt. She literally pre-judges, and the series validates her prejudices by showing that she never errs in her "instincts," as Keene always describes this alarming mental process. By making Nancy's prejudices one site of her inspirational perfection, Keene implies bigotry as one of the constituting factors of Nancy's splendid personhood. A champion of classist white supremacy, slavish modesty, and perfect other-directedness, Nancy is not only a poor substitute for a real feminist, she actually personifies several of America's most retrograde beliefs about race, class, and sex. Small wonder that the "radical notion" of this teen girl's personhood excited no public criticism; the only radical element of the series, it is so heavily cloaked in tropes of static social hierarchies as to appear entirely non-threatening. Perhaps the strongest of those social hierarchies is that between parent and child, making Nancy an obedient and adoring daughter to her equally adoring, perfect patriarch.

Nancy's Heart Belongs to Daddy

When Adams's interviewers asked about feminism in the Nancy Drew series, she sometimes cited Nancy's loyalty to Carson Drew as a strong counterargument. Indeed, the idealized relationship between Drews, *père* and *fille*, allows Nancy both to support and to reject patriarchy, presenting a double message about a girl's proper role in her society. This double message allows readers to see Nancy as a powerful figure while also seeing that she never "talks back" to authorized patriarchs, a paradox which also, significantly, applies to Harriet Adams's own complicated relationship with paternal authority.

Over the years, Adams's public statements to the press conveyed a complicated duality in her memories of Edward Stratemeyer. On one hand, she saw herself as following in his masterful footsteps; she credited him with providing the example upon which she modeled herself, praised his tremendous achievements as an author and businessman, and generally seemed "still in awe of her father," as one journalist noted.[84] She frequently spoke of her plans to write Stratemeyer's biography, a project she worked on for years without completing. On the other hand, she lost no opportunity to publicize her triumphant surmounting of the obstacles her father had placed before her. The single most frequent remark Adams publicly made about Stratemeyer was that he had been "strict" with her when she was a child, and that he refused to let her work for the Stratemeyer Syndicate, as she had fervently wished to do after graduating from college. Instead, Stratemeyer would allow her only to edit manuscripts that he brought home from the office. Adams's interviews reveal that the conflict-free and mutually supportive relationship between Nancy and Carson Drew was a wish fulfillment for *her*, as well as for her readers: "My father was quite old-fashioned and very strict. I put my Nancy Drew much more out on her own [than I was]. She is what I would have liked to be."[85] Another interview revealed her feelings even more suggestively:

> Adams is fond of describing the teen-age sleuth as her "fiction daughter." But Nancy Drew is more Adams's alter-ego than her offspring. "Oh, I would have loved to have been a teen-age detective and solved mysteries," Adams says wistfully. . . . Adams says Drew is no women's liberationist. "She has great respect for her father and she would never overrule him," she maintains. . . . "My mother was never very well, but we were raised very strictly," she recalls. "My father thought I should stay home and learn to keep house. He never encouraged me in writing."[86]

Adams's remarks suggest a consciousness split between a belief in proper filial duty (not "overruling" the father) and grief at what that duty cost her. By the time Stratemeyer died, Adams's post-graduation ambitions had diluted with the passage of years, and with her transition into a fulltime wife and mother of four. She and her sister attempted at first to sell the Syndicate, but found no one willing to make such a purchase in 1930, the first year of the Depression. Eventually they assumed control of the business themselves and Adams quickly warmed to the task, taking pride in running her father's business—a venture made all the sweeter by his early discouragements. In her final interviews before her death, when mental frailties began to replace her characteristic decorum with a more unfiltered expression of emotions, she sometimes made rather catty remarks about having surpassed her father's accomplishments.[87] Like Nancy Drew herself, Adams followed in her father's professional footsteps; but the Drews' professional camaraderie bore scant resemblance to Stratemeyer's negation of his daughter's ambitions, or Adams's muffled resentment.

Mildred Wirt often told a somewhat parallel story. While she seldom spoke about her father, she noted that he had discouraged her career ambitions, telling her that she would never make a sufficient living as a writer.[88] Wirt, in fact, is the Keene who developed the series' exceptional father/daughter bond; Edward Stratemeyer's original outlines specify that Nancy and Carson collaborate on cases, but do not delineate the unusually warm and loving rapport between them, which became a defining element of the series in the hands of Wirt and Adams.[89] It is tempting to read this fantastic(al) relationship as a kind of therapy for both authors, as well as for their readers, many of whom have singled out this filial/paternal harmony as one of their favorite aspects of the series. As one writer notes, "Much to the envy of those of us who were forced to compete for our father's attention, Nancy was left motherless ... without a sibling in sight."[90] Another writer attributes part of her own childhood love of the series to the fact that Nancy "has—sex aside— all the advantages of being a wife and a daughter with none of the corresponding disadvantages. She lives in an Oedipal dream come true."[91]

As this reference to Oedipus suggests, distinctly romantic undertones inflect the mutual admiration between father and daughter, for Nancy's boyfriend places second to Carson in the contest for her affections. The few times when Nancy displays emotional vulnerability, it is usually directed toward her father, and the same is true of his reactions to her. When Nancy spends considerable time and money having her portrait painted as a gift for her father's birthday, he receives it with profound appreciation:

> For several minutes Carson Drew was too moved to speak.
> "You like it?" Nancy asked softly.
> "Like it! Nancy, the word doesn't half express my feeling. As long as I live, I'll treasure this wonderful portrait of you," he said, a slight catch in his voice. ... "So that's what you have been doing with your spare time of late," he teased. "I was rather alarmed by your frequent unexplained absences from home."[92]

His emotionalism and his "teasing" reference to her whereabouts make Carson sound as much like a smitten husband as a father. Later in the same novel, he and Nancy both survive a plane crash, but are separated. Frantic in her efforts to find "Dad, dear old dad," Nancy approaches hysteria, an extremely unusual condition for her. Finally locating Carson in a hospital, she is so overcome with emotion that she must lie on his bed with him until her dizziness passes.[93] In another volume, while visiting a seaside resort, Nancy encourages Carson to join her in a midnight swim, for "the moon is full . . . and the beach will be beautiful." Though reluctant at first, "after a ten-minute dip in the bracing sea he was glad he had listened to his daughter's plea, for he felt alive in every part of his lean body. He raced Nancy back to the dressing room."[94] The series' general refusal to acknowledge Nancy's embodiment makes surprising this sensual description of the paternal body. Moments as suggestive as these do not occur often in the series, but they bespeak a quasi-romantic conception of fatherhood that flavors every volume.

Some of Adams's authorial decisions about her characters' domestic and romantic lives seem designed to strengthen a bond with her own father. Edward Stratemeyer did not include a boyfriend for Nancy Drew in his original outlines; his daughters added this character in the seventh volume, and named him Ned—a well-known nickname for Edward. Nancy, a character with whom Adams explicitly identified, thus dates a man named for Adams's father. Similarly, when devising the Dana Girls series, Adams gave the two orphaned sisters an aunt and uncle—elderly siblings who live together—named Harriet and Ned, after herself and her father. These decisions suggest that Adams sought ways to inscribe her father's presence into these series along with her own (either through Nancy, as her self-described "alter ego," or through Adams's actual first name), casting father and daughter as cooperative partners. By writing him into her work, paralleling him and herself, and heightening the sweetness between Nancy and Carson—who are also partners in their work—Adams repeatedly smoothes out the wrinkles that marred her history with her own father. That so many fans have especially loved this father/daughter relationship suggests implicitly that the lack Adams felt was a lack common to many girls. In patriarchally structured societies like the United States, where traditional divisions of labor make mothers the primary caretakers of children, conflicts can arise from a father's estrangement from his child's inner life. By redressing her own problematic filial feelings in the Nancy Drew series, Adams "ministered unto" her readers in ways she may not have consciously intended.

Reading the components of the father/daughter relationship in the Nancy Drew series as a sort of "medicine" can, then, suggest what ailments Nancy's readers (and her creators) found in their own experiences as the daughters of fathers, and suggests how readers as well as authors can use the creation and consumption of popular fiction to fill experiential gaps. But there is a shadow-side to this perfect father/daughter nexus, as well; one result of the glorious Drewian harmony is that Nancy's independence is not really all that sound. In fact she is overwhelmingly father-identified, another potent reason why claims of her feminism fall short. Close analysis proves that her freedom is actually a perquisite for her successful defense of patriarchy. The Nancy Drew series is not alone in literalizing the link between the Father and the Law known so well to psychoanalytic critics; many of the narrative cycles about teen characters that flourished between the 1930s and the 1960s similarly position the teen as the offspring of an attorney or a judge, usually to maximize the dramatic conflict between social order and "teen craziness." But the Nancy Drew series presents no conflict whatsoever. Dad is the ultimate font of all the powers and privileges that Nancy enjoys, and she follows so neatly and carefully in his footsteps that she is never "crazy" and therefore earns the total freedom he gives her.

By modeling a heady alternative to typical American family life, Nancy's apparently perfect relationship with Carson Drew could have a somewhat subversive effect on the real-life family dynamics of Nancy's readers. In 1971, journalist Jim Treloar wrote an article about Nancy Drew and Mildred Wirt, whom he had discovered to be the series' original ghostwriter. Five years earlier, Treloar had proven himself a fan of Stratemeyer Syndicate books in a nostalgic article about the Tom Swift series, which he wanted to share with his young son.[95] But when writing about Nancy Drew and Wirt, Treloar's tone shifts to one of sharp resentment and reveals some of the tensions between fathers and daughters. He begins by recalling that he'd found his daughter, Rebecca, reading a Nancy Drew book in her messy bedroom:

> In the most kindly way, I suggested she might find something more stimulating than Nancy Drew—and that she might clean up her room before reading anything. She turned on me like a cornered animal: "Nancy Drew never has to clean up HER room! HER father treats her like an ADULT!"
>
> This is not one of your Sunnybrook Farm type of Rebeccas.
>
> But there you have it.
>
> Parents keep buying Sunnybrook Farm–type books because that's the kind of daughter we dream of having; while Nancy Drew is what every 13-year-old girl dreams of becoming.

Treloar prefers a nineteenth-century image of the dutiful and sweet little girl (which, ironically, Rebecca of Sunnybrook Farm was *not*—he errs in this characterization) to the emerging independent thinker in his own house, who resists his paternal authority to tell her what to read and how to live. He expresses jealousy of Carson Drew, the father to whom his own fractious daughter compares him negatively: "[Nancy's] daddy was the witty, urbane, tweedy, pipe-smoking type of daddy the rest of us daddies instinctively despise." Motivated by his home experiences, Treloar tracked down Mildred Wirt, "the creator of Nancy Drew and 'daddy.'" Not surprisingly, the resulting interview contains a tone of belligerence toward its subject; Treloar draws parallels between Wirt and Nancy Drew to pointedly suggest that Wirt is neurotic and unbalanced. Surprisingly, he fails to recall that his beloved Tom Swift, too, had had a perfect daddy (one of the prerequisites of a Stratemeyer series). It is only in regard to the *daughter* that this daddy feels inadequate and touchy about his privileges, and Treloar clearly blames "Carolyn Keene" for exacerbating his paternal strife.[96]

This article is a rare testament to the potentially disruptive effects of Nancy and Carson's domestic harmony, and as such it offers a unique insight into how this fictional bond could appeal to readers. Because "HER father treats her like an ADULT," there is no (apparent) sacrifice in being daddy-identified in this series, no loss of autonomy, because Daddy wants her to be autonomous, too. But this adult treatment has a subtle price that does not emerge as clearly to young readers, perhaps, as its reward does. How autonomous is Nancy, really, when the powers that allow her to sleuth all derive from her father and are wholly father-oriented in their goals?

Although Nancy is the primary mystery-solver in the Drew home, her talent is often described as an inheritance from Carson, making his own acumen an indispensable factor in Nancy's success. Ghostwriter Walter Karig delineates this relationship in *The Password to Larkspur Lane* (1932): "Many a problem which had baffled professional mystery-solvers had been cleared up by her keen mind, coupled with what Nancy herself called 'a sort of sixth sense, probably inherited from father.'"[97] This sixth sense frequently manifests in the odd bursts of sudden "insight" that lead Nancy to her fast conclusions about people. But although these processes look a great deal like intuition, the series can continue its purported privileging of reason and logic because the taint of "feminine intuition" is skirted by the claims that Nancy's gift is a paternal legacy. When dealing with difficult authority figures, Nancy often relies upon her father's power. Her confrontation with the River Heights postmaster, quoted earlier, offers the satisfying sight of the postmaster's contrition upon learning that she is "THE Nancy Drew"—but it also reveals that his concern has as much to do with Carson's fame as Nancy's: "[T]here was a tone of respect in his voice when he spoke again. Carson Drew was a power in politics, and his daughter was not one to treat with disrespect."[98] Scenes like these appear often throughout the series; it is her father's name, not her own, that rescues Nancy when all else fails.

Carson's implicit trust in Nancy stems from her total acceptance of his values, which privilege paternalistic social institutions as the highest moral goods. For the progeny of a lawyer and a "power in politics," being a good daughter is the same as being a good citizen. We have already seen that Nancy's decisions about whom to help are based upon hegemonic notions of social hierarchies. The nature of her work, too, supports the values of hegemony and patriarchy, not just in upholding the law, but in the early volumes' most frequent subplots: Nancy spends a great deal of time supporting heterosexual unions and the nuclear family as social institutions. In the first twenty volumes or so, Nancy often rescues mistreated minors from cruel or criminal guardians and places them, when possible, with lost blood relatives. A small but significant gender difference colors the portrayals of parents and guardians. Foster parents of both sexes are usually evil, as are male guardians or stepfathers. But as long as he is related by blood, a father is *always* good; the same is not always true for mothers, who can be careless or misguided. Fatherhood is the only unassailable condition, as long as it is supported by the all-important bloodline.

The significance of bloodline is best displayed in *The Mystery of the Brass-Bound Trunk* (1940), in which Nancy works on two interconnected mysteries, both of which involve young girls in conflict with their fathers. One girl has a criminal stepfather, and Nancy's capturing him allows the girl to escape his domestic tyranny. But the other girl fights her *real* father, who aims to force her into a marriage with a man she dislikes. Nancy befriends this girl, but works behind the scenes to effect a gradual persuasion; solely through Nancy's efforts, this beleaguered young woman finally sees that her father knows best, and willingly consents to marry the man she formerly rejected. By book's end, Nancy can rest comfortably in the knowledge that she has preserved the power of domestic patriarchy. Never, at any point in the series, does Nancy separate a nuclear family or gainsay the word of a true father.

But true fathers, other than Carson, are rather rare in the series; for the most part their privilege is protected through invisibility. By contrast, false fathers (unfailingly bad) seem to turn up under every rock. This means that even while Nancy's entire mission is patriarchally oriented, the more immediately visible message of the series is that bad or false fathers must be fought and beaten. In five of the first seventeen volumes, Nancy protects helpless young wards from evil stepfathers, male guardians, or adoptive fathers, in scenes made particularly memorable by their sometimes high level of physical confrontation. Here we see another appealing manifestation of Nancy's unusual self-possession and certainty of her rights: where real teenage girls might cower or hesitate, Nancy does not think twice before grabbing a whip away from the man who beats his ward (*Mystery of the Ivory Charm*, 1936), or climbing a ladder to wrestle with an evil, muscular man at the window of the room where he imprisons his foster-daughter (*Sign of the Twisted Candles*, 1933). Tellingly, both of these dramatic scenes were selected in their respective volumes for visual representation as one of the four full-page, glossy illustrations that appeared in each book. In the latter case, Nancy's wrestling match occurs by moonlight and she is dressed all in white, "glowing" angelically while grappling with the evil father figure.

The series further suggests an oppositional relationship between girls and patriarchs through its attitude toward adult men in general, a population barely present in the series. I've already suggested that the milieu of River Heights is a feminized world of tea parties and Victorian elegance; another aspect of its femininity is its exclusion of able-bodied or "manly" men. Most of the victims Nancy helps are women, and the few males are somehow stripped of their virility: they are either very elderly, partly disabled, or employed in a feminized profession like theater, music, or art. In *The Clue of the Tapping Heels* (1939), Nancy is assisted by a professional male detective; his presence undercuts Nancy's power and deprives the story of some of its usual satisfactions, and the Syndicate did not repeat this tactic until many years after the period analyzed here. For the most part, the series' good men are weak men, except for those in Nancy's inner circle, whose masculinity poses no threats because they never pull rank on her and always defer to her wishes.

The frequent assaults upon bad or false fathers, and the scarcity of men who are simultaneously manly and good, give the Nancy Drew series a distinct tinge of sexual segregation, echoing the themes of sacred interiority mentioned earlier and providing a kind of *hortus conclusus* that protects virgins by keeping men out. The Nancy Drew series embodies one of the foundational philosophies of women's colleges like Wellesley, Adams's alma mater: girls thrive best with no men to distract or upstage them. Even the recurrent presence of bad male criminals does not alter this logic, for the series' structure makes it inescapably predictable that every bad man will eventually be subjugated in quivering defeat. Like the confrontation and fight scenes, the books' scenes of defeat are narrated in great detail and become vivid set-pieces that fire readers' imaginations. Not only does Nancy deflect projections, she swiftly punishes those who cast them, metaphorically grinding her dainty heels into their faces: as Lee Zacharias colorfully puts it, "Nancy's victory has an element of revenge, proving to the criminal that she's not just any girl. . . . She has a compulsion to reduce her villains to broken old men. The attractive young sleuth is a ballbuster!"[99] The paradox of the unrealistically perfect father/daughter relationship and the books' avoidance of normative masculinity allow Nancy herself to appear the dutiful daughter in every respect, while letting the series as a whole seem to "kill the father" symbolically.

As the numerous examples here have suggested, both of the primary

Carolyn Keenes in the 1930s and 1940s used personal experience and personal commitment to inform their work. As Adams cared about Nancy's "ministering" to others, so she and Wirt "ministered" to their readers in ways both conscious and unconscious, reflecting their efforts to obtain personhood (the freedom to define one's own identity and agency) in their own lives, despite the discouragements of social and domestic patriarchs. The Nancy Drew they established thus presented to female children the "radical notion" that they, too, could be people. But Nancy also demonstrated that her rights paradoxically depended upon upholding the oppressive values represented by the very patriarchy with which her personhood placed her in opposition. She could thus appear to "talk back [and] fight," as Kismaric and Heiferman state, without really assaulting the fundamental power structures that uphold race, class, and sex privilege. The comments of various fans repeated here indicate that Nancy's toxic relation to the status quo denied some readers the identification process which led to the enjoyment of personhood; but they also show that even some Othered young readers could glean an inspiring sense of empowerment from this unusual heroine.

Nancy Drew's loyalty to the patriarchy prevented this series from appearing too radical, and thus offered a balance that allowed the series to placate protectors of social order while also allowing girl readers to find a space in which to establish their own right to talk back, as Jim Treloar's daughter did. The series, more often than not, created cracks in the armor of patriarchy that girls could use to sustain their own dreams of power. But this presentation only worked while the series was aimed at an audience of little girls, readers to whom Wirt and Adams felt a conscious commitment. Eight years after Nancy Drew's debut her audience widened, to her detriment, when Hollywood turned its sights on Nancy and created a series of films about her. The following chapter argues that the loss of producers with strong commitments to their girl audiences, and the widening of that audience to include males and adults, destroyed nearly all the subversive potential of Nancy Drew and left only a broad caricature of female adolescence, expressing patriarchy's dismissive attitude toward the too-radical notion of young girls' personhood. In these films, Nancy crystallizes the stereotypes of teenage femininity that would prevail, and increase, in the years to follow.

2

"Pretty Baby"
Nancy Drew Goes to Hollywood

She makes mistakes. We all adore
her.

—Kathleen Norris, 1938

 In 1938 Warner Bros. Pictures pur-
chased the rights to the Nancy Drew
series from the Stratemeyer Syndicate
and began filming a series of B-pictures
based on Nancy's adventures. In doing so, the studio sought to capitalize
on a new trend toward teenage protagonists which, though recent, had
already proven lucrative. In January 1937 Universal Studios had released
Three Smart Girls, the first of their popular vehicles for Deanna Durbin,
a fifteen-year-old with an operatic soprano voice. In the spring of that
same year, Metro-Goldwyn-Mayer released *A Family Affair*, the first of
the Andy Hardy series (starring Mickey Rooney), which would become
one of the highest-grossing film series in history. Meanwhile, serial B-
films about detectives were a staple of both Warner's and its rivals' productions.

The Nancy Drew movies, then, were modest attempts to capitalize
on genres and trends already in place, and they performed adequately.
Reviewers judged them mostly favorably, given their secondary status as
"programmers" (films to fill out a theater's program for a double feature),
and the series might have endured beyond its four installments had its

star, Bonita Granville, not left the studio in 1939. In themselves, these films offer nothing remarkable—until one compares them with the books that provided their inspiration. Very little of Carolyn Keene's Nancy remains in the films. Instead, the Nancy offered by Warner Bros. is markedly younger, more inept, and generally less admirable than her literary counterpart. Filmic Nancy pointedly lacks the personhood inherent in literary Nancy, creating an astonishingly abrupt alteration of the character's meaning. The fundamental difference between these two Nancys depends largely on the difference between their audiences, and on their respective producers' creative decisions based upon their assumptions about those audiences. While the books were written solely for children—and primarily girls—the films would reach a wider audience because the medium of film had a broader cultural visibility than children's fiction, and thus had to address adults' desires as well as youths'. Before World War II, the film industry imagined its audience as a cross-section of "everyone," and crafted its stories with the idea of pleasing a broadly general aesthetic. Not until after the war did studios conduct the sort of demographic research that revealed the distinct size of their youth audience, and at that time, studios accordingly began shifting their focus onto film styles and topics aimed specifically at young people.[1]

In the 1930s, however, Hollywood did not make systematic distinctions between fare for adults and for youth. Contemporary reviews indicate a general understanding that the Nancy Drew films were primarily aimed at "the juve element," as *Variety*'s reviewer described children,[2] but the films fell under an adult gaze in several ways. Some parents or other adults might accompany their young wards to a Saturday matinée—indeed, the press book for *Nancy Drew—Reporter* (1939) blazoned its product as a "family-patronage feature."[3] More generally, the movie industry had for many years been closely scrutinized by a variety of social, educational, and religious groups. Their negative attentions put pressure on the film industry to bow to the morality of the general public in all films. The famous Payne Fund studies, undertaken by a group of educators and reformers, had been fueled initially by suspicions that this new mass medium might harmfully influence children and youth. The findings of those studies, as summarized in the popular book *Our Movie Made Children* (1933), seemed to corroborate the worst fears of concerned adults, indicating that youngsters absorbed questionable or immoral messages from films.[4] Children were not the only focus of concern; during the 1920s, the Dionysian revelries of movie stars received much negative publicity, prompting a backlash from a middle America disgusted not only by actors' crimes and debaucheries, but also by the sensationalist content of movies. In an effort to fend off external censorship, the Hollywood studios invited Will Hays, who had been postmaster general in President Harding's administration, to serve as the film industry's internal watchdog. The Hays Office devised a set of morally sound "dos and don'ts" for filmmakers which, by the late '30s, had solidified into the long-standing Production Code of the motion picture industry.

In addition to forbidding nudity, profanity, and gory violence, Hays's document also forbade the depiction of anything that might offend an ideologically conservative mentality. Acknowledging that "[i]t is difficult to produce films intended for only certain classes of people. . . . Films, unlike books and music, can with difficulty be confined to certain selected groups," the Code required the industry to produce all films—even ones intended primarily for children—with regard for the sensibilities of the general (adult) public. Eschewing any material that might "lower the moral standards of those who see it," the Production Code exhorted filmmakers to present "correct standards of life," a goal which included upholding "the sanctity of the institution of marriage and the home."[5] This stipulation could bear directly upon portrayals of gender relations. While the Nancy Drew books contained nothing immoral, their non-normative vision of girlhood (including Nancy's preference for hard work and the company of her girlfriends over boys), did not adhere to the dominant gender ideologies implicit in the Production Code.

Show-business lore has it that producers ask, "Will it play in Peoria?" when anxious about the reception their productions might meet in middle America. This chapter analyzes Warner's translation of Nancy Drew to suggest that its alterations to her character reflect national concerns about the proper forms of teenage femininity in 1930s America. These films provide a model of girlhood that conforms almost exclusively to traditional gender expectations, reassuring consumers of the ultimately harmless frivolity of youth, and tacitly instructing girl viewers in how to personify a patriarchally sanctioned version of femininity. Warner Bros. performed radical reconstructive surgery on Nancy Drew to make her successfully "play in Peoria." Using specific ideologies of class and gender privilege, the film studio abandoned Nancy's status as a perfect agent in order to foreground her status as the perfect foil for an embattled and anxious middle-class masculinity.

A Descent from Goddess to Little Girl

The script Warner's staff chose to inaugurate its series, *Nancy Drew—Detective* (1938), was closely based on the 1933 mystery *The Password to Larkspur Lane*, the tenth volume in the Nancy Drew series. Ghostwritten by Walter Karig, *Larkspur Lane* provides one of the series' clearest articulations of Nancy's quasi-divine omniscience and omnipotence. In Kenneth Gamet's screenplay, however, Nancy's character deviates considerably from its literary origin. One of the most consistent elements of Nancy's portrayal in fiction is her vast knowledge: she is rarely shown in the act of learning, but seems always already to know with perfection. *Larkspur Lane* highlights Nancy's intellectual acumen in the very first scene. As she strolls through her lush flower garden, picking larkspurs to enter in a charity exhibition, Nancy offers a brief lecture on history and horticulture to the Drews' housekeeper: "'If I had lived two thousand years ago, I should have been a Grecian maiden,' [said] Nancy. 'And right now I should be praying at the temple of Apollo in Delphi. . . . These larkspurs are also called "delphinium" because they were the sacred flower of the temple at Delphi,' Nancy explained. 'I believe they have other names, too.'"[6] Nearly every novel in the series offers juvenile readers brief instruction in some arcane pocket of knowledge, usually delivered from Nancy's own lips rather than from those of an adult male expert. Her disquisition about Greece and delphiniums is merely the first of several such edifying conversations throughout the novel.

Within moments the clue to a new mystery literally falls out of the sky when a wounded carrier pigeon lands at Nancy's feet bearing a cryptic message about "blue bells." Her all-encompassing knowledge helps her decide a course of action: "I have a plan! . . . I'll telegraph the number stamped on the ring the bird has on its leg to the American Pigeon Club. . . . They'll know who the owner is, because they have records of carrier pigeons by their numbers" (5). Nancy's knowledge provides an intellectual link between her and her attorney father, shown in the series' frequent portrayal of the two as co-workers. Karig delineates the foundation of this mutual partnership: "Carson Drew had always been close to his only daughter, whose mother had died many years before, and often discussed his legal work with her. At first he did so just for the sake of reasoning aloud. Then, as Nancy Drew grew into her 'teens he learned that her advice was often very valuable, regardless of how involved the cases were" (13). As noted in the previous chapter, the intuitive gift that complements Nancy's logical mind is "probably inherited from [her] father," so that Keene never describes it reductively in the cliché of feminine intuition. Nor does Nancy use her gift in the mundane scenarios in which women were popularly imagined to employ intuition—to read the emotions of loved ones, or to scheme against a female competitor for a boy's attentions. Nancy is all business, displaying an unflappable calm and maturity which never waver, no matter how dire the circumstances.

These qualities of omniscience and steady calm emerge forcefully in the novel's lengthy climax. Nancy and her friend Helen disguise themselves to infiltrate a *faux* sanatorium where a criminal gang, posing as medical personnel, imprison elderly women to swindle them of their money. After locating the woman she has come to rescue, Nancy dispatches her and Helen to freedom, staying behind for further sleuthing. Caught by the criminals and subsequently dumped into a deep cistern, Nancy does not even consider the possibility of panicking. Feeling along the slimy walls in total darkness, she uses sharp debris she finds on the floor to dig grooves in the rotting mortar; she can thus climb to the stone-covered outer rim. Karig's description of this scene emphasizes the courage and strength of this teenage heroine, who is cold and tired and has "had nothing to eat for several hours": "Gritting her teeth, the girl exerted herself . . . to move the stones overhead. Dirt and rubbish cascaded down upon her. At last . . . she managed to make an opening big enough, she estimated, to allow her to thrust her head through. Carefully she released her hold on the wall and raised her arms until both hands gripped the edge of the cistern. Then, straining every muscle in her body, she wormed her way to freedom" (207).

Once above ground Nancy scribbles SOS messages, attaches them to the gang's carrier pigeons, and sends them off to fetch help, before applying her energies to the sabotage of the gang's getaway vehicles. Nancy "raised the hood [of their car] and felt for the cylinder of the gasoline filter. She unscrewed the butterfly bolt which held it in place, and as the glass came off in her hand, gasoline gushed over her fingers" (208–209). Her skillful, confident handling of exotic machinery offers thrills to young girls who have probably never heard of a butterfly bolt, let alone a "cylinder of [a] gasoline filter." Nancy then vandalizes the gang's airplane, twisting the exhaust pipe so that it catches fire when the criminals attempt to escape; their ringleader, Dr. Bull, sustains a burned leg. As the gang's plans crumble into chaos, police airplanes, alerted by the carrier pigeons Nancy sent, arrive bearing officers as well as Nancy's father and boyfriend:

> Panting and almost falling, Nancy reached the group.
> "Ned!" she cried. "And Father! Oh, how glad I am!"
> She stumbled, and fell into Carson Drew's outstretched arms.
> "Nancy, dear Nancy," he said. "Are you hurt? You are covered with dirt."
> "Never mind that, Father." She hugged him, assuring him that she was un-
> harmed, although practically exhausted. (215)

These lines could easily appear in any hackneyed melodrama about an endangered heroine who faints with joy and gratitude at the moment of rescue. But Keene alters their meaning through the knowledge that these men have not rescued Nancy; she alone has rescued both herself and the moral order of her universe. Only after displaying atypical heroism does Nancy revert, briefly, to typical femininity.

Ghostwriter Karig stages one of his characteristic confrontation scenes to highlight Nancy's self-possession and gracious aplomb. As the police lead them away, two criminals pause to face the girl they thought they had left to die, marveling that Nancy "must be a witch" to have escaped the cistern. She counters their outraged incredulity with galling politeness:

> "I bet you gummed up our airplane too," Bull raged savagely.
> "I did my best," Nancy said. "I am sorry if it caused you serious injury."
> "Sorry—bah!" hissed Dr. Bull. "To think of being foiled by a mere slip of a
> girl!"
> "I told you so," cackled Thorne. "I told you she was dangerous, but you were
> too conceited to believe a girl could fool you."
> "Oh, take me away and lock me up," Bull groaned. "Lock me up in a lunatic
> asylum. Put me in a strait-jacket—anything! Do something, do something—I'm
> beat out!" (217)

It is not just his destruction, but the particular fact of its delivery by a "slip of a girl," that reduces this arch-criminal to a broken husk and drives him to the brink of insanity.

No such "witchy" power remains in Bonita Granville's portrayal of Nancy on film. Rather, *Nancy Drew—Detective* establishes Nancy immediately as a teenage girl of merely life-sized proportions. Where the books allow Nancy to exist magically beyond the realities of school or employment, the film's opening shot establishes that Nancy attends a private girls' school. In keeping with her schoolgirl status Nancy has no special knowledge or skills, with minor exceptions (an early scene implies that Nancy fixes her own flat tire, but does not show her doing it). On a few occasions Nancy demonstrates knowledge of some general points of law and detective procedure, but the knowledge obviously derives from an authoritative source, such as her father; Nancy knows nothing unusual by herself.

The scene introducing the carrier pigeon offers an instructive example. Nancy does not enjoy the position of discoverer or interpreter of the strange event, as she did in the book; instead she functions as a fussy, hyperfeminized bystander while boys exhibit agency and intelligence. Her boyfriend (renamed "Ted" in the films) now lives next door to Nancy, and she happens upon him just as he hurtles into her garden after tackling his football practice dummy. Nancy berates him in a schoolmarmish tone for ruining her flower bed, while he rolls his eyes dismissively. Another boy, a friend of Ted's, dashes in holding a wounded pigeon he has found, asking Ted's help in discerning its provenance. Nancy baby-talks to the pigeon: "Poor little precious," she coos, for which the boys mock her. Ted, not Nancy, knows that the numbers on the bird's leg identify it as a carrier pigeon. Enthused, Nancy asks Ted to start his radio to "find out who owns this bird." But he knows a better way to glean information: "Aw, you don't have to do that. All racing pigeons are registered with the American Pigeon Association. Just send them this number." Throughout *Nancy Drew — Detective* many insights and deductions attributed to Nancy in Keene's text are reassigned either to Ted or to Carson Drew, with Nancy reduced to the role of cheerleader ("Gee, Ted, that's plenty sharp!"). Nancy herself becomes the real wounded pigeon, her wings neatly clipped by Warner's staff.

In every critical or dangerous situation, Ted's gender-specific technical knowledge reappears as the means of Nancy's deliverance, while Nancy retreats into timid dependence. In *Larkspur Lane*, Helen unwittingly reaches for a fence that Nancy recognizes as electrically wired; stopping her friend in the nick of time, Nancy instructs Helen in how to distinguish electrified fences. But *Detective* replaces Helen with Ted as Nancy's partner in crime solving and transfers to him the knowledge that Nancy had possessed in the novel, undermining her prowess: now it is *she* who nearly touches the fatal fence and Ted who warns her of its dangers. In the wide-eyed, breathy delivery of the rescued maiden, Nancy thanks him for saving her life. The film thus reverses the whole point of this scene in the book: that Nancy knows more and can do more than other girls, without needing male assistance.

The film similarly replaces the scene of Nancy's solo escape from the cistern with a more mundane imprisonment of both Nancy and Ted in the sanatorium's cellar; at no point in the four-film series does Nancy investigate or suffer capture alone, as she frequently did in the novels.

Furthermore, where Keene's Nancy did not hesitate to feel her way along pitch-black, gooey walls, Warner's Nancy reacts with dainty disgust upon touching a dusty railing and says tremulously to Ted, "I'm scared. . . . I should've listened to Dad—and you." But Keene never turned Nancy against herself in such self-abnegating surrender; part of literary Nancy Drew's awesome personhood came from her sure-footed trust in her own instincts, and the novels' subsequent validation of them. In the cellar, while filmic Nancy frets, Ted ingeniously rigs an old x-ray machine to send distress signals in Morse code, replacing Nancy's use of carrier pigeons in the novel.[7] Adding insult to injury, Warner's Nancy performs a mechanical task extremely badly: getting hold of one of the gang's guns in the final melee, she squeezes her eyes shut and shoots wildly, proving that she has plenty of "moxie" but no skill. Her inept shooting expresses a kind of temporary insanity, which becomes apparent when the arrival of the authorities breaks the spell of Nancy's panic. As she realizes that she has been playing with a dangerous toy, more suited to adult men like the police who now supersede her, she performs the ultimate feminine gesture to apologize for her transgression: she rolls up her eyes and faints.

Nancy's hyperfemininity and ignorance bring her derision from the adults and males surrounding her. While Ted mocks her fussy airs and hyperactive behavior ("it's an eternal mystery to me how anybody as smart as your father could raise such a dizzy daughter"), the authorities dismiss her as a "little girl." Unlike Keene's novels, the films do not use these dismissals as fodder for scenes of swift retribution; whereas readers are cued to feel a flash of annoyance when some foolish man derides Nancy as a "girlie," audiences of the film are instead encouraged to sympathize with the disdainful men, for Nancy's behavior warrants little respect. Keene's Nancy thwarts her detractors by pulling herself up to the height of her dignity and leveling them with a cold stare and a stream of calmly stated facts, but Warner's Nancy stamps her feet and tosses her head, making indignant faces and bratty remarks. When the thick-skulled police captain Tweedy patronizingly suggests that Nancy should leave the case to real detectives, she later refers to him in a fit of pique as "that conceited tweet-tweet!" demonstrating the very childishness for which adults and boys scorn her. Worse, she displays an over-blown sense of personal dignity that, lacking corroboration from others, makes her appear absurd; while Keene's Nancy was legendary throughout River Heights, Warner's Nancy is a legend in her own mind. In narrative conventions, such a swollen self-image sets Nancy up for deflation.

Her only assets are described in distinctly feminized, and hence devalued, terms; where literary Nancy is tenacious and brave, filmic Nancy is good at "snooping." Where literary Nancy has a cool and logical mind, filmic Nancy is emotional and easily flustered. Where literary Nancy has "a sixth sense" inherited from her father, filmic Nancy's hunches get no such heightening; in *Nancy Drew — Detective*, Carson Drew belittles his daughter's hypotheses and asks her why she is so certain of them. "I don't know," Nancy replies and then voices the very cliché that the books pointedly avoided: "I guess it's just my woman's intuition. Every woman has one, you know." Her father sounds bemused: "Yes, I know." Only her boyfriend and her father possess true rationality, and the film contrasts them with Nancy frequently, driving home the message that a girl detective is something like a bearded lady at the circus: an entertaining freak, sufficiently powerless to let us find her amusing. As one scholar has noted, Nancy's father and boyfriend "do not encourage her sleuthing. They appear merely to tolerate it and humor her because if she gets her own way she is likely to be less of a nuisance."[8]

Nor does Carson Drew hesitate to assert his authority. Far from being equals, filmic Carson and Nancy enact an affectionate but one-sided power dynamic in which Nancy tests her father's authority and he reins her in sharply. Although proud of her when she succeeds, Carson very clearly treats his daughter like a daughter, not a partner, and does not hesitate to put her in her place. In turn, she thrives on his patronizing authority even while pretending to sulk, for she is drawn as a devoted "daddy's little girl," complete with the semi-romantic nuances inherent in that identity. *Nancy Drew — Troubleshooter* features an extended subplot about Nancy's jealousy when her father dates an attractive woman, highlighting her filial devotion in erotic terms. Eros tints the father/daughter relationship as well in *Nancy Drew — Reporter* when Nancy stays up past her bedtime, awaiting Carson's return so that she may discuss a case with him. A cozy domestic scene ensues; Nancy kneels before Carson to help him put on his slippers and perches companionably on the bathtub to talk with him while he changes into a robe and washes his face. He grouses when he accidentally grabs her drying stockings while reaching for a towel. After performing his ablutions Carson insists that Nancy go to bed, even though she is still deeply involved in her dialogue about a boxer with a "funny" (cauliflower) ear, who she suspects is a criminal.

Nancy: Dad, I felt all along that that man with the funny ear was a clue. I think you ought to do something about him.

Carson: I'm going to do something about a girl with a funny face. Come on, baby, you're going to bed. [He lifts and carries her to her bedroom]

Nancy: [squealing] Oh Dad, put me down! I'm no baby.

Carson: You'll always be your daddy's baby.

Nancy: I won't be anybody's baby!

Carson: [singing] "Everybody loves a baby, that's why I'm in love with you, pretty baby; pretty baby."

As Nancy giggles and shrieks, Carson vigorously tucks her into bed, silencing her when she tries to speak. While father and daughter cooperate in the books to protect patriarchal law, they cooperate in the films to protect paternalism—a related but very differently inflected goal.

Nancy does not go entirely without heightening; the films trade upon her class and color (as did the books) to imply that Others are less ra-

Figure 1. Nancy's father exercises more authority over her in the films than in the book series. Here, he forcibly puts his pretty baby to bed. *Nancy Drew— Reporter* © 1939 Turner Entertainment Co. A Warner Bros. Entertainment Co. All Rights Reserved.

tional than she. Thus the eye-rolling, chicken-thieving black handyman in *Nancy Drew — Troubleshooter* provides comic relief, while hysterical Effie, the housekeeper, makes Nancy look efficient and collected in comparison, just as the slow-witted efforts of working-class Captain Tweedy provide a foil that heightens Nancy's deductions. But the truly admirable characters in these films—the voices of reason and common sense, the possessors of rightful dignity and sympathetic perspectives—are the middle-class white men, Ted and Carson. They enjoy the benefits of full personhood, while those who do not share their color, class, and sex receive less narrative respect. The only moments in which Nancy appears to triumph over the white, middle-class male are those in which, comically, her schemes humiliate Ted by requiring him to cross-dress, or in one memorable instance, to lose his pants altogether when Nancy inconsiderately demands his belt as a makeshift measuring stick.

Images of man's humiliation at the hands of a scatterbrained woman proliferate in comedies of the period, and present a paradox: while clearly putting the man at a disadvantage as the object of ridicule, such scenes do not uniformly endorse the woman's emasculating operations. Indeed, if the man in question is a character with whom the film shows sympathy and agreement in other moments, scenes of his gendered humiliation can function as cautionary tales about the potential evils of feminine agency, inviting a measure of sympathy for, rather than unalloyed ridicule of, the embarrassed man. In the case of the Nancy Drew films, the protection of masculinity supports a doubly patriarchal logic by privileging the adult over the teenager: Ted can be stuffed into a dress or left pantless, but Carson Drew never suffers any humiliating event, let alone one that destabilizes his masculinity. Among the white middle class, the young appear more risible than adults, and Nancy's many moments of deflation—though much less dramatic or overt—outnumber Ted's, revealing that the gender/age nexus could leave a young female stuck in the most powerless position of all.

For countless little girls sitting in theaters across the country, the ostensible mystery in *Nancy Drew — Detective* must have paled next to the mystery of who kidnapped the real Nancy Drew and left this limp imposter in her place. Diana Beeson explains these jarring alterations with reference to the "screwball mystery," a hybrid genre popular in the 1930s that combined the formulae of the detective story and the screwball comedy. Classic screwball comedies of the 1930s like *My Man Godfrey* and *It Happened One Night* routinely featured "working-stiff," average-guy heroes and spoiled, flighty, upper-crust heroines who enacted a battle between the man's sensible worldview and the woman's "screwy" one. Beeson persuasively traces this same pattern in the relationship between Ted and Nancy, arguing that the imperatives of the screwball genre wholly explain the films' radical departure from the books. But this argument, while explaining a good deal, omits the influence of another trend in 1930s filmmaking: the popular interest in adolescence, which was rapidly growing during these years. These generic influences cooperated to construct a Nancy Drew who catered to Depression-era fantasies about gender and generation.

Hollywood Grapples with Youth and Girls, 1900–1937

Teenage heroines were nothing new in Hollywood. Such girls had featured in the stables of stock characters in many studios since the earliest days of the silents; D. W. Griffith, for example, used his star Lillian Gish to project an idealized personification of female youth as an abstraction of purity and beauty. In early cinema, youth often functioned more as an abstract concept than as a historical category; that is, there was no depiction of an age-specific, era-specific "youth culture" in pre-1920s films. Ingénues were either plucky little urchins (Mary Pickford, the original "America's Sweetheart," played scrappy adolescents until well into her thirties) or else ethereal innocents, often played by actresses with allegorical names like Blanche Sweet, Bessie Love, and Pearl White.

In the 1920s Hollywood began to portray a specific youth culture, responding to a sudden, nationwide interest in the new generation of college-aged "flappers" and "sheiks." As Paula Fass has shown, the 1920s saw large increases in enrollment in colleges, where the lack of parental supervision and the converging of like-minded peers fostered a thriving youth culture that commanded national attention. The 1920s gave Americans their first systematic images of "flaming youth," the title of a popular 1923 book and a catchphrase for much of the decade. College-aged youth shocked and titillated their elders by embracing such stylistic innovations as the "lowly" musical form of jazz, daring fashions for girls (short skirts, bobbed hair, rouged knees), and crazy campus activities like flagpole sitting and goldfish swallowing. Much as it would a generation later, the conclusion of a world war led to popular perceptions that the younger generation had been badly warped, and now might lead the country straight to hell. Youth's peer culture circulated in the media the way all popular panics do: as a source of anxiety and pleasure simultaneously, offering viewers the opportunity to consume provocative stories and images while allowing them also to feel superior to those they read about.

Much of the public conversation about youth focused specifically on the modern young female, known as the flapper: "During the 1920s, a flapper was generally characterized as a young woman who sported a cynical attitude and a candid interest in sex, smoking, dancing, and jazz music."[9] Representative of this genre of public commentary was "Flapper Americana Novissima," an article published by youth authority G. Stanley Hall in the June 1922 issue of the *Atlantic*. Hall provided a taxonomy of this "newest American flapper," adopting the scientific tone and Latin terminology of a lepidopterist classifying a new species of butterfly. This authorial stance cast female youth as a strange breed to be pinned down and labeled from a rational adult perspective. Public discourse about girls would continue to use this tone for decades to come.

Hollywood responded with a crop of movies about college-aged people with a lively, modern sensibility. Noting that movie attendance played a large role in 1920s youth culture, Cynthia Felando has argued that this period marked the film industry's first efforts to reach a youth audience, by offering youth-friendly fare about college antics (e.g., *The Plastic Age*, 1925) and wild young flappers and sheiks (e.g., *Our Dancing Daughters*, 1928).[10] But the precise market for these films may not have been carefully differentiated by age factors; while Hollywood strove to capitalize on "young" audiences, the filmgoers who matched that description might range from twelve to thirty. An understanding of the divisions among youth was not yet widely available either to the film industry or to the public at large.

Both Fass and Schrum have shown that the peer culture thriving in colleges nationwide had its counterpart in high schools as well, although the antics of younger teens did not often appear in films. One possible explanation for this exclusion may be that college students had more freedom than high school students, who still lived at home; the jazzy new youth culture involved illicit activities, and thus could be most thoroughly lived only by youngsters with mobility and a lack of parental supervision. The rare 1920s films about high school youth placed their characters in wholesome settings like a soda fountain, rather than in the speakeasies, late-night parties, and wild car rides that characterized many of the flapper-and-sheik movies. Only the older "kids" had the freedom and means to enact a dramatic break from prewar standards of propriety. And, to the adult eye, that license may have been the films' greatest selling point: adults watched youth to find signs of social decay or, at the very least, social change.

The flapper and college movies of the 1920s died at the end of the decade, when the crash of the stock market and the ensuing Depression made images that celebrated rollicking, hedonistic wastrels seem not only obsolete but in poor taste. Film studios stopped making products that showed youth leading the world into hell, perhaps sensing that American moviegoers of the 1930s already felt themselves to be living a hellish existence. If anything, youth were the only way out, as the "bright promise of tomorrow." Consequently, the popular interest in youth, which continued unabated, shifted to portrayals that elicited pity, concern, or affection, rather than prurient indignation or shock. The 1930s thus intensified a trend toward depictions of very young children which had begun in the silent era, when comic actress "Baby Peggy" and Jackie Coogan, who played more serious roles, were extremely popular.[11] The *Our Gang* series of shorts, which began in 1922, found increased popularity and its most enduring fame starting in 1932—one of the harsher years of the Depression—when the precocious "Spanky" McFarland became a lead character. In that same year the juggernaut of Shirley Temple was unleashed upon the world in a series of shorts called *Baby Burlesks*. By the middle of the decade, as the star of feature films at Twentieth Century–Fox, Temple was the single largest box-office draw in Hollywood and far more popular worldwide than any previous child star had been, purveying optimistic fantasies about youth's redemptive benefits for dispirited adults.[12]

In the mid- to late 1930s, while new child stars continued to draw healthy audiences, some veteran child actors were reaching their teens. This often meant the end of their careers, but for a few, a new trend in entertainment began to allow continued stardom in adolescence, as young actors began surfacing as the protagonists in films of all kinds. Freddie Bartholomew, one of the era's most successful young male performers, found meaty leading roles in such dramatic films as *Captains Courageous* (1937) and *Kidnapped* (1938), playing boys in perilous and adventurous circumstances. Other dramas that presented adolescent boys in threatening situations (thus arousing emotions of concern and care) included films about youngsters' susceptibility to criminality and homelessness in the absence of stable families: *Dead End* (1937), *Boys Town* (1938), and *Little Tough Guy* (1938), among others. Mickey Rooney, one of the most prolific of this period's male teen actors, bridged both drama and comedy; in addition to starring in *Boys Town*, his comic turn at the center of the Andy Hardy series presented the era's clearest enunciation of youthful masculine energy as the harbinger of a bright future.

The primary girl-centered films of this period were those of Shirley Temple and of Deanna Durbin, who often played sunny, well-to-do ingénues in a wildly popular string of musical comedies from Universal Studios. Both Durbin and Temple, though representing different ends of the "youth" spectrum, played roles with similar functions: girls more saintly than human, who solve the crises of troubled, disconsolate adults. So hungry were audiences for these comforting images of youth that the revenues from Temple's and Durbin's films were credited (somewhat hyperbolically) with single-handedly rescuing their respective studios from bankruptcy. Recognizing the role of sunny youth in raising the nation's spirits, the Academy of Motion Picture Arts and Sciences awarded Shirley Temple a miniature special Oscar in 1934, and gave similar honorary awards to Durbin and Rooney in 1938, for their "significant contribution in bringing to the screen the spirit and personification of youth, and as juvenile players setting a high standard of ability and achievement."[13]

Just ten years earlier, the "spirit and personification of youth," as presented in the flapper-and-sheik films, had meant something entirely different, proving Austin and Willard's formulation of youth's dual roles as either our "best hope for the future" or "the vicious, threatening sign of social decay."[14] Cultural definitions of youth depend largely on adults' needs in a given historical moment. In the 1920s, a period of relative affluence and enthusiastic expansion, the very essence of youth itself had been figured as inherently wild and oppositional to adult culture. This anxiety about youth flourished in a moment when other anxieties diminished, when science and industry thrived, and the increased enrollments in colleges attested to the growing affluence among middle-class families. But the Depression's attack on American optimism led to images of youth that emphasized its positive potential, imagining a mutually loving, comforting relationship between youth and age. Kathy Merlock Jackson tells us that "[a]s Americans endured their economic struggle, they looked two ways: to the past for the security of tradition and to the future for hope in a better world. Children, who are the continuation of past generations and the key to future ones, represented both of these comforting perspectives."[15]

Not all youthful roles were overlaid with honey and sugar. Bonita Granville, as a contract player at Warner Bros., earned distinction in the mid-1930s by playing fractious and mean-spirited girls in dramatic films like *These Three* and *Beloved Brat* (in the latter case, her brattiness results from poor parenting, and the film ends with her redemption once her parents see the error of their ways). With the Nancy Drew series, Granville moved into a more upbeat set of roles. Granville, born in 1923, was part of the new breed of "in between" actors whom Hollywood (and society at large) was still having some difficulty codifying. A movie magazine in 1937 described her as "right up there with . . . the rest of the young girls who don't come in the baby class, nor yet are they with the adolescents."[16] Granville was fourteen at the time of this article, an age that qualifies for adolescence by any definition today. The confusion surrounding the applicability of this term suggests the degree to which the categories of youth were still mutable in popular 1930s discourse. That they loved seeing kids on screen, audiences knew; how to establish a stable discursive field around such creatures was still a bit of a mystery, however, and the popularity of screen teens suggests that moviegoers used cinema as a way of resolving some of their curiosity about what "youth" meant in the post-flapper era.

Granville herself commented on the relative novelty of the screen teen in an interview she gave to *American Girl* magazine in July of 1939. Asked her opinion of working in the Nancy Drew serials, Granville remarked,

> I'm certainly glad I'm on the screen now, instead of ten or fifteen years ago. Until lately very few child actors had a chance to go on to grown-up parts. They didn't make pictures about the "awkward teens" then, so, when a child grew too old and gawky to play cute children parts, he was still too young to play adult roles. By the time child actors were old enough to go back into pictures, the public had forgotten them. But now Deanna Durbin, Judy Garland, Mickey Rooney, and Jackie Cooper are among the high ranking actors, and are all in the "awkward teens." The reason they can stay popular is that they're playing parts of boys and girls their own age. So you see, I'm glad of a chance to play something like the *Nancy Drew* series for a while.[17]

The "awkward teens," as many contemporaries referred to them, began to draw increased public attention during this period. The growing visibility of high school students contributed to this development, just as the increased visibility of college students during the 1920s amplified the public's interest in them.

High school attendance was not universal during the early years of the twentieth century; enrollments began to rise during the 1920s and then the Depression became a sort of Great Leveler amongst teens as hopeless job prospects forced more of them to remain in school full time than ever before in American history.[18] Their forced proximity fostered a distinct teenage subculture, allowing the events of high school life to shape common experience along an age axis that ameliorated differences in geography, class, or ethnicity that had more rigorously separated youth in previous years. Gradual signs of a certain "youth culture" that fully encompassed precollege youth began to infiltrate the wider culture, particularly in the mid-1930s when swing music, an offshoot of jazz, began drawing large and highly visible audiences of youngsters. As Grace Palladino notes, "swing music reoriented teenage social life and high school style," bringing to both a new level of public recognition from the wider adult culture.[19] Cultural attention to high-school-aged youth would continue to grow in the last years of the 1930s, assisted by film cycles like the Hardy series, the Durbin musicals, and the Nancy Drew comedy-mysteries.

Building the Perfect Girl

In 1938, when Warner Bros. confronted the issue of how to translate Nancy Drew into films, it had both a wealth and a dearth of precedents from which to draw. Durbin's and Rooney's films provided the most immediate impetus, but those series did not fully establish a firm set of discursive rules for Warner Bros. to use. A gender differential caused a rift in types of images. Andy Hardy, though definitely an idealized youth, still seemed "real" enough to pass for a plausible "boy next door." Durbin, however, played parts less real than angelic. Teen girls in 1930s films tended largely to be cast as "saviors and matchmakers," in Georganne Scheiner's phrase, and in nearly all her films Durbin portrayed a spotless force for moral good, using her gentle demeanor and operatic voice to create harmony from chaos.[20] Durbin's image said less about real girls than it did about fantasies of wealth, and of the redemptive innocence and beauty of youth. Judy Garland's screen persona had more fragile vulnerability to it than Durbin's; she, too, used her beautiful voice to project ideals of sweetness and innocence, particularly as Betsy Booth, a recurring role she played in four of the Andy Hardy films. Betsy made her first appearance in the series in 1938, the same year that the first Nancy Drew film was released, as a wealthy socialite with girl-next-door values—the best of both worlds.

When crafting Nancy Drew, Warner Bros. sought to create a more typical image of adolescent girlhood. One method it devised to learn about realistic contemporary teen culture involved consulting Bonita

Granville and Frankie Thomas, the series' lead actors, for their impressions of the dialogue that screenwriter Kenneth Gamet had written for them. One publicity release recounted producer Bryan Foy's confidence that *Nancy Drew — Detective* "would appeal to theatre-goers of all ages and classes"—until he asked his teenage stars to look over the script:

> When the reading was finished [Foy] turned to Bonita and Frankie for their opinion.
>
> "The story would chap a monk," said Bonita, her eyes shining, "but the dialogue is a dilly."
>
> "I beg your pardon?" said Foy, politely.
>
> "She means the story's smooth," explained Frankie, "but the dialogue's a lot of pap."
>
> "You interest me," Foy said. "I didn't know that."
>
> "Yes," continued Bonita, "the story is thrilling and amusing and swell entertainment. But the dialogue for Frank and me and the rest of the kids in the picture is all wrong. It sounds like a grownup talking for us. High school kids nowadays have a slanguage all their own."
>
> "I think you've got something there," Foy said, pulling his chair closer. "Tell me some more."[21]

The ensuing lesson in teen "slanguage" resulted in several changes to Gamet's script after the studio double-checked its new information: "hundreds of high school students were queried" to assure the authenticity of slang phrases.[22] But even more noteworthy than the teens' colorful argot is the narrative framework applied to this anecdote; it establishes teenage customs as ineffable, bizarre, and disruptive of adults' plans—for Gamet, Clemens, and Foy had been perfectly happy with their script until the "teeners" burst their bubble. More than just curiosity about a new trend, this document reveals a trace of anxiety that the world, soon to be entrusted to these odd-sounding little aliens, is changing so quickly that the adult producers in a major industry might become obsolete.

As well as learning modern slang, the studio tried systematically to establish "realism" by producing a questionnaire about the habits of teenage girls, which it circulated to people it deemed experts in such matters, including actual teenagers.[23] Its aggressive attempts at determining "typicality" in this survey indicate the degree of the studio's confusion about female adolescence, its sincerity in trying to approximate reality in its series, and the general state of contemporary ideas about teenage girls. Warner Bros. included some newspapers on its list of recipients for the questionnaire. The *New York Evening Post* reproduced the questionnaire on its "Woman's Page" under the headline, "Want to Help 'Type' the Sixteen-Year-Old Girl?" The article quotes Robert Taplinger, head of the studio's publicity department, explaining why the survey was necessary: "Motion pictures have grossly neglected the female adolescent with the result that very little is known about what is typical of a sixteen-year-old girl."[24] Herman Lissauer, head of Warner's research department, made similar observations in the letter he sent to the professionals whose advice he sought: "It is intended by the studio that Nancy Drew shall be the actual girl of sixteen living in 1938. When I was asked to describe the Nancy Drew of 1938, I had to confess that I did not know anything about her. . . . I feel that the correct presentation of the typical American girl of today is a pretty serious responsibility and I would be grateful if you would help me to obtain a good picture of her."[25]

Although these studio staffers had no clear idea of a female adolescent, they certainly had preconceived ideas about the questions critical to ascertaining her nature. The questionnaire itself reveals the lines along which Lissauer was already thinking, as certain topics are highlighted so as to suggest what, to his mind, were the crucial issues surrounding female adolescence:

1. Does she smoke? Openly? On the sly?
2. Does she use lipstick and rouge?
3. Does she have a boyfriend? A steady?
4. Does she go out nights? Unchaperoned?
5. How late is she permitted to stay out?
6. Is she athletic? Musically educated?
7. What is her musical taste, "swing" or the classics?
8. Does she have her own spending money? How much?
9. Does she buy her own clothes? Or does her mother help her choose them?
10. Is she allowed to drive a car?
11. Does she belong to any clubs? Girl Scouts? What other clubs?
12. Does she plan a professional career?
13. Does she look forward to marriage?
14. Has she any political opinions? Are they conservative or radical?
15. What is her attitude toward her parents? Mother? Father?
16. Is she tomboy or "crinoline" feminine?
17. Does she discuss sex? As a great mystery? Or does she know all about it?
18. What are her literary tastes?

19. Is she practical and matter-of-fact? Is she aggressively indepen-
    dent?
20. Can she cook? Is she trained for a career as a housewife?

Combined with the questions about tastes and hobbies are questions that
get to the heart of all the usual anxieties about youth, particularly girls:
sexual sophistication, obedience or disobedience to authority, and adherence to gender roles.

But while some of these concerns have attended adolescent femininity
across the decades, others were unique to, or especially sharpened by,
the Depression; these seemingly innocuous questions reveal contemporary concerns about the social roles of young women. The opposition
between swing music and the classics, for example, speaks directly to a
contemporary debate about youth culture. Many types of music were
popular in the late 1930s, not only the two arranged oppositionally in
the questionnaire. But swing music, one of the most visible markers of
a separatist adolescent culture, provoked an anxious reception that often
focused on its destruction of the presumably better values of classical
music. In 1939 *Newsweek* reported that swing music had "invaded the
sacrosanct" by appropriating classical melodies for swing-band arrange-
ments, revealing the editors' pronounced bias.[26]

Classical music was not, as one might assume, separate from youth
culture in the 1930s; youngsters of a certain class (or whose families had
certain class aspirations) often received training in classical instrumen-
tation and had at least some familiarity with an array of classical composers. Indeed, the outrageously popular films of Deanna Durbin traf-
ficked almost exclusively in classical music; the songs she performed were
often selections from operas. While Durbin's fan base encompassed all
ages and both sexes, young girls were among its most devoted members.[27]
Such classically inclined girls allowed conservative adults to look upon
the rabid consumers of swing music (particularly the girls who were beginning to be called "bobby-soxers") as lowly aberrations from a preferred, imagined norm. Fans of swing, which was closely related to jazz,
were criticized in terms similar to those used earlier to scold flappers and
sheiks who consumed that music. Several magazine articles cast a with-
ering glance on the pop-culture fads and pastimes of 1930s youth, for,
as Palladino reminds us, "conscientious parents [felt] a duty to steer
youngsters away from addictive time wasters like swing music, radio
broadcasts, and movies."[28] Lewis Erenberg has described the cultural
threats posed by swing music; its attraction of mixed-race and mixed-

class audiences, and the seemingly sexual dances that accompanied it, were seen to represent an assault by youth on values associated with white culture and the upper classes.[29] To ask if a girl prefers "swing or the classics," then, is to ask a coded question about her adherence to class allegiance, racial separatism, and sexual conservatism. Nancy Drew, both in the books and on film, has all the qualities associated with classical music in this dichotomy, but the studio wanted its Nancy to be a modern girl as well as a good one. Consequently, when the studio publicized Bonita Granville's own responses to the questionnaire, they said that she liked both kinds of music.[30]

The questions about planning a professional career or "look[ing] forward to marriage" are an even keener example of the questionnaire's references to contemporary debates, for this topic caused much controversy during the 1930s. Many women, encouraged by the social and political gains of the 1920s, continued to pursue professional lives despite the Depression's general cultural pressure upon women to stop competing with men for the few available jobs. Women were often categorically fired during the 1930s, and the general attitude toward the shrunken labor market revealed a strong disparity in gendered conceptions of labor. Men were expected to win the bread, and women who attempted to find or hold employment during this period of job scarcity were castigated sharply. Historian Peter Filene charts some of the typical attacks:

> Married women workers, proclaimed a Chicago civic group, "are holding jobs that rightfully belong to the God-intended providers of the household." Working wives with adequately employed husbands "cannot be dignified by the name of workers," agreed the (unmarried) president of the Massachusetts Women's Political Club. "They are deserters from their post of duty, the home," she continued. Congresswoman Florence Kahn agreed that "woman's place is not out in the business world competing with men who have families to support." . . . In a Gallup poll of 1937, 82 per cent of Americans agreed.[31]

That extremely high level of agreement reflects the widespread assumptions that breadwinning was a male responsibility and prerogative, and that women who attempted it were not only foolish but "deserters from their post of duty"—an interestingly military metaphor in a time when the battle against poverty could feel like a war.

The emphasis on reserving the few available jobs for men reveals what was really at risk: not just the financial stability of families, but specifically the status of American men. Writing of adolescent dating rituals during the 1930s, Mary McComb and Beth Bailey have used a financial metaphor to suggest that the "economy of dating" pitted girls against each other as competitors for the "goods," men. The underlying concern behind these codes was a nationwide crisis of masculinity in which male youth, facing a financially insecure future, felt inadequate to function in the traditionally prescribed male role as breadwinner.[32] Michael Kimmel tells us that unemployed fathers during the Depression "saw themselves as impotent patriarchs. . . . With their economic power eliminated, their status as head of the household [was] eroded and with it their sense of manhood." Nor were these perceptions confined to the minds of men; wives and children, raised with the same expectations of masculine breadwinning, often felt ashamed or even scornful of the provider who could not provide.[33]

More than just an expression of concern for individual men's status in their homes, the emphasis on restoring men's breadwinning role was a group project with *national*, not merely personal, implications. This crisis of masculinity took on a broad significance within the national imaginary, creating a perception of a dangerous loss of virility from society at large. The United States had always defined itself in accord with certain stereotypes of masculinity: the rhetorics of discovery, conquest, and the "taming" of various wildernesses—rhetorics on which every American public school pupil has historically been raised—rely overwhelmingly on images of the masterful male. A "crisis of masculinity," then, could disturb Americans' faith in their national identity.

Public discourse attempted to compensate for America's lame-duck masculinity by prescribing a version of femininity concomitantly weakened and hollowed-out; no matter how small Man was, Woman had to be made even smaller to preserve the balance of power. Prescriptive literature for youth, including mass-marketed advice manuals and textbooks used in high schools and colleges, discouraged girls from competing with boys and urged them instead to compete with *each other* to win the ultimate prize, a boy. Placing boys at the center of girls' lives and efforts "reinforc[ed] male dominance in gender relations [and] would bring about an end to the crisis of masculinity."[34] One of the worst ways to violate this dating code was to appear too intellectual in school, for, as McComb reminds us, "[a]ggressive female students threatened male dominance in the classroom and were seen as potentially menacing people who might decide to compete with men for employment in the limited job market." Moreover, stellar academic achievement might cloud a girl's good judgment; if she became too excited by her studies, she might neglect her duty to catch a man, which would have the terrible result of making her an "old maid"—a fate girls were taught to dread.

Bearing in mind the public attitudes recorded by Filene and the prescriptive texts studied by McComb, the reassignment of Nancy's clever ideas in *Larkspur Lane* to her father and her beau in *Nancy Drew — Detective* seems not only logical, but overdetermined. The drives toward consensus and obeying popular prescriptions deemed "normal" would indeed have dictated that a likeable film heroine not outshine her men, since popular and expert opinions militated against such behavior at a time when masculine authority seemed in such jeopardy. The Nancy Drew films, then, can be seen as socializing agents, participating in the same discourse propounded in prescriptive manuals and textbooks, as well as serving the worldviews of the adult watchdog groups whose gaze extended to children's movies. The press book for *Nancy Drew — Reporter* proudly blazoned the endorsement letter Warner Bros. had received from Youthbuilders, an organization devoted to "bringing up a generation of fair-minded and courageous citizens." The group's executive director praises the first of the Nancy Drew film series as excellent fare for young audiences: "In a day when lurid and sensational forms of entertainment claim an undeniably large part of our children's attention, parents would be especially grateful for films, such as NANCY DREW— DETECTIVE, which offer the excitement and action all children crave— without any adverse or unhealthy social attitudes."[35] Nancy's intellectual diminishment, relative to middle-class white males, wholly matched dominant culture's belief in the evils of female "competition" with men, and thus counts among the supposedly healthy "social attitudes" promoted by the series.

Posters and other ad materials for all four of the Nancy Drew films, displayed in the press books, repeatedly emphasize Nancy's intellectual flaws. Not content merely to downplay any competition with males that might be implied by good schoolwork, Warner's publicity department took pains to portray Nancy as a virtual dunce. Her only mental gift is an ability to sleuth, which is presented as comical and freakish. The series' advertising posters bore such slogans as

> Her homework may not be so hot . . . but her police work is 100%!
> If it's murder, she'll solve it right . . . If it's homicide, she'll spell it . . . wrong!
> Report Card: Algebra . . . 60%; Latin . . . 50%; Snooping . . . 100%.

Nancy flunks her school subjects, but in the time-honored tradition of constructing women as gossips and busybodies, she excels at "snooping." One poster for the first film proclaimed, "You'll cheer Nancy Drew, the demon detective! She's just sweet sixteen and she's never been . . . baffled . . . except by her . . . homework!"

Figures 2–4. Advertisements for the Nancy Drew films use signifiers of youth and folly to diminish their heroine's competence. Used by permission of the USC Warner Bros. Archive.

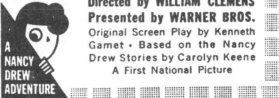

Warner's efforts hollowed out Nancy considerably, but even these measures were not sufficient for some men who were hypersensitive on the issue of masculine power. The series' very premise—that a girl could solve mysteries better than the police—threatened traditional ideas about men's superior competence. In reviewing *Nancy Drew and the Hidden Staircase*, a writer for the *Kansas City Star* ignored much of the film's plot, production values, and cast in order to focus on its menace to manhood:

Just so the masculine sex won't feel too assertive this week, the Mainstreet [theater] follows an "A" feature in which the leading man disappears in the second reel, with a "B" feature in which a little girl makes monkeys of a masculine murderer and a masculine police force. The fact that her boy friend lends valuable assistance is all that prevents patrons from feeling that masculinity has gone the way of the mustache cup, the dinosaur, and high button shoes. Apparently man isn't through yet. He still enjoys a limited sphere of usefulness as mother's little helper.[36]

The rest of the review extols that savior of a boyfriend: Frankie Thomas, playing Ted Nickerson, is the only actor named and the only one whose talents receive mention. It seems surprising that Warner Bros.' hollowed-out, diminished Nancy should incite such nervousness, especially since the worst of the Depression was over by 1939. This reviewer's words remind us that patriarchal fears of girls who "make monkeys" out of men are deeply entrenched, even to the point of outpacing common sense; like cacti, they thrive on little nourishment.

But fear of competent or self-reliant females, though widespread, was not universal. The very same harsh economic realities that made Americans wary of girls' "competition" also made that competition necessary, for clearly not everyone could count on being supported by a husband; what about single girls who had to eat and pay rent? Another form of prescriptive literature, columns for teenagers in women's magazines, offered one answer to that question. In *Good Housekeeping*'s column "The Terrifying Teens," author Marjorie Hillis addressed this topic one month before *Nancy Drew — Detective* arrived in theaters. Titled "Job Ahead," this installment advises girls frankly of the need to supply their own economic security. Demonstrating that the assumptions of former generations had been irreparably exploded by the Depression's ravages, Hillis argues that a middle- or upper-class social status should not justify a girl's complacency; after all, even some millionaires had been flattened in recent years. Hillis also attacks the comforting notion that men could rescue women from poverty: "But you hope to get married and not have to work? . . . [Y]ou'd better not overlook the truth that hundreds of romances today can end in marriage *only* if there are two salaries to support them. Or that thousands of husbands have left widows who, not knowing how to lift a finger, found it pretty agonizing to learn after forty."[37]

Careers and economic self-sufficiency proved a steady theme of Hillis's columns. "Your Own Money" (January 1939) emphasized the necessity of girls' learning to budget their finances, while "Dream It and

Do It!" (April 1939) encouraged girls to parlay their dreams into careers (although one of the "careers" she names is that of "the successful house-wife"). Taken together, Hillis's columns offered eminently sensible ad-vice for young women, made rather poignant by her sincerity. But despite the unassailable truth of her comments, they were not the stuff that most Americans wanted to hear—or more accurately, they were not the stuff that America wanted its daughters to hear. It may or may not be a co-incidence that "The Terrifying Teens" vanished from the pages of *Good Housekeeping* after a fairly brief run. While pragmatism dictated that girls should plan for careers, the preferred cultural narrative reinforced tra-ditional gender roles instead of challenging them. The actual teens War-ner Bros. purportedly interviewed reflected this confusion; many appar-ently said that they intended *both* to have a career *and* to marry, although the chronology of these events, as girls imagined them, remains unclear.

Nancy Drew — Detective includes a line about ambition: at Nancy's school, a teacher overhears a classmate's remark about Nancy's desire to follow in her father's footsteps and become a lawyer. "I didn't know you were planning to be a lawyer, Nancy," the teacher says in surprise; Nancy replies, "I think every intelligent woman should have a career." But while Nancy mouths this line seriously, the film undercuts its implications by portraying Nancy as a member of the upper middle class, for girls of that status or higher—known at Nancy's age as "sub-debs"—were ex-pected to marry well and rarely, if ever, worked after marriage. In fact, class status is one of the biggest keys to the films' portrayal of Nancy because, as I suggest in the following section, it ranked among the most crucial symbols, not only of a girl's character, but also of her father's affluence.

Sub-Debs and the Specter of Social Decay

The phrase "sub-deb" technically indicated a high-society girl in her early to mid-teens, too young as yet for the "debut" or "coming out" party that would mark her officially as a debutante. Throughout the 1930s and early 1940s, the figure of the sub-deb—gracious, well-to-do, and largely decorative—was the dominant image of the teenage girl in popular culture, despite the fact that, during these years of national crisis, fewer girls than ever had legitimate expectations of moving in society circles. *Life* magazine ran an article about "sub-deb" clubs in the nation's high schools in 1941, noting that the term no longer referred strictly to rich girls.[38] This shift in meaning probably occurred during the 1930s, when "sub-debs" and "debs" were appearing as the only alternatives to (rare) images of girls either destitute or delinquent. But why should the term be used at all? Why evoke the image of upper-class leisure as a pervasive label for all white girls at a historical moment when the label was least accurate? Precisely because so many real-life girls lived in states of financial distress, popular entertainment denied that reality as vigorously as possible. Far more than boys—for whom no category comparable to the sub-deb existed—the teenage girl had to "keep up appearances" in order to reassure Americans that, as long as there were leisure-class daughters with wealthy fathers, God was in his heaven and all was right with the world. The sub-deb, like a fairytale princess, evoked romantic fantasies which directly influenced the Nancy Drew film series.

The image of "the little princess" has traditionally been central to the construction of the father/daughter relationship as portrayed in popular culture, and even as enacted, often, within real families. Clichés of this relationship cast it as quasi-romantic, with both participants cooperating to foster a paternal view of a little girl as an "angel" or a "princess," two common nicknames that fathers use for their daughters even today. Few have questioned this pervasive system of appellation, although it very noticeably differs from the system applied to boys, whose fathers, according to the same clichés, call their sons names like "buddy," "little man," or even just "son." Significantly, daughters are not imagined as their fathers' buddies or as small adults, and are rarely addressed simply as "daughter." Rather, the young daughter's symbolic emotional significance to her father demands that she be described in non-human, magical, or fantastical terms.

Valerie Walkerdine has noted this tendency in father/daughter relationships, and rightly pulls the phenomenon outside of its literal manifestation among actual individuals to locate it at a broader level, as part of shared cultural narratives. This mutual fantasy allows daughters to participate willingly in a fanciful construction of themselves, in order to sustain a bond with their fathers. Walkerdine's own father called her "Tinky," short for "Tinkerbell" (the miniature fairy in *Peter Pan*), and she locates a similar phenomenon in one of her case studies, the Cole family, in which the father called his daughter Joanne "Dodo":

> Tinky and Dodo were fathers' fantasies about their daughters: a fairy with diminutive size but incredible powers on the one hand and a preserved baby name (Dodo, as a childish mispronunciation of JoJo) on the other. But a dodo is also an extinct bird, or for Mr. Cole, that aspect of extinction which is preserved in his fantasy relationship with his daughter: a baby. Joanne is no longer a baby;

babyhood, like the dodo has gone, but it is preserved in the fantasy of Mr. Cole's special nickname for his daughter, and in so designating her, he structures the relationship between them: she remains his baby.[39]

Walkerdine traces the origin of her own father's nickname for her to a family photograph of her "dressed as a bluebell fairy. This is where I won and 'won him over': my fairy charms reciprocated his fantasy of me, designating me 'his girl' and fueling my Oedipal fantasies." Walkerdine pinpoints the mutual agreement between fathers and daughters to envision their bond as romantically inflected, a fantasy which requires the man's position as protector of his "little" girl—her being his *baby*, not merely his offspring, matters. Walkerdine might also have noted that "dodo" is a slang expression for a stupid person; it thus doubly applies to my argument here about the need to diminish a girl in order to heighten the distance between her father's position and her own, as a prerequisite for their symbolic romance.

This phenomenon, "daddy's little girlism," often functions through signifiers tinged with class associations; fairy tales are, after all, often about rich people or the attainment of wealth by poor people. In the father/daughter dynamic, the little girl is often imagined not just as a small, non-human creature, but specifically as a "fancy" or elevated creature—as Walkerdine indicates in her story about dressing up as a bluebell fairy, and as implied by the familiar nicknames "princess" and "angel." The fantasy of daddy's little girl mandates that the girl embody a quality higher and more glowing than mere pedestrian reality. That quality elevates her symbolic power—her function as an object for desiring (male) subjects—while diminishing her own subjectivity. We should recall here the arguments of James Kincaid, summarized in the introduction, about the erotic appeal of the innocent and somehow "empty" child—not entirely human, not invested with personhood, but rather emptied of subjectivity, hollowed out to make space for adults' fantasies. As Walkerdine suggests, little girls who love their daddies gladly participate in this process, because the romantic fantasy can appeal to them as much as to the adult. Thus, "daddy's little girlism" thrives as a cultural trope and continues across generations.[40]

The gender specificity of this phenomenon is revealed when we attempt to reverse the terms; the "mama's boy" is also a well-known trope, but not a desirable one. Because of the cultural insistence upon heterosexuality, and because heterosexual masculinity is popularly imagined to forge itself through separation from feminine influence, a boy over-identified with his mama transgresses against gender expectations; he too might be considered a "fairy," but a scorned kind. The same heterosexual insistence in the perception of parent/child relations makes the "daddy's girl" as normative as the "mama's boy" is deviant, because our collective fantasies of heterosexuality posit a diminished female paired with a dominant male. "Daddy's little girlism" is not a pathology; it merely intensifies our normative cultural construction of heterosexual love. The standard codes of that romance borrow from the discourse of the father/daughter relationship, and, concomitantly, portrayals of fathers and daughters in popular culture often employ signifiers of courtship.

"Daddy's little girlism," in sum, is a gender-specific fantasy that operates by diminishing the girl in relation to her daddy, by figuring her as an unreal, "high" embodiment of abstract ideals, and by placing both father and daughter in a heterosexual juxtaposition that mirrors the erotic male/female meta-narrative. The girl is to be protected, unsullied, preserved in childhood like a delicate insect preserved in amber. This partly explains why, in another familiar cliché, a son's sexual activity may make a father proud, while the same activity by his little princess causes intense panic; in addition to the threat of pregnancy, sex destroys the fantasy of purity and the innocence that needs daddy's protection, thus suggesting that the daughter is no longer "his girl," in Walkerdine's phrase. It also sheds light on why American culture has for so long reacted to girls' chastity, or lack thereof, with intense interest and panic; a good deal of recent scholarship on the history of girls and young women has focused upon legal and cultural anxieties about sexual purity. In the realm of popular culture, Georganne Scheiner's survey of adolescent girls on film shows that fears of sexuality attach to girls consistently in every decade; moreover, the discourse surrounding juvenile delinquency has historically bifurcated along gender lines, with sexual promiscuity defining delinquency for girls, but not for boys. In the eyes of the "societal father," the patriarchy, a girl's innocence allows her to symbolize the fantastical, ethereal qualities that serve as her father's and her society's link to the mysteries of the divine. Images of ideal girls, then, must highlight their inhuman, or superhuman, innocence—their lack of corrosive knowledge.

Although the tropes of "daddy's little girlism" are neither era-specific nor limited to the United States, they took on a particular urgency here during the Depression. In 1930s popular culture the "little princess" had more than ever before to seem a *literal* princess: a sheltered, adored creature whose perfection surpassed the limitations of everyday life. The insistence upon this image suggests that it performed a crucially important kind of cultural work for a patriarchal nation in a time of masculine "crisis." Coincidentally, a perfect example of the nature of that work comes to us indirectly through Nancy Drew herself. Harriet Adams, head of the Stratemeyer Syndicate, often told interviewers that her father had denied her wishes to enter the family business when she was young: "His standards were strict and he didn't believe women should work. If they did it was a disgrace and meant their fathers couldn't support them."[41] Any employment she might undertake would say little about her own abilities or competency, but rather would be read as a reflection upon the status of the man in charge of her. The phrase "trophy wife" has entered English slang in recent years to signify the decorative but otherwise insignificant spouse of a successful businessman; Adams's story shows how the same logic operated with younger females. The "trophy daughter" signifies little beyond her father's wealth, and she is among its most important signifiers. The "trophy daughter" idea thrived in the Depression, when the proliferation of sub-deb images in popular culture addressed the perceived crisis of masculinity by suggesting that Daddy was still a real man—that his masculinity was not entirely in crisis as long as he could protect his angelic little girl.

The sub-deb dominated representations of girls, even though the vast majority of American girls did not conform to this mold—and many, significantly, lived in distressed circumstances at the opposite end of the spectrum. A 1934 volume, *Boy and Girl Tramps of America*, reported that the Depression was forcing thousands of teenagers, including girls, to run away from poverty-stricken homes and turn to a hobo life on the railways.[42] Some necessarily resorted to prostitution to support themselves. In 1936, a previously established night court for adult prostitutes developed into a court for female juvenile delinquents, suggesting an increase in such cases.[43] Sexual activity—either solicited or as the result of predation—attended the lives of many girls forced to live without homes or guardians. As Miriam Forman-Brunell states, "thousands of teenage girls . . . slept on park benches in New York City" during the Depression,[44] a fact which many Americans found too disturbing to dwell upon; there is surprisingly little coverage of such girls in the popular press of this period. What little coverage did appear, however, made the plight of impoverished girls disturbingly clear.

In March of 1933 the National Committee on the Care of the Transient and Homeless surveyed the people seeking shelter from local relief agencies on a single night in eight hundred cities across the country. The results of that survey revealed a staggering number of homeless women and girls, many of whom traveled alone. The *Ladies' Home Journal* published two editorials about these survey results in consecutive issues, July and August of 1933, to arouse civic-minded concern among its middle- and upper-class readership. It reported that of the 12,681 homeless females who sought shelter on the night the survey was done, fifteen percent—or 1,480—were under twenty-one. Of the 14,187 individuals making up the *families* that sought shelter, 2,708 were girls between the ages of fifteen and twenty, while 5,544 were children of both sexes under the age of fifteen.[45] This survey presented one of the few discussions of homelessness specifically among underage girls, while the plight of vagabond boys had already received a good deal of public attention and discussion; the female version of adolescent indigence seemed harder to discuss. Popular ideals of gender roles may account for this discrepancy; masculinity is traditionally assumed to forge itself through upward struggle, the "proving of manhood," which allowed even the miseries of homelessness for boys to have at least a faint tinge of the usual narrative of maturity. But for girls, traditionally associated with domesticity and private space, homelessness violated the precious interiority inherent to ideals of femininity; it literally forced girls outside, into the corrosive and dangerous public realm that would eradicate their innocence—and thus irrevocably diminish the girls' value in the economy of national gender ideologies.

Both editorials in the *Ladies' Home Journal* took pains to prevent their readers from assuming that "homeless" automatically meant "morally corrupt," emphasizing that girls who lived on the streets were not callow thrill-seekers who had willingly abandoned their homes; rather, the majority of them were "good" girls from "good" families who wandered out of necessity and who faced unavoidable dangers of sexual exploitation— particularly the poorest girls, who could not afford public transportation and had to hitch-hike instead: "The practice [of hitch-hiking] has been discouraged for obvious reasons—indeed, is against the law in many states—with the result that most of the hitch-hikers now travel by truck. The truck driver is often making a return trip with an empty van in which a stowaway can easily be concealed. He does not own the truck, and he is a ready accomplice for the runaway or wandering girl."[46] Unspoken but implied is the specter of what, besides concealment, might transpire in the back of that truck between a penniless fifteen-year-old and a "ready" truck driver. Even a girl of slightly greater means, who traveled alone by bus, faced the risk of having to accept a "date" to pay for whatever miserable lodging she might procure. The *Journal*'s second editorial recounted the story of a girl who found herself stranded in a new city when a job prospect had fallen through. The girl "hesitated for a moment and then, stepping up to a man on the corner, asked him if he could tell her where she could find a room for the night. . . . The man . . . looked her over, and after a moment offered to take her to his boarding place."[47] Both editorials frame the crisis of female homelessness as a threat to girls' chastity, and in so doing, reveal the ideological stakes of the innocence of the "nice" girl. The real horror that haunts these editorials is less the fact of poverty than the fear of girls' sexual corruption. While homeless boys and girls both went "tramping" as hoboes, only girls risked becoming *tramps.*

The plight of homeless girls received some coverage in media articles about juvenile state homes, reform schools, and other such institutions for wayward girls. *Life* magazine profiled a school that looked relatively homey in 1937, but *Time* magazine wrote in 1938 about one institution in Kansas which punished disobedient girls by sterilizing them.[48] The popular media provided a small but steady stream of evidence that real-life teenage girls came in all moral shades, all classes, and all ranges of safety or endangerment. Yet while news of impoverished or sexually compromised girls received some public discussion, by far the greater portion of public conversation and concern addressed the fathers of those girls: the middle-aged men—many of them veterans of World War I—suddenly reduced to unemployed, enfeebled patriarchs. In April of 1932 President Roosevelt, in a radio address to the nation, spoke urgently of "the forgotten man at the bottom of the economic pyramid."[49] His words tapped into a widely shared anxiety and instantly became a popular catchphrase. "The forgotten man" permeated all venues of public discourse, even co-starring in some of the era's most popular films; *Gold Diggers of 1933* concludes with the lengthy, sobering musical number "Remember My Forgotten Man," while Gregory LaCava's screwball comedy *My Man Godfrey* opens on a scene of self-absorbed socialites breezing through a city dump in search of "a forgotten man" for their scavenger-hunt party. Ironically, the forgotten man was hardly forgotten; no one could stop talking about him. Meanwhile, his daughter remained silently in the shadows, eclipsed by the largely fictional, but spotlighted, sub-deb. Any erosion of the "little princess" fantasy would force Americans to face their fear that the princess's Daddy had lost his scepter.

This fear directly relates to the dominant portrayal of teen girls as comfortable innocents in 1930s popular culture. Georganne Scheiner notes that 1930s films offered an overwhelmingly one-sided portrait of teen girls: they were nearly always angelic "Miss Fix-Its," and only a small handful of films depicted them as runaways or delinquents; little in between seemed to exist. Scheiner also notes that, while female sexual delinquency was a near-constant theme of 1920s films, that topic all but disappeared in the Depression, during which most films about delinquency centered on boys.[50] This striking discrepancy fits the pattern delineated here: the image of the perfect little angel seemed to function like an ideological pacifier for traumatized Americans to suck on, and the worse the trauma, the bigger the pacifier. The very few "bad girl" films that Scheiner names in the 1930s—like 1938's *Girls on Probation*—did not reap the highest box-office receipts or the most enthusiastic public response. Those honors were reserved for the kinds of films made by Deanna Durbin and Shirley Temple. One of Temple's most popular roles was, tellingly, in *The Little Princess* (1939).[51]

The preference for the image of the princess-like sub-deb—the "trophy daughter" of patriarchy—may have been responsible for killing the "Terrifying Teens" column in *Good Housekeeping*, rife as it was with gritty realities about budgets, jobs, and career planning.[52] We cannot take its disappearance as evidence that teen-girl columns, in themselves, had no audience; the *Ladies' Home Journal*'s comparable column began in 1928 and ran steadily into the 1950s. But the *Journal*'s teen column was called "The Sub-Deb," and that title indicates a crucial difference. While "The Terrifying Teens" addressed girls of several classes and spoke of brutal fiscal realities, "The Sub-Deb" addressed only an imagined upper-middle-class audience and dealt with such burning issues as whether or not to make one's next party a formal affair. The tone and content of the *Ladies' Home Journal* overtly privileged the perspectives, styles, and assumptions of "society," while the homier *Good Housekeeping* had a middle-class orientation. Both magazines enjoyed wide circulation, but the higher-class fantasy seemed the preferred one as long as the subject was daughters. In the worldview of "The Sub-Deb" column and other texts with similar topics, a daughter is obliged—as Harriet Adams had been—to reflect flatteringly upon the wealth of her father, and by extension, the family unit of which Father is the head.

This cultural emphasis on the well-to-do teen girl surfaced in the replies Warner Bros. received to its research questionnaire about the "typical girl of sixteen." The studio's press releases allude to several replies, but their archives preserve evidence of only two, those of Kathleen Norris (a popular novelist and frequent contributor to women's magazines) and Emily Post, the renowned expert on etiquette.[53] Norris had a slightly rowdier image of the teenage girl than Post had; she felt that the typical girl of sixteen used makeup, smoked on the sly, dated a steady boyfriend without a chaperone (but usually in the company of a group of friends), drove a car, discussed sex freely and knowledgeably, and was not "trained for a career as a housewife." However, Norris also noted that, trained or not, housewifery was more likely to be in the girl's future than full-time work: "A professional career is more attractive at sixteen than twenty. Then she is looking forward to marriage." She closes with these revealing lines: "I'm assuming that your girl is of the finest class, [the] country clubs, private school, summer in Europe class. She is spoiled, generous, fine, impulsive, vital. She makes mistakes. We all adore her."[54]

Norris imagines that a girl of the leisure class will marry and put career dreams behind her. Nancy Drew's portrayal as a private-school pupil in the opening scene of the first film—the kind of girl Norris delineates—thus makes it all right for the studio to insert Nancy's line about "every intelligent woman" 's planning a career. They can afford to let her give lip service to the idea because the "finest class" of girl is expected to outgrow this ambitious phase. Emily Post's vision matched Norris's rather closely; she too imagined that the "typical" sixteen-year-old girl drove a car, for example—a telling detail in a period when many families could not afford a car. Post apparently ignored the question about careers, but stated that the typical girl "expects to marry." Publicity for the film maintained that, in addition to the adult experts, "hundreds" of actual teenagers were queried as well; although their responses seem not to have been recorded, or at least preserved, the studio claimed that the girls' answers closely matched the experts': the majority of all populations it interviewed said that girls dreamed of ultimate marriage.

Warner Bros. adhered closely to these imperatives in its construction of Nancy Drew. One of the most overt articulations of this link between Nancy and the discourse of sub-debs appears in a bit of cross-promotion in which the studio leased the name and likeness of Bonita Granville to the Lane company, a manufacturer of hope chests. Lane used the images of various teenage actresses in its advertisements for many years; in 1939 the company named one of its new models after Granville and placed her face prominently on a large flyer it circulated among girls in graduating classes. The link between hope chests and graduation is made explicit in the large headline: "When school days end . . . romance begins." The text leapfrogs over any plans for college or careers that some girls may have been formulating, suggesting once again that girls of this class were expected not to labor for money. At the top of the flyer, Granville's smiling face appears next to the headline, "I'm just starting my Lane Hope Chest, too." The caption identifies Granville as "Warner Brothers' *Debutante* Star of the Popular Nancy Drew Pictures" (my emphasis). The back of the flyer lists the items necessary for any complete hope chest, including such class-specific items as "1 dozen finger-bowl doilies," and "1 dozen tiny tea napkins." Clearly, the world conjured by this advertisement would never be more than a fantasy for many of the girls who saw the ad—but, thanks to "low prices and easy terms," some middle-class graduates could reasonably aspire to the product Lane sold, and its attendant fantasy.

Promoting Granville as a debutante took a bit of nerve on her publicists' part. Granville, although blessed with the golden-white prettiness of an American princess, was born to parents who worked in vaudeville; the family were "show people," as 1930s high society would have disdainfully called them. Nonetheless, in the magic cauldron of Hollywood publicity, a person could enter as a sow's ear and emerge as a silk purse, and that transformation was fairly easy in Granville's case. When *American Girl* magazine interviewed her on the set of *Nancy Drew—Troubleshooter*, it presented her persuasively as a cross between a debutante and a fairytale princess. A photo shows her playing the piano, and she speaks gushingly of her favorite classical composers, thus signaling an allegiance to the Western canon of "good" music. Other photos show her engaged in such leisure-class pastimes as diving into a large swimming pool (presumably her own) and horseback riding. Stagehands, interviewed on the set, extol her charms like village serfs praising the gracious daughter of the feudal lord. Readers learn that Granville retreats to her private dressing room between takes to knit sweaters for her father figures on the set (director William Clemens and actor John Litel, who played Carson Drew). The journalist even makes an explicit reference to a fairytale by framing the entire article as a pun on *Alice in Wonderland*; titled "Bonita in Movieland," the article refers often to Lewis Carroll's novel, positioning Granville as a beautiful innocent in a whirlwind adventure.[55] This association of debutantes with Nancy Drew caught on rather easily; at least one reviewer described the Drew films as a "sub-deb detective series," an ambiguous phrase that could refer equally to the film's star and its audience.

But there is a darker side to the image of the debutante, too; as Norris says, "She makes mistakes. We all adore her." Granville's skill at horseback riding and knitting notwithstanding, the filmed character of

Nancy Drew, as we saw earlier, has little skill at anything. In the 1930s discourse of the leisure-class girl, her charm derives partly from her lack of practical competence: she is a lovely, lively, quick-witted "flibbertigibbet" who is also a bumbler, a scatterbrain, and a creator of mild chaos. The juxtaposition of "mistakes" and "adoration" in Norris's statement implies a causal relationship between the two: we adore this darling creature *because* she makes mistakes. A girl who enjoyed all the privileges of the leisure class combined with perfect self-possession and practical efficacy might terrify adults instead of entertaining them. A girl like that could take over the world—as, indeed, Nancy Drew could easily do in her superhuman literary incarnation.

The combination of Nancy Drew's gender-transgressive activities as a detective, and the studio's desire to render her "realistically" vis-à-vis modern teens, brought the character closer to earth. These films are thus meaner to their heroine—making her the butt of several jokes— than are the films of Granville's teen-girl contemporaries, Judy Garland and Deanna Durbin, whose characters frequently embody the more clearly approved ideals of iconic sweetness in adolescent femininity. Because a "realistically" portrayed teen-girl crime fighter must step off the pedestal of the little princess, the films recontain her subversions even while exploiting them as a source of humor. Thus we have the spectacle of Carson Drew in *Nancy Drew—Reporter* literally putting Nancy in her place: hoisting and carrying her to bed, tucking her in tightly, silencing her discussion of the mystery she works to solve. And as he does so, he sings a song that suggests another of the methods of recontainment applied to Nancy: the heightening of her sexual appeal to a patriarchal gaze.

"Pretty Baby"

As he hauls his daughter off to bed, Carson Drew sings a few lines from the chorus of "Pretty Baby," a Tin Pan Alley song from 1916 which remained popular for many years. In this song, the speaker celebrates the qualities in his lover that most arouse his admiration: "Your cunning little dimples and your baby stare / Your baby walk and baby talk and curly hair / And that is why I'm sure that I / Will always love you best of all." In the chorus, he invites his girl to "come and let me rock you in my cradle of love / And we'll cuddle all the time." Although frequently spoken by lovers of both sexes, the nickname "baby" is used in popular culture more frequently by men to name women, and though we usually think of it (when we consciously think of it at all) as expressing a sweet care-taking impulse, it also carries a connotation that the woman's desirability is connected to her infantilization. That meaning is explicit in the song "Pretty Baby," in which the speaker identifies his girl's oddly infantile walk, talk, and stare as the roots of his admiration: "And *that is why* I'm sure that I will always love you best of all."

We have seen that images of the father/daughter relationship in popular culture can mirror the relation between patriarchy and young female subjects in the broader social context. I want now to explore the implied mandate of a binary that makes diminution a catalyst for sexual consumption. Because she is shrunken in popular culture, the teen girl cannot help becoming sexy; the two conditions operate mutually. Examining 1930s prescriptive texts for youth, McComb finds that they "place intelligence and sexual allure in binary opposition to one another,"[56] reminding us that binaries have the unfortunate consequence of creating artificial either/or choices: by forgoing intelligence in its portrayal of Nancy, Warner Bros. emphasized her sexual allure. The ten-to-fifteen-year-old girls who made the Nancy Drew books best-sellers did not need to find their heroine sexually alluring; admiring her and wishing to emulate her were enough. The heightening of her girlish attractiveness in the film speaks to two concerns: first, to address the patriarchal values inherent in the traditional family structure (for this was a "family patronage" series), and second, to create a character who could act as a social prescription for girls.

The films subtly assert the importance of Nancy's appeal to the opposite sex by eradicating all the female friends with whom she sleuths in the books and reducing her social "circle" to her boyfriend, who accompanies (and berates) her in all her activities. But the advertising campaigns reveal the clearest links between Nancy's character and sexuality. Not only do the ads diminish Nancy intellectually, they also dangle her sexuality overtly before the public's eye, and the link between the two seems to be that of cause and effect. For example, one poster displayed in the press book for *Nancy Drew — Detective* connects stupidity and man-catching: "She may get the wrong answers in school . . . but she gets the right men . . . in jail!" The coy ellipses forestall the reader's recognition of the words "in jail," allowing us to absorb the juxtaposition of getting wrong answers and right men. Keene's Nancy "gets" men only in the crime-fighting, not sexual, sense; her possession of the bland and obedient Ned allows her to have the necessary accoutrement of the boyfriend without performing any seductive acts of self-display. Indeed, as suggested in the previous chapter, the series consistently punishes any girl who allows her attractiveness to "shine" too brightly. Nancy herself is wholly oblivious to the existence of sex, beyond her chaste friendliness toward Ned and her occasional interest in reuniting separated lovers. The films' publicity similarly implied a sexual obliviousness in Nancy, but constantly invited the gaze of others to assess her as a cute dish. As we shall see in subsequent chapters as well, the construction of America's media "sweethearts" in this period—and across the twentieth century— consistently derides *subjectively sexual* girls in favor of *objectively sexualized* ones who are innocent enough to avoid sexual aggression, but knowing enough to incite men's aggressive interest.

In the advertisement for *Nancy Drew—Detective* which claimed that Nancy is "just sweet sixteen and she's never been . . . baffled . . . except by her . . . homework!" the first phrase evokes a well-known cliché: "sweet sixteen and never been kissed." This aphorism took on epic significance in Warner Bros.' construction of Nancy Drew; it emphasizes the centrality of sexual innocence to the image of the debutante, and provides another link to the "economy of dating" that McComb describes. That system of emphasizing the single-minded pursuit of popularity reinforced an older tradition in which girls must deploy their sexuality in a careful guise, struggling to be deemed desirable without resorting to the lowly tactic of "petting." Displays of sexual drive or aggression were unladylike and would destroy the very popularity the girl strove so hard to achieve. This was the specifically high school version of the old madonna/whore dichotomy, and the discussions of "how far is too far" that appeared in 1930s magazines and prescriptive books indicate that the boundaries of a girl's chastity were an issue of some concern in popular consciousness.

It certainly seemed important to Warner Bros. When seeking extras and secondary characters for the Nancy Drew series, the company's casting call specified "sweet sixteen and never been kissed" as the quality it wanted the actresses to project. The press book for *Nancy Drew—Reporter* contains an article titled "Read This to Discover What Happens to Girls Who Were Never Kissed." It describes the efforts of "an investigator" (whether a legitimate journalist or a studio employee is not made clear) to interview the young actresses who played extras in the film:

> Sweet sixteen and never been kissed? Don't you believe it! . . .
> An iconoclastic investigator visited the set of *Nancy Drew—Reporter* to inter-

view one hundred and twenty-five 16-year-old extra girls engaged [for the film].

Direct in his methods, he asked bluntly, "Have you ever been kissed?" There were hurried consultations with mothers, agents and chaperones. All but five hands were raised. Only five had never been kissed.

Pursuing his inquiry further, he asked about petting. Sixty-two girls answered in the affirmative. One out of every two 16-year-old girls have petted, at least once, he concluded. . . .

Returning to the five young ladies who had never been kissed, the implacable investigator handed them each a scroll.

"Cherish these," he said, "they signify your charter membership in the Hollywood Liars' Club, Nancy Drew Chapter."

This cynical and mean-spirited piece was intended, remarkably, to be printed in newspapers. In this paradoxical game, it was important not to go too far; the publicity department discarded or edited less desirable material before distributing the press kits. In one example, an early draft of a blurb in the *Nancy Drew — Detective* press book stated that

Not all of the two hundred young ladies who responded to Warner Bros.' call for eight 16-year-old girls who had never been kissed could live up to the qualifications. At least one of them was a wife and mother. She left her baby asleep in her car while she went to the studio casting office to register as unkissed sixteen.

Upon final publication of the press book, this passage was omitted. As the relative cultural silence about vagabond girls already suggested, the public did not seem equipped to contemplate the existence of total sexual knowledge in a teenage girl (even if she was a "wife"). Projections, however, were a different issue entirely; as long as the girl was the passive recipient of a leering gaze, it was perfectly fine to link her image with a limited, one-directional sexuality. Both the published and the unpublished articles score comic points off the backs of teenage girls by judging and consuming their sexuality.

Neither Nancy herself nor the actress playing her escaped this exploitation. The anxious curiosity about sixteen-year-olds' kissing status resurfaced in publicity for *Nancy Drew — Troubleshooter*, during the filming of which Bonita Granville turned sixteen years old. The studio made much of her arrival at the traditional kissing age; they determined to insert a love scene between Granville and Frankie Thomas into the film. This would be Granville's very first screen kiss, her "chrysalis moment."[57] Granville herself contributed to the fray by agreeing to this scene, and to the ideology it represented, according to one article in the film's press book:

> Celebration of her sixteenth birthday recently held unusual significance for Bonita Granville.
>
> In honor of her natal day her mother, Mrs. Bernard Granville, officially sanctioned screen kisses for the first time. And that day, for the first time, Bonita received a screen kiss.... Director William Clemens thought it fitting and proper that the first scene to be filmed on her birthday should be the one in which Bonita's leading man, 17-year-old Frankie Thomas, would kiss her.
>
> The sixteenth birthday kiss met entirely with Bonita's approval.
>
> "I wouldn't want to be known as sweet sixteen and never been kissed," she said.[58]

Granville's and her mother's approval, and the director's decision that it was "fitting and proper" to shoot the kiss on her actual birthday, bespeak a shared assumption that a girl's sexual initiation is a public act, and more broadly, that the story of sex is the main story to be told about a teenage girl. No matter what else she does, her heterosexuality must dominate the discussion. Diminution contributes to her proper heterosexuality, rendering her the dewy innocent who speaks, sees, does, and knows no evil, allowing men to take the lead. The dumbing down and sexing up of Nancy were mutually cooperative actions.

Warner Bros.' intense preoccupation with the osculatory status of "the typical girl of sixteen" is a complex phenomenon with varying implications depending on the audience. Much of the studio's publicity was aimed specifically at young girls, and emphasized an image of adolescent femininity that allowed for a little modernity, but which rested on a bedrock of sexual conservatism. This is how the films functioned, in part, as socializing agents, interpellating young females into a conservative sexual ideology. One full page of the press book for *Nancy Drew— Detective,* headlined "Special Publicity for the American Girl—'Nancy Drew Club,'" reveals that the studio launched a social club for teenage girls, with a charter chapter at nearby Hollywood High School. The press book recommends that exhibitors promote the films in their communities by encouraging local girls to start their own chapters of the Nancy Drew club. Members would receive a photo of Bonita Granville as well as a membership card and badge. The club's values hewed to the "majority answers" the studio had received to its questionnaire, and membership depended upon meeting the criteria outlined in the studio's composite of the typical teen girl. The rules included

1. Must have steady boyfriend, in the sense of a "pal"
2. Take part in choosing own clothes
3. No smoking, drinking or petting
4. Pay their share on dates with boys own age.

The decision-making role of choosing one's wardrobe and the implication of financial equality with boys incorporate progressive sensibilities about girlhood, but the rules mandating only a "pal" as a steady boyfriend and the abstention from any form of sex play or substance use clearly reveal some wishful thinking. In trying to accommodate what they knew of "reality" to what they, and other adults, found appropriate, the studio crafted a composite that implied near-total sexual innocence. Since no one could pretend that sixteen-year-olds don't kiss, the rules simply forbid "petting," in all the glorious vagueness of that term.

Interestingly, the publicity department did not adhere to consistent standards when incorporating its survey results into the films and publicity articles; rather, it privileged any answer—even if it was not "the majority" 's—which supported conservative behavior. Realities of modern teen life were fine in virtually any other topic, but not regarding vice. For example, the researchers found—or at least admitted to—only one glaring difference between the responses received from teens and those from adult experts: while the experts agreed that teen girls smoked, the majority of girls said they did not. In that instance, the studio used the teens' opinion as the norm. In the instance of sexual behavior, however, the studio ignored the information it gleaned from the 125 girls queried in the piece quoted above, fully half of whom had admitted to petting. Notwithstanding the likely differences between the lives of Hollywood starlets and girls in other parts of the country, a rate of fifty percent suggests that a little sexual experimentation must have been happening in the lives of many American sixteen-year-olds, not just those in Los Angeles. Privileging the conservative replies, the studio's project ultimately was less about studying actual teen life than it was about finding evidence to grant the filmmakers "authentic" permission to continue promulgating wholesome images of teen-girl sexuality. While the primary function of the prefabricated "Nancy Drew Club" was naturally to increase ticket sales for the films, a secondary function was to disseminate a strictly monitored code of adolescent femininity to actual adolescents.

Warner Bros.' "sweet sixteen" articles about kissing and petting are clearly written from and for an adult perspective. How, then, might an adult react to these repeated narratives of sixteen-year-old girls and their kissing status? With some worry, perhaps—but also with some desire. By discussing and manipulating Nancy's/Bonita's chastity at such length, Warner Bros. held it up as a spectacle for public consumption. If the studio desired to project only the girlish innocence it saw as an ideal, why not ignore the kissing issue entirely? Nancy Drew did not kiss her boyfriend in the books until well into the 1960s, and her readers did not seem to mind this absence of overt sexual display. But the studio did not only seek to address young girls; touted as a "family" series, and subject to the general cultural standards which influenced all Hollywood products, the Nancy Drew films conformed to the expectations of a general patriarchal gaze. That gaze, as I have suggested throughout, found an invitation to sexual consumption in the presentation of a girl's innocence; as the "blank" screen, the inexperienced and naïve girl provides space for the projections of adult consumers.[59]

Nancy is completely innocent—not just virginal, but also "hollowed out" of knowledge and, because of her youth, of full personhood. As we saw in the introduction, the empty or diminished girl invites the probing erotic gaze that clamors for a chrysalis moment—the initiation that dramatizes the girl's entrance into the mature sexual marketplace. The innocent offers patriarchy a challenge that provides self-definition through conquest; it is the same appeal as the unclimbed mountain, the uncharted terrain, or the unblazed trail. Annette Kolodny famously argued that the United States has historically constructed its self-image as that of a conquering hero, and that which it has conquered—the wilderness, the frontier—has routinely been described in literature as a female body; the United States was partly built on a rhetoric of sexual conquest.[60] Tales about the domination of "virgin land" have permeated many of our national myths, in myriad incarnations; as such, they have influenced the minds of Americans of both sexes for multiple generations. It is neither difficult nor intellectually unfair to assert that virgin-defloration is a central metaphor in American nationalist narratives, or to remind ourselves that virgins, most often, are figured as young girls. The greater the innocence, the more significant (and delicious) its destruction. This chain of associations would come as no surprise to purveyors of child pornography, or to such sexual caterers as publisher Larry Flynt, whose monthly *Barely Legal* specializes in extremely young-looking models, and is one of the most profitable in his empire of magazines.

No sexuality beyond kissing appears in the Drew films or their publicity, but Nancy's/Bonita's sexuality is "showcased," displayed as a plea-surable object for a male gaze. Mrs. Granville's permission neutralizes the display of the girl's sexuality, clearing the way for uncomplicated vo-yeurism. Mama Granville, baby Granville, and director Clemens coop-erate to turn Bonita's initiation into a public performance from which all profit, setting in motion a collective fetishization of her innocence—because, after all, the fabled logic of whorehouses holds that virgins fetch the highest prices. That same theme structures Louis Malle's no-torious 1978 film about a pubescent girl named Violet, a prostitute's child who loses her virginity in the New Orleans brothel where she and her mother live. When she reaches age twelve, Violet is carried around the parlor on a litter while the assembled customers bid at auction for the rare treat of deflowering her. This drama ostensibly bears no resem-blance to any of the Nancy Drew films, yet both depend upon the same ideologies, albeit to different degrees. The title of Malle's film reveals the link: *Pretty Baby*. That song tinkles from the brothel's piano in sev-eral scenes, and Malle uses the phrase both to describe his beautiful child star, Brooke Shields, and to underscore the mentality that finds virginity arousing.

When Carson Drew sings "Pretty Baby" to his own baby while shush-ing her and carrying her to her bedroom, he naturally does not express sexual desire for her; this bedroom symbolizes sleep and silence, not sex. But that scene also cannot help evoking the larger assumptions of a pa-triarchal culture, which, as we saw in the introduction, has often figured girls' sleep and silence—what Bram Dijkstra calls "inanition"—as an in-vitation to sexual conquest. To be silent, diminished, and rendered with-out full personhood is to be a "pretty baby," sexually attractive and ju-venile. By hollowing out its heroine, Warner Bros. made her passively seductive and hence a satisfying figure of social parables about the invi-olability of male dominance. While the studio's publicity hails the series as "straight from the famous Carolyn Keene books, with a mass appeal de luxe," it unwittingly bespeaks the central problem: a Nancy "straight from" the books would not have had "mass appeal" to any audience besides female children, because she was too much of a person to appease contemporary gender anxieties. Kathleen Norris said of the typical girl of sixteen, "She makes mistakes. We all adore her." As written for child readers, Nancy Drew earns adoration by making *no* mistakes. Screen Nancy, however, needs a diminished intellect and hyperbolic, childish behavior to stake a claim to adult adoration: once infantilized, she can be "pretty." A crisis of masculinity thus prompted the evisceration of a literary heroine who was inspiring millions of young readers. In the contest for cultural attention, the nightmares of fathers outranked the dreams of little girls.

3

"Delightfully Dangerous" Girls in the 1940s

And why do I sew
Each new *chapeau*
In a style they must look positively grim in?
Simply between us—*entre nous*—
I . . . hate . . . women!

—"Anatole of Paris"

 These lines are sung in the 1947 film *The Secret Life of Walter Mitty* when Mitty (Danny Kaye), an inveterate day-dreamer, imagines himself as "Anatole of Paris," a world-famous Parisian milliner. In Mitty's fantasy, he sings the wickedly clever lyrics while perambulating among a group of smiling models who wear his monstrous creations (one beauty sports a Venetian gondola on her head). Punctuating his remarks with a maniacal giggle, "Anatole" concludes with this joke about the *haute couture* industry: surely anyone who could design such moronic garb and peddle it as "stylish" must secretly despise the very customers he claims to glorify.

The spirit of this song hovers, too, over the popular string of comic teen narratives which continued to proliferate after the 1930s. During and after the war, virtually every medium of popular culture—fiction, theater, radio, film, and magazines—featured comic narratives with teen-agers in starring roles. In addition to the still-growing roster of Andy Hardy films, consumers could frolic with *The Aldrich Family, A Date with*

Judy, Junior Miss, and *Meet Corliss Archer,* among others. These entertainments shared a puzzling paradox. All of them presented young people
as fundamentally good-hearted, idealistic, energetic, and earnest. Yet at
the same time, writers habitually rendered teens as maddening creatures:
mentally unstable, irresponsible, clumsy, ignorant, insatiably hungry, and
incessantly troublesome to their long-suffering parents. Arrayed in the
finery of wholesomeness and sentimentality, these teenagers were simultaneously draped in the rags of contempt. Surveying this oddly clad crop
of grinning goons, one is tempted to conclude that their producers shared
Anatole's sadistic logic: they hated teenagers.

This chapter is about the strange, conflicted love story between
American audiences and the adolescent, a creature whose public visibility
reached new heights on the eve of World War II. By 1941, American
public discourse had already begun to focus attention on all things teenage; by the middle of the decade, that discourse had formed so firm and
distinct a set of representational codes that the word "teenager," recently
coined, could conjure a fully articulated image in the minds of consumers
of the news media in print, radio, and newsreel films. These discussions
presented teens in the familiar paradox noted in the introduction: either
as "the bright promise of tomorrow" (citizens-to-be embodying the idealistic optimism that augured well for the nation's future), or else as
neglected delinquents whose moral development, compromised by the
war's disruption of home life, heralded social decay. This discourse influenced mass entertainment; two of the most popular girl-centered narrative cycles of the war period, *Junior Miss* and *Meet Corliss Archer,* present the zenith of a paradoxical portrayal of girls as the simultaneous
saviors and destroyers of the American way of life.

Junior Miss, a comedy by Jerome Chodorov and Joseph Fields, opened
on Broadway on the evening of November 18, 1941. Its protagonist,
thirteen-year-old Judy Graves, lives in New York City with her parents
and her sixteen-year-old sister, Lois. Most of the play's action centers on
pubescent Judy's creation of chaos in the Graves household in a series
of slapstick fiascos ranging from simple headaches to the loss of her
father's job. Pronounced a hit in the city's newspapers the next morning,
the play ran for nearly two years, finally closing on July 24, 1943.[1] So
enthusiastically did New York clutch *Junior Miss* to its heart that the *New
York Times* gave the play two reviews: one a standard critical assessment
published the morning after opening night, and the other an extended
rumination on the play's themes, published on November 30. Renowned
critic Brooks Atkinson wrote both reviews, and concluded the second

one with his explanation of why Judy Graves, her sister Lois, and her best friend "Fuffy" were such a welcome addition to the Broadway season: "They are all good girls, though, it must be confessed, a sore trial to their well-behaved parents. And that, in turn, is one of the basic jokes of North America."[2]

Seven days later, the Japanese bombed Pearl Harbor. The nation's leading general magazine, *Life*, had little time to respond; while its December 15 issue included a seven-page spread on the attack, the cover—perhaps already gone to press by December 7—showed only the smiling visage of teenage Patricia Peardon, star of Broadway's *Junior Miss*. Inside, the magazine's Theater section profiled Peardon and the popular new play. The juxtaposition of teen-girl antics with America's violent entrance into a world war may have struck that week's readers as rather incongruous, yet it heralded the tone of things to come. American audiences would prove repeatedly over the next several years that they found the perfect antidote to war anxieties in that "basic joke of North America." Adults had been using entertainment images of youth as anxiety-antidotes for several years by then; in the mid-1930s, Franklin D. Roosevelt offered this homage to Shirley Temple at the height of her fame: "When the spirit of the people is lower than at any other time during this Depression, it is a splendid thing that for just 15 cents, an American can go to a movie and look at the smiling face of a baby and forget his troubles."[3]

The smiling faces of teens served a similar function during the war years, although teen-centered comedies first appeared much earlier. At the turn of the twentieth century Booth Tarkington made several popular contributions to the genre with his Penrod stories and his novel *Seventeen*, both of which sparked early narrative cycles, adapted into plays and films. Aurania Rouverol's *Skidding*, a 1928 Broadway comedy about adolescence, introduced the characters who later appeared in the Andy Hardy films made by MGM.[4] Not until the late 1930s, however, did teen-centered comedies emerge as a prominent and frequent subgenre of popular entertainment. In 1938 Clifford Goldsmith's play *What a Life* debuted on Broadway, a comedy about a hapless high school student named Henry Aldrich. Running for over a year in 538 performances, the play was so successful that its characters spread to other media; *The Aldrich Family* debuted on radio while *What a Life* was still on Broadway, and remained on the air for fourteen years. Paramount Pictures launched an eleven-film series about Henry Aldrich (1939–1944), and *The Aldrich Family* later became one of the earliest successful television comedies (1949–1953).[5]

As these examples suggest, the teen narratives adored by mass audiences were usually about boys. The first girl-centered cycle to garner national attention, *Junior Miss* contains numerous genealogical resemblances to the boy-centered cycles that preceded it; the *New York Daily News* was one of several papers to report that *Junior Miss* was a distaff version of Tarkington's old tales of adolescent boyhood: "Booth Tarkington would, I think, have been one with the cheering section at the Lyceum Theatre last evening. '*Junior Miss*' was there revealed as the best of the adolescent visitations of the season, and it is decidedly in the Tarkington tradition."[6] But *Junior Miss* also reveals significant departures from the boy-centered texts in tone and style of representation, departures which signaled contemporary attitudes about teenage girls. Rising public awareness of adolescence as a site of subcultural separatism—a youth culture that departed from the standards of adult culture—manifested in a paradoxical attitude, combining fears of change and generational tension with a growing capitalist discovery of youth's potential as an untapped, highly lucrative market. Both the subcultural separatism and the massive consumption represented by teen culture were shown, in the media, to flourish especially among teenage girls, sometimes known as bobby-soxers because of the style of socks they wore. These girls were at the center of a new teen culture adults found fascinating yet alienating, and girls' portrayals in popular entertainments reveal contradictions of intrigue and anxiety that mirror those found in the news media.

The Conventions of Adolescent Comedy and *Junior Miss*

Teen comedies, as a genre, strive to present something that looks recognizably average. They take pains to draw an idealized portrait of normalcy and to hail their audience into that identity, so as to create an impression of timelessness—the inevitable, comforting sameness of "growing pains" and their effects on the family unit. In the opening scene of the film *Janie*, a popular 1944 teen comedy, a voice-over narration tells us that Janie and her family live in Hortonville, "an average, homey little town, like yours or mine." In the inaugural episode of the *Meet Corliss Archer* radio series, the announcer tells us that teenage Corliss "could be in almost any family, and in almost any town."[7] These reiterations of familiarity participate indirectly in what Lary May has identified as a creation of consensus in 1940s films, when "government leaders called on the film industry to promote an unprecedented class and cultural consensus as the very essence of the American way."[8] May concentrates on films more obviously nationalist in their content, with plots about war or government, but the teen-centered comedies foster a consensus as well—one based specifically on discourses of home and family life, powerful nationalist symbols in America's wartime propaganda. Images of home and family celebrated the essence of American values, the building blocks of the nation. Teen comedies embody this vision of the family, but also complicate it by portraying teens as their parents' ultimate headache; the films thus build consensus in two ways at once, both by celebrating the democratic American family unit and by interpellating audiences into the supposedly common identity of the exasperated parent. Surely, these stories imply, "we all" know the strains of sharing a house with a teenager. Henry Aldrich exemplifies teens' dual roles: the Aldrich cycle, set in a fictional town with the revealing name of "Centerville," usually focuses on hapless Henry's creation of mayhem. But the cycle's fundamental support of the nuclear family and its all-American values remains consistent and appears even more forcefully in *The Aldrich Family Gets in the Scrap*, one of Paramount's short propaganda films exhorting audiences to participate in the war effort. In both their worst and best guises, teens symbolized the bonds that united Americans.

To underscore the accessibility of this "centered" averageness, the families in these tales occupy the default identity of American families in popular culture: white, Christian, and comfortably middle-class. In order to express the idealism that Mickey Rooney (quoted in the introduction) attributes to teen comedies and the cultivated appearance of normalcy that informs this genre, the families are usually financially secure but not so wealthy as to damage their claim to averageness. Anchoring the stability and solid morality of these homes, the father often holds a position of social authority: doctor, newspaper editor or publisher, college professor, or, most frequently, attorney or judge. Such teen characters as Andy Hardy, Nancy Drew, Judy Graves, Henry Aldrich, and Corliss Archer all had fathers in the legal profession.[9] Adding to this uniformity was the film industry's tendency to typecast actors in certain roles, so that Henry Aldrich and Nancy Drew even shared the same father: actor John Litel played the attorney-parent in both film series.[10] Casting Dad as a representative of law and order reinforced the patriarchal tone of this genre, for when the father enforces the laws of the land, the teen's filial behavior symbolizes his or her behavior as a citizen of a patriarchally organized society. This pattern also provided comedic opportunities to juxtapose sober fathers with their lunatic children—for all teenagers in this genre flirt with lunacy. Energized by naïve earnestness and cockeyed optimism, teen protagonists embark on schemes designed to procure lofty results, but destined to go as painfully awry as possible before the tidy conclusion.

Narratives about boys often followed in the tradition of Booth Tarkington's highly popular fictions. *Seventeen* centers on William Sylvanus Baxter, who suffers tribulations in his struggles for a good suit, a girlfriend, and a little dignity. This mold shaped nearly every subsequent boy-centered comedy for decades thereafter; central to all of them is a good-hearted and earnest lad who suffers setbacks and public embarrassments that thwart his desire to be considered manly. The financial comfort of the teen's family does not extend to the boy himself; one of the most common plots in this genre concerns his lack of adequate funds. Because he is the one expected to pay for dates and for repairs to his wheezing car, the protagonist's uphill climb toward solvency teaches him self-sufficiency and responsibility to others. The overwhelming tone of boy-centered comedies thus balances humor derived from the boy's youthful folly with respect for his innate impulse toward manliness; while his struggles elicit laughs, they also elicit sympathy and draw upon the traditional trope of adversity as the young man's path to maturity. Boys in this genre always have sound values and good hearts; the Andy Hardy series, in particular, frequently emphasizes its hero's strict moral code. Although his youth and naïveté cause him to miscalculate in crucial instances, the series suggests that Andy's youth is all that's wrong with him—and youth, fortunately, is temporary.

Boy-centered teen tales are often produced from a nostalgic perspective, evoking viewers' sentimental identification with youth. Perhaps for this reason, the boyhood portrayed in this genre usually remains temporally vague; the boys' daily activities rarely adhere so strictly to generational specifics as to preclude adults' sense of recognition. In the Andy Hardy series, for example, high school boys work on the school newspaper and the senior class play, drink sodas in malt shops, take country walks to "spoon" with their girlfriends, attend dances, fix their cars, and build short-wave radio sets. None of these activities occurred exclusively in the period of the films' production. Indeed, they might have derived from the boyhood memories of the tales' adult producers; the thrill of short-wave radios, for example, had been exploited by Edward Stratemeyer with the launch of his Radio Boys series in 1922. The activities that constitute youth culture in these films thus offer a comforting message of continuity over time. Audiences seem to have accepted this intergenerational invitation to affectionate recognition, for the Andy Hardy series set box-office records nationwide with adults and children alike. Ezra Stone, who played Henry Aldrich onstage in *What a Life*, also enjoyed a cross-generational appeal; he received fan mail from adults praising the play for bringing back happy memories of their own adolescence, while letters from teens—including girls—thanked Stone for portraying the agonies of high school with such accuracy.[11]

The real innovation in 1930s and 1940s popular culture, however, was the sudden proliferation of teen cycles that focused on girls: beginning gradually in the late 1930s, girl-centered cycles quickly multiplied in the 1940s with *Junior Miss*, *Janie*, *A Date with Judy*, and *Meet Corliss Archer*. As we saw in the previous chapter, in 1938 Warner Bros.' research department had been puzzled about how to define and codify the "typical girl of sixteen." Over the next few years the puzzlement disappeared. Produced by artists who watched and learned from each other's efforts, the teen-girl tales crafted a rapidly solidifying set of stereotypes about adolescent femininity. If the boy-centered tales rely on an aura of timelessness to foster identification with the hero, the girl-centered tales do almost the opposite, emphasizing contemporary details that foster an adult's sense of alienation from the heroine. Girls' pastimes and activities, while sweetened and idealized in comic teen films, tend to focus on the irritating effects of contemporary popular culture; teen heroines are distinctly drawn as either jive-music lovers or movie fans, with the names of specific stars frequently dropped into the scripts. The chaos caused by girls is sometimes linked to their immoderate consumption of popular culture—a continuation of the arguments put forth in the 1930s' Payne Fund studies of the corrupting influence of movies on young minds, but narrowed to a girl-specific context. Since the film industry understandably would not want to portray itself as a social evil, the "fault" is applied to the young heroines in question: it is their biological identities of age and sex that make them pathologically susceptible to the romantic suggestions of art and culture. If all teenagers were "wacky kids," the wackiness could only increase when the teen in question had a female brain (less rational) and female body (more sexually disruptive).

Freud famously asked, "What does a woman want?"[12] But in the teen-centered entertainment of the 1940s, the more pertinent question seemed to be "what are little girls made of?" as various artists anatomized the styles and habits associated with teen girls, using them to conjure a specific story about girls' identities. Those stories, usually narrated through an adult, male perspective (even, sometimes, in scripts written or co-written by women), revealed a degree of anxiety and mistrust of teen girls surprising in its departures not only from the norms of boys' representations but also from the recent images of girls as helpful "Miss Fix-Its" and idealized angels. In 1941's *Andy Hardy Meets Debutante*, Andy, in a slightly dated plot device, pined for a remote and glamorous New York socialite; but in that same year, Jane Withers played a sassy and tomboyish *Small Town Deb* in a role that would soon come to typify girls' images. Teen heroines of the 1940s tend to be slangy, sarcastic, disobedient to authority, aggressive, and determined. Although Deanna Durbin's 1930s film characters had often shown a girlish and charming form of aggression, it was always in the service of a higher good, usually a figuratively or literally patriarchal project.[13] Teen heroines of the 1940s, by contrast, enact their aggression in self-pleasuring pursuits, usually to the detriment of their father's (or their community's) peace of mind. Sass and aggression did not imply self-sufficiency or maturity; bobby-soxer texts often show their protagonists as silly creatures who cause astronomical, if accidental, damage to their fathers' stability. Driving every adult around them into righteous fits of fury, teen girls were now *Delightfully Dangerous*, as the title of one 1945 film proclaimed.

The most frequent plot of the girl-centered comedies turns on some kind of sexual misunderstanding, either a father's fear that his daughter has lost her virginity or a daughter's fear that her father is having an extramarital affair. Tellingly, sex is always the story to be told in relation to girls, specifically a kind of sex that juxtaposes them tensely with their fathers. In tone, these narratives sympathize more with the father than with the daughter, even while she is the central protagonist. Fathers routinely have common sense on their side but are overanxious and easily flustered, while daughters appear relatively cool and wrong-headedly confident in a worldview based on hyperemotional folly. One theater critic described Judy Graves as "a higgledy-piggledy child whose values are distorted by the wildness of her imagination. . . . When Judy and [her friend] Fuffy put their heads together they can turn the ordinary affairs of the world into complete insanity. For what they see is dyed in the gaudy colors of screen romance."[14]

Portrayals of girls suggested that adolescence is a more dangerous phase for females than for males, because it mixes the follies of youth with the inherent vulnerabilities of the female mind (one reviewer of the first Corliss Archer film described Corliss as "a compound of girlish innocence and female perversity"[15]). The genre consistently figured girls as guilty of inconstancy, petulance, vanity, affectation, and moral relativism. Writing in the 1980s, L. E. Ward offers a concise summary of these films' negative moral judgments of bobby-soxers:

> Such girls were always too big for their britches. With stars in their eyes, they often fell head over heels in love with an older, single man. . . . Such 'crushes' were merely that, a result of too many visits to the local malt shop, too many issues of movie magazines, too much leisure time, and too much pampering. They were still, after all, fundamentally dependents of their parents, as well as non-adults in almost every way. . . . They disdained 'boys,' but their [*sic*] was always a nice boy-next-door to take their put-downs, complaints, and to provide a happy ending in spite of everything.[16]

Spoiled and absorbed in the whirlwind of exciting peer culture, such girls challenge the values upon which American patriarchy and capitalism rest. They don't know their place, or the value of a dollar; they lack discipline, principles, and skills. Everything that's wrong with them is the result of "too much"—malts, magazines, leisure, and pleasure. Suffering from superfluity, they are superfluous themselves. Their dependency on their parents, combined with their frivolous behavior and excessive consumption of popular culture, makes them "non-adults," and therefore inferior to the boys who "provide a happy ending." Ward's summary includes examples that span a brief but varied array of films, though not all instances of the genre equally manifest the traits he names. The first widely successful narrative cycle based on a girl, *Junior Miss* has a younger heroine than would become typical; at thirteen, Judy Graves is a shade too young, according to narrative conventions, to exhibit the extremes of vanity and boy-craziness Ward describes. But much of her behavior matches his descriptions, which is why the *Times*'s critic could call her a "sore trial" to her parents, and thus part of "the basic joke of North America."

Judy's original creator, writer Sally Benson, hardly had such a joke in mind when penning her short stories for the *New Yorker*. The first, "Junior Miss," appeared in the issue for October 28, 1939.[17] Based on a scene Benson witnessed on a New York City bus, in which a young adolescent girl was berated by her mother and elder sister for dropping their fares,[18] "Junior Miss" is a sensitive story about an awkward girl, the object of her family's criticisms, whose dreams of a stylish new coat are thwarted by her pubescent body: too large for the children's sizes, she is not mature enough for the "Junior Miss" styles that target older teen girls. The existence of "junior miss" fashions was itself a recent phenomenon in the 1930s, adding a topical element to the story and linking the girl to modern-day consumer culture, a detail that figures only marginally in Benson's fiction but which haunts the stage and screen versions of *Junior Miss*, as well as the bobby-soxer genre at large.[19]

Benson's use of the third-person narrative voice allows her to concentrate on Judy's starry-eyed perspective while also showing how others, more cynically, perceive her. Neither a children's story nor a joke for adults, "Junior Miss" demonstrates Benson's signature style: understated prose and a perceptiveness that makes her adept at stripping away her characters' self-delusions even while empathizing with them. Her fiction was thus more challenging than most of the magazine fare of her day; commenting on her distaste for that market, Benson told an interviewer that "what they really want are healthy, clean-limbed, hearty young people on a raft, and that isn't for me."[20] The *New Yorker*, a discerning literary magazine, appreciated complex, three-dimensional characters— and, it should be noted, was not commonly read by children. In later years, the collected volume of *Junior Miss* stories became a favorite among girls: published initially in 1941 by Random House, it was reprinted by Scholastic, a children's publisher, and a 1959 survey of school and public libraries revealed that *Junior Miss* remained one of the ten most popular books for young adults.[21] As *The Catcher in the Rye* would later, *Junior Miss* became known exclusively as an adolescent's book, even though its first enthusiastic audience had been sophisticated adults. The *New Yorker*'s readers responded so favorably to the initial short story that Benson was invited to write more of Judy Graves's adventures, and when the collected volume was published, it quickly became the Book of the Month Club's choice for June 1941.[22]

The popularity of Benson's stories inspired playwrights Jerome Chodorov and Joseph Fields, who had successfully mined the pages of the *New Yorker* for earlier Broadway entries, to apply their restructuring talents to the Judy Graves tales. The play *Junior Miss* had a successful run from November 18, 1941, to July 24, 1943. It sparked the creation of a radio series (1942–1954, sporadically) and a film in 1945, based closely on the play. The play and film depart significantly from the tone of Benson's texts; it took some hammering to shape her subtle short stories into a linear, plot-directed narrative, and the process had the unfortunate result of "hardening the delicacy" of Benson's prose and "creat[ing] a popular stereotype," in the words of a latter-day reviewer.[23] That stereotype resulted from the play's shift to a paternal perspective, and the concomitant diminishment of Judy. No longer a narrative about a pubescent girl, the play *Junior Miss* became a narrative about the effects a girl has on her father. The trajectory of the Junior Miss cycle—much like that of the Nancy Drew cycle—suggests that a female character's transition from fiction to film could recast her as an object rather than a subject and thereby diminish her personhood.

In describing filmmakers' approaches to portraying youth subculture, Thomas Doherty has employed a colonialist metaphor, finding that "teenpics fall readily between two pillars that might be labeled 'imperial' and 'indigenous,' aligning themselves with either parent culture or teenage subculture." Unfortunately, the revised edition of Doherty's study omits the rest of what followed this sentence in the first edition, where the original paragraph included this useful explanation: "Ethnographers speak of an analogous dichotomy in the 'etic' and 'emic' methods of making sense of alien cultures. The etic investigator applies his own frames of reference to the host culture; the emic investigator . . . adopts the host culture's own frame of reference. To the etic observer, the tribesman who ingests peyote engages in debilitating escapism; to the emic he participates in a religious reaffirmation of tribal values."[24] This anthropological metaphor applies perfectly to *Junior Miss* and other bobby-soxer texts, all the more so because of its reference to ingestion; as we shall see, "consumption" of various kinds proved one of the issues that most clearly illuminated the tensions between imperial/etic and indigenous/emic interpretations of youth.

As fiction, the Junior Miss stories respected and empathized with Judy Graves's subjectivity, offering, if not quite a wholly indigenous portrayal, at least one that privileged indigenous over imperial interpretations of Judy's actions. But in the dramatic and filmic texts, Judy's subjectivity diminishes in proportion to her role as a foil for her father, and for a patriarchal, imperial narrative perspective. In other words, with every step that *Junior Miss* took away from a specialized medium (literary magazine) toward more mass media (stageplay and film), it took a concomitant step toward further denigration of its ostensible heroine. As *Junior Miss* grew to be a genuine phenomenon—incarnated in several media outlets, popular with consumers of all ages—Judy became the first truly mass-culture heroine to personify the stereotype of female adolescence as an abject condition.

The different perspectives on Judy offered by the serio-comic prose and the purely comic theatrical and filmic texts surface even in minor changes of dialogue. In "Les Temps Perdus," a story in the *Junior Miss* collection, Judy reads aloud to her family an autobiography she has written for a school assignment. Her mother takes issue with a bit of Judy's poetic license:

> Judy cleared her throat and began to read. "It was exactly on the stroke of midnight on the twenty-first of September that I was born."
> "Judy!" Mrs. Graves said. "How did you get it into your head that you were born on the stroke of midnight? You were born at eight in the morning."
> "A few minutes after eight. Almost ten past, I think it was," Mr. Graves said. "I remember I got to the office about nine-thirty."
> "It isn't so very important," Judy said.
> "In an autobiography," Mrs. Graves told her, "one should be accurate."[25]

Here is the same scene as written by Chodorov and Fields:

> *Judy:* (reading) "My Life So Far" by Judy Graves. "It was exactly on the stroke of midnight, on the twenty-first of September, that I was born."
> (Harry and Grace [Graves] exchange a look.)
> *Grace:* How did you ever get it into your head that you were born on the stroke of midnight?
> *Harry:* You were born at six o'clock in the morning! And made plenty of trouble for everybody![26]

In Benson's version, this scene highlights a gap between filial and maternal attitudes toward imagination; in the play, it instead establishes Judy as a "troublemaker." There is no reason to change the hour of her delivery from eight to six A.M., except to imply that the defining purpose of her existence is to inconvenience her parents. Tellingly, Mr. Graves's inconvenience is privileged in these scripts—a striking fact, given that labor and childbirth are obviously harder on mothers. Mr. Graves's line in the story, above, seems merely to establish a matter of fact, while in the play his word choice and the use of exclamation marks reveals that he speaks with great annoyance. In the stories, Mr. Graves appears uninterested in his girls' foibles and therefore has few opinions about them, leaving the primary parenting to his wife. In the theatrical and filmic versions, his version of parenting consists mainly of angry outbursts. Paternal suffering, rather than adolescent suffering, becomes the play's dominant locus of empathy; Mr. Graves emerges as the pitiable, overburdened victim of his offspring.

In fiction Judy also has a vexed relationship with her father, but Benson presents the vexation more equitably as affecting both partners in the relationship. Harry Graves's well-intentioned vagueness toward his daughters bespeaks an utter lack of interest in them, but given the choice, he prefers Lois because she is more mature and prettily feminine than his awkward younger daughter. The story "Daddy Dear" treats Judy's failed efforts at forging a sentimental bond with her father. After seeing a movie about a ringlet-haired Victorian girl who adores her dashing soldier-father (an allusion to Shirley Temple's film *The Little Princess*), Judy emerges from the theater determined to re-create the mutually wor-shipful father/daughter relationship she has just seen on screen. But when she returns home, a clash between fantasy and reality awaits her:

> Her thoughts were so filled with a blurred image of her father, who had obligingly donned the uniform of a British officer, that it was rather startling to find him actually sitting in the living room reading a paper when she got home. She walked softly over to his chair and shook her head at him playfully. Her hair hung in a thick, straight line to her shoulders, and no soft curls bobbed about at the movement. "Good evening, Daddy dear," she said.
> Mr. Graves lifted his eyes. "Oh, hello there, Lois—Judy," he answered.[27]

So remote from his children that he cannot keep their names straight, Mr. Graves is a poor object for Judy's efforts at romantic reconstruction. As she shakes her head at him, vainly trying to mimic Temple's bouncing curls, her father asks, "What do you keep shaking your head for? . . . Have you got something in your ear?" But he is not really unkind; when he sees how badly Judy wants to walk with him around Central Park the next day, he indulges her, although he soon regrets it; still playing the adored and adoring moppet, Judy swings on his arm with the full weight of her pudgy body.

> He shook her off. "Stop wiggling, for Christ's sake, and *light!*" he exclaimed. "And step on it, because I'd like to have time to snatch a drink before dinner."
> Judy dropped his arm . . . and her feet, in their brown oxfords, dragged heav-ily. It was not usual for her father to mix drinks before Sunday dinner, and the soldier-father in the picture certainly hadn't reached for a bottle after a brief session with his idolized little daughter. As she stumped along, keeping step with her own father, she decided that it was not easy to become the apple of someone's eye.[28]

Benson's prose elicits the reader's sympathy for both characters. There is no hero or villain in this story, only the yawning chasms of age and sex which doom father and daughter to mutual disappointment. Judy's disappointment, however, receives greater attention, and Benson creates a strong tone of empathy for this clumsy, illogical heroine who longs in vain to be the apple of her father's eye.

"Daddy Dear" inspired the plot of the play *Junior Miss*, yet none of its events occurs in the play. The only narrative elements that survive are Judy's attempts to model real-life relationships on cinematic fictions and her father's subsequent irritation. The play introduces J. B. Curtis, Mr. Graves's boss, and Curtis's daughter and secretary, Ellen, whose strained relationship with her father constitutes the subplot. The play thus telescopes the fiction, minimizing the roles played by Judy's mother and elder sister and highlighting instead the juxtaposition of two vexed father/daughter relationships. These patterns would resurface in every girl-centered narrative for the rest of the 1940s: this genre makes the girl her father's defining, necessary enemy; each is the other's Other, the second term which gives the first term its definition through juxtaposition and conflict. No yin without yang; no black without white; no teenage girl without a suffering father.

The suffering in *Junior Miss* follows from Judy's status as a consumer, and a minor conflict arises from Judy's literal consumption: her ceaseless snacking irritates everyone in the house. Mr. Graves cracks jokes about the size and health of Judy's "tapeworm" while the housekeeper berates Judy for sampling leftovers as they clear the table: "Why don't you just hold your mouth open and I'll scrape all the plates into it?" But the more serious conflict stems from Judy's consumption of movies; the playwrights and screenwriter insert numerous lines to demonstrate the girl's obsession with cinema. As Mrs. Graves feels Judy's forehead one evening, worried that her daughter's bizarre behavior might indicate illness, her husband sarcastically reassures her: "It's not yellow fever, it's just the double feature. Tonight she's Stella Dallas," naming the heroine of a famously sudsy melodrama. Cinematic hyperboles become Judy's dominant paradigm for interpreting real events, resulting eventually in the near-destruction of the Graves family's stability.

Harry Graves works in a law firm for the blustering J. B. Curtis and Curtis's daughter, Ellen, a browbeaten young woman who slaves for her dictatorial father. In a moment of sympathy Graves gives Ellen a chaste kiss. Judy secretly watches this exchange and filters it through her extensive mental catalog of film plots. Because she has seen *Wife vs. Secretary*, in which Clark Gable finds himself torn between the titular women in his life, Judy jumps to the conclusion that her father is having an affair with Ellen.[29] Enlisting the help of her friend Fuffy, Judy determines to save her parents' marriage by distracting Ellen with a new suitor. The perfect solution presents itself in Judy's Uncle Willis, a mysterious figure whose past the elder Graveses refuse to discuss. We ultimately learn Willis's secret—he has been gone for several years while overcoming alcoholism—but, deprived of this information, Judy again uses movies to explain Uncle Willis's absence and sudden reappearance: she reasons that he must have served a stretch in prison, like Tyrone Power in *Johnny Apollo*. Associating him with her movie idol, Judy briefly transfers her crush on Power to her Uncle Willis: saying her final goodnight to him on the night of his arrival, she closes her eyes and tilts her face up, inviting a romantic kiss. Willis deliberately kisses her forehead, but plays along as Judy walks, dazed, into her bedroom: "Good night, my dear," he calls after her; "We shall meet again." Viewers hear the humor in Willis's voice; Judy does not. Convinced that he is an irresistibly romantic figure, and brim-full of the reformer's zeal, Judy believes that introducing Willis to Ellen will have the doubly happy result of speeding his rehabilitation while curing her father's imagined infidelity.

Ellen and Willis obligingly fall in love, and Judy feels proud of her ingenuity, as she cheerfully informs her father's boss when he pays a call. But J. B. Curtis has no desire to lose Ellen, his daughter-servant, especially when Judy blurts out that Ellen's intended is (as she believes) an ex-con. Curtis tongue-lashes Judy cruelly in both the play and film, calling her a "little brat," a "little idiot," and a "little monster." He promptly fires her father, a blow that will surely destroy the Graves home; no longer able to afford their apartment, their housekeeper, or the girls' private-school tuition, the family will have to split up. Mrs. Graves and the children will live with her parents in another state, while Mr. Graves searches for a new job and starts at the bottom again. Weeping inconsolably, Judy apologizes for destroying everyone's lives; "I don't blame you for hating me," she sobs, and even offers to let Lois slap her. Her abjection seems appropriate for the horror she has wrought.

Despite the critics' comparisons, this plot is much harsher than any in Booth Tarkington's stories, or in most other male-centered teen comedies. Temporary inconvenience, embarrassment, or expense are usually the worst that the father of a boy suffers. In girls' stories, however, teen chaos often threatens not just fathers' peace of mind, but their very livelihoods, and thus the stability of the father-centered nuclear family. The girl's magnified threat evokes a magnified punishment: while Henry Aldrich and Andy Hardy often suffer humiliations, Judy Graves goes through real hell, crushed by guilt and shame. The scenes of her tearful apologies act as a sort of dramatic spanking; the playwrights punish Judy for her movie-corrupted imagination, her foolishness, and her meddling in adults' affairs, the ultimate transgression for a girl-child in a patriarchal home. If the play were to end at this moment it would be a tragedy, and a particularly frightening one for having been caused by the ravings of an idiot savant—a daughter who doesn't know her place.

But this is a comedy, and after the playwrights have beaten some contrition into Judy, they can afford to lift her up and wipe her tears away. The last scene magically restores order: mistakenly believing that Harry Graves plans to steal a valuable client when he leaves the firm, J. B. Curtis hurriedly rehires Graves and promotes him to "junior partner" (juxtaposing the father and his "junior miss" daughter). Judy appears, at first, to catalyze these adult events: Curtis's misunderstanding stems from Judy's preparation for her first party-date that evening with a boy named Haskell Cummings, Jr., son of the client whom Curtis fears losing. Hearing only that someone named Haskell Cummings is on his way up to the Graves's apartment, Curtis jumps to his fortuitous conclusion, and remains magnanimous even after learning the truth of the mix-up. Both he and Graves, formerly united in their rage at Judy's meddling, now praise her for having restored peace and order.

When Judy emerges from her bedroom dazzlingly arrayed for her first date, she symbolically emerges from her chrysalis of childhood into young womanhood: "Looking freshly lovely in her first evening dress, she is a heroine of which any play should be proud," said the *New York Herald Tribune*.[30] Formerly a hoyden in the bobby-soxer's uniform of sweater and skirt, Judy now appears as a lovely, demure young lady, and every male in the room—young Haskell, Mr. Graves, and J. B. Curtis—is awed by the transformation. "Young man," Curtis says to Haskell in the play's final line, "you're going out with a hell of a girl!"[31] In the film version, Mr. Graves adds hyperbolic praise by calling his daughter "one of the outstanding personalities of our time, and very probably the first woman president of the United States." The film further heightens Judy's glory in this scene by playing the melody of "Somewhere over the Rainbow" on the soundtrack, Judy Garland's landmark song from *The Wizard of Oz* (1939). Evoking the audience's memory of that other Judy as a lost darling for whom "there's no place like home," the song underscores Judy Graves's transformation from hellion to "a hell of a girl."[32] Bedecked in splendor for her inauguration into the world of dating, and serenaded by a sentimentally loaded melody, this Judy, too, reaffirms the joys of "home": the ideologies of heterosexual romance, eventual marriage, and devotion to the patriarchally organized family. She has, moreover, preserved her father's status as breadwinner and thus restored the security of her family. Now that her bobby-soxing sins have been cleansed by confession and acts of contrition, Judy, initially an enemy of the status quo, suddenly becomes its ultimate icon.

A remarkable fact about the ending of this play and film is its absolute lack of irony in suggesting that Judy has somehow saved the day—and the critics reinforced this reading. But has Judy really accomplished anything to merit being called "a hell of a girl," let alone the future president of the United States? All throughout the play, her efforts at agency are mocked and scolded. In the final scene she does nothing but put on a dress; no agency of hers solves anything. The narrative's real savior is patriarchy itself, through the system of patronymics: Mr. Graves gets his job back, quite simply, because Haskell Cummings, Jr., has the same name as his powerful father. This is patriarchy at its clearest, inheritance through the male line and the male name. Young Haskell's status as Judy's escort is merely the luckiest of coincidences, for they met through mutual friends; Judy had no knowledge of their fathers' connection, and therefore can claim no credit for the happy outcome. How, then, could anyone assert that Judy "is able finally to straighten everything out and take the last curtain handsomely arrayed and thrillingly triumphant," as one critic said?[33] The handsome raiment is the answer, for characters and critics alike were dazzled by the power of Judy's chrysalis moment. So eagerly does the logic of this play push toward recontainment of the dreadful bobby-soxer that everyone, both inside and outside the fiction, considers Judy's transformation into obedient heterosexuality the necessary proof of her inherent goodness. This act alone gives Judy the patriarchal seal of approval, a trick which allows the play to appear "a glorification of the American youngster"[34] while actually leaving intact its disdain for Judy's behavior. The writers and directors of *Junior Miss* show Judy only slightly more beneficence than "Anatole of Paris" shows toward the women he secretly hates, while publicly adorning and adoring them.

What this play really glorifies, albeit indirectly, is fatherhood itself. Not only does patriarchy solve the play's problems, it also receives validation through the play's narrative perspective and through the characters of J. B. Curtis and Ellen. Curtis's domineering cruelty to his daughter allows Mr. Graves's bellowing sarcasm toward Judy to appear almost loving by comparison, a neat sleight of hand that further encourages audiences' allegiance to Mr. Graves. Sally Benson's "Daddy Dear" had allowed readers some sympathy with the father's irritation, but underscored the poignancy of Judy's futile yearning to be "the apple of [his] eye." The film, by contrast, makes explicit Judy's status as the enemy of adult males in its very first scene: as Mr. Graves enters his New York apartment building at the end of the day, he learns from the weary elevator man that Judy's roller skates, which she carelessly abandoned in the lobby, caused another man to fall and spill his groceries. The elevator man, too, suffers from Judy's ill-advised behavior: to beautify the building, she has stuck posters of Tyrone Power on the elevator's walls. Even before we lay eyes on Judy herself, we are prepared for her entrance by a framework of adult men's exasperation and anger.

Why does Judy become increasingly insulted and diminished in each textual incarnation, as she moves from fiction to stage play to film? What made the play's and film's producers think that mass audiences would respond best to a portrait of a teen girl as a chaotic menace, rather than the sympathetic, awkward sweetheart of Benson's fiction? For that matter, why would they portray Judy Graves with a degree of mockery that surpassed that in the prior boy-centered tales? During the 1940s girls became increasingly culturally visible in ways that inspired complex, sometimes hostile reactions from adult observers.

Victory Girls, Bobby-Soxers, and Shifting Perceptions of Teens

Aggressively critical portraits of teen girls represented an interesting shift from the 1930s images of girls as helpful angels. Several factors influenced this change from divine to disruptive protagonists, particularly the end of the Depression and its crisis of masculinity. After America's entry into World War II, the abstraction of national masculinity was no longer in question; servicemen deployed all over the world reinvigorated a faith in the virility of the United States, while the booming war industries solved the problems of the breadwinner who stayed a civilian: "Fathers who went begging for work in the 1930s now had a variety of high-paying jobs from which to choose, and with work men gained a new sense of manhood."[35] The reestablishment of American masculinity meant that cultural images of girls no longer had to do compensatory work; with symbolic fatherhood restored to its ideal strength, girls and teens could be portrayed with some of the same aggression and rebelliousness that characterized images of flappers and sheiks during the affluent 1920s. Texts characterizing teen culture as threats to established order can thrive, perhaps, only when the established order seems secure enough to weather such an assault.

But even while the war restored masculinity in military and industrial arenas, in the domestic arena it clearly weakened the institution of fatherhood, which required more than merely breadwinning. With fathers deployed in the armed services, or working in defense plants sometimes geographically distant, new concerns arose about the absence of paternal authority from children's lives.[36] Juvenile delinquency became a common topic in public discourse, as many worried that a lack of parental supervision would erode youngsters' obedience to authority. One historian has counted no fewer than 1,200 newspaper and magazine articles in the first six months of 1943 alone, warning Americans of a supposed tidal wave of juvenile delinquency on the horizon.[37] Authorities reported that girls' delinquency was rising, relative to boys': while the ratio of male to female delinquency hovered around 6:1 before the war, "after World War II . . . the ratio began to narrow. By 1949 girls represented one out of every four juvenile court cases."[38] Media consumers had an array of evidence that the current crop of teens, particularly girls, demonstrated a degree of aggression and disregard for authority that seemed to surpass earlier generations' youthful rebellion.

At the same time, a certain measure of increased aggression and independence among women on the home front matched exhortations from government and industry. Magazine articles, advertisements, and public service announcements on radio and in film encouraged civilians to screw their courage to the sticking place and take an active role in helping the war effort in every way they could. The famed image of Rosie the Riveter signaled increased employment opportunities for women in sometimes physically demanding jobs vacated by men. Even fashion trends pointed to a new emphasis on female strength and vigor, as both women and girls began adopting styles with masculine nuances: while women wore broad shoulder pads, suggesting that they could shoulder the burdens of homefront life, teenage girls began wearing actual men's clothing. A 1944 photo essay in *Life* magazine showed girls posing in men's pants, shirts, and pajamas, explaining that "after school and on weekends. . . . [t]heir favorite fad is wearing men's jeans and shirts which they borrow from father, brother and each other or buy in boys' wear departments. They defend this costume on the grounds of its great comfort and practicality, reasons which also lead quite logically to low heels and shirt-tails left flapping."[39] Women's adoption of masculine roles and signifiers provoked a paradoxical reaction; although in some guises it clearly fulfilled a patriotic purpose, it also raised uncomfortable questions about boundaries and propriety. In the popular press, women who took war jobs found themselves alternately praised as patriotic servants and excoriated as bad mothers whose work made them neglect their children. Those neglected children, in turn, were the focus of the delinquency panic.

Culture looked anxiously at women and youth, perhaps, because they ideally represented the all-American home, an ideological construct that took on extra significance during the war. Teenagers functioned in this discourse of domesticity as future family-builders and citizens. Sentimental images of home and family abounded in all forms of public discourse, symbolizing the bulwark of American values, the backbone of democracy, and the perfect icon of what American soldiers fought to protect. In a radio broadcast called "To the Young," produced by the U.S. government's Office of War Information, a boy and girl in love exchange these lines:

> *Boy:* That's one of the things this war's about.
> *Girl:* About us?
> *Boy:* About all young people like us. About love and gettin' hitched, and havin' a home and some kids, and breathin' fresh air out in the suburbs.[40]

The precise link between fighting a war and "gettin' hitched" is muddy at best, but the fatuous logic of the claim did not stop its circulation or undermine the ineluctable power of its appeal. The American household and family blatantly symbolized the American polity, a synecdoche of home and nation. In this construct, strict distinctions between the male as breadwinner and the female as homemaker reinforced the conservative celebration of tradition and continuity that gave the icon of home its emotional power; "The war became not only a war against fascism but, more fundamentally, a war in defense of the American home and its traditional division of labor."[41] With such ideological emphasis placed upon the home, the realm with which women and girls were most associated, an apparent reduction of femininity in girls' fashions and behavior seemed to signal a worrisome rebellion against the traditional values upon which ideologies of "home" rested. Those values seemed even more directly threatened by the reports of rising delinquency rates among girls.

Significantly, the suddenly widespread rhetoric about juvenile delinquency manifested differently according to gender. Reports of male delinquency focused mostly on violence and property damage, but sex was the "delinquent" activity most associated with girls. Under the familiar double standard, boys' sexual activities did not arouse widespread accusations of their moral decay or criminality, as girls' did. A new breed of girl, known variously as "victory girls," "V-girls," or "khaki-wackies," who dated soldiers and sometimes had sexual relations with them, were decried in the press as a threat not just to national morals, but even to national safety; promiscuity could spread venereal diseases among America's fighting force. Many girls, frustrated by their inability to contribute to the war effort directly, considered it a patriotic right and duty to entertain lonesome soldiers; the harmless form of that entertainment meant volunteering at a USO canteen. Although some girls did include sexual relations in their concepts of caregiving, America was not overrun by a horde of syphilitic floozies, as the press implied; delinquency panics, even when founded in fact to some degree, are usually exaggerated in the media.[42] In the case of victory girls of the 1940s, the exaggeration reflects the extent to which such girls challenged normative notions of femininity. Not only did they controvert the belief that "nice" girls are less sexual and better behaved than boys, they also seemed to threaten the war effort by felling American servicemen with spirochetes, waging a sort of biological warfare.

Girls' dual roles in the popular imagination, as potential delinquents and as icons of the idealized home, merged in several bobby-soxer entertainments. *Janie*, a successful cycle that followed quickly in the tracks of *Junior Miss*, featured a slightly older heroine than Judy Graves; at sixteen, Janie Conway is old enough to participate more directly in a sexually inflected story. Based on a novel, the play *Janie* debuted on Broadway in September 1942. Critics generally compared it negatively to *Junior Miss* (one reviewer recounted the lobby gossip of opening night, when witty playgoers joked that the show should have been called "Junior Missed"[43]). Its flaws apparently did not deter the public from embracing *Janie*, for it ran until January 1944, and subsequently became a popular film. The film's plot revolves around a father's nervous reaction to his daughter's sexual coming of age: hearing that a military base is coming to town, Mr. Conway strenuously objects that the soldiers' presence will encourage misbehavior among the town's girls. Janie seemingly validates his fears by falling in love with one of these soldiers, casting off her high school boyfriend. When the discarded boyfriend learns that Janie and her new love plan a private party, he vindictively spreads word around the military base, with the consequence that dozens of boisterous soldiers invade the Conway home and turn the party wild.

After the usual shouting—from Janie's father, the police, and the soldiers' commanding officer—Janie restores harmony by tearfully delivering a noble speech about the importance of giving servicemen the comforts of an all-American home: "All the USOs in the world can't take care of all the boys in your army. I'm glad there were so many. When a soldier has to live in a tent and take orders for weeks and weeks he ought to have a chance to see what a home looks like. I know just about everything is going to happen to me, but I don't care. If only when the going gets tough those boys can look back and say 'Gee, that was a swell party we had that night in Hortonville.'" These rather banal words magically infuse the uniformed men surrounding Janie with a glow of sentimental patriotism and a new appreciation for a young girl as the bearer of national ideals; one of them even compares her to Joan of Arc. Janie's invocation of the sanctity of American domesticity proves she is a good girl after all—indeed, the very best possible girl—and her father's fears of promiscuity were unfounded.

Filmed as the victory-girl panic spread, *Janie* is one of the first texts to voice paradoxes of pleasure and anxiety surrounding a bobby-soxer's sexuality; the film's tagline, "She's the gleam in the eye of every G.I.," has at least two meanings, depending on how one interprets the "gleam": either Janie is the all-American sweetheart, inspiring our fighting boys to heroism, or else she is a victory girl who makes their eyes gleam with sexual interest, for the idiom "a gleam in his eye" often refers to lubricious desire. The *double entendre* expresses a double reaction to teen girls, mixing sentimental fantasies with a fear of unbridled sex. Teen comedies routinely treat this fear as a mistake, for they paint idealized portraits of adolescent purity; as Scheiner says, "[s]creen teens seem almost blissfully ignorant of the finer points of sex,"[44] even though real-life teenagers come in all shades of innocence and experience. This fantasy of total innocence allows the entertainments to exploit the titillating possibilities posed by a young girl's budding sexuality without offering a real threat; the blankly innocent girl becomes a pure white screen onto which anxious adults can project their desires and fears, exemplifying James Kincaid's observation that "the asexual child is not . . . any the less erotic but rather the more."[45] Audiences could have their girl and eat her, too.

If popular narratives can allay contemporary anxieties by containing them within reassuring comic conventions, the news media often strives for the opposite effect, inciting anxieties by heightening the appearance of danger. Teens defined as delinquents or victory girls were described in periodicals as pervasive threats, as in the May 1943 issue of *Reader's Digest*. Author Eleanor Lake's opening salvo indicates her central concern: "A year ago, 75 percent of the venereal infection in the armed forces in the United States could be traced to professional prostitutes. Today, 80 percent of it comes from young casuals and amateurs. . . . The post surgeon at a large midwestern air base reports: 'Good-time girls of high school age are the army's biggest problem today as a potential source of venereal disease.'" Lake denies the inherent unfairness of blaming only one half of the sexual couple, for she explicitly raises such objections only to dismiss them: "It's too easy to blame service men for our zooming delinquency. Men don't change when they get into uniform." As the ones who have "changed," girls deserve the criticism, and Lake suggests two causes for this unhappy occurrence. First, like many others, Lake grabs the opportunity provided by the delinquency panic and uses it as a stick to beat guilt into working mothers: "The hard fact is that most girls go astray because their mothers are too busy or indifferent to keep them out of trouble." The exaggerated delinquency panic thus provided a double service for patriarchy, allowing critics to scold daughters and mothers alike for the same "crime": leaving the house. But the second cause that Lake cites points to a significant wartime development in girls' increased consumer habits: "These 'victory girls' and 'cuddle bunnies' who go uniform-hunting . . . are just ordinary kids who have been swept along by a torrent of wartime excitement and *free spending*."[46] Apparently, opening one's purse might lead to opening one's legs.

Teens' spending, and its potentially subversive effect on their obedience to moral and social order, became a contentious topic during the war. The booming wartime economy allowed rising rates of teen employment; some teens dropped out of high school to work full-time, but more worked only part-time, which allowed them both the financial means and the time to participate in the leisure culture of high school peer groups. Fully one third of all adolescents between fourteen and eighteen held some form of paid employment during the war, which granted teens some financial autonomy and encouraged the development of consumer goods aimed at the youth market.[47] Teenagers' access to more money, and the leisure goods they spent it on, sometimes challenged the hierarchies and boundaries of the status quo. In the 1950s the moral panic about juvenile delinquency often blamed popular culture for corrupting youth, but the issue in that instance was the *content* of popular culture;[48] in the 1940s, it seemed rather that the *fact* of teens' consumption gave them too great a sense of entitlement. Numerous commentators wondered if teens' increased financial autonomy, and the ever-growing array of frivolous goods and activities aimed at them, might make them too big for their britches. "Youth in Crisis," a 1943 installment of the *March of Time* newsreel, shows a scene of a father scolding his son for staying out late and coming home "all liquored up." Sneering that he now earns the same salary as his father, the son asserts his independence and his right to have fun. Youths who can finance their own activities, the newsreel implies, can no longer be controlled by domestic patriarchy.

As it had in the 1920s, the public complemented its fears of youth with an intense interest in youth trends. In addition to their relatively new status as well-paid employees and active consumers, teens' growing numbers in the population helped make them more culturally visible. Increased birth rates during the economic boom years of the 1920s produced, by 1940, a crop of 9,720,419 Americans between the ages of fourteen and seventeen, a larger number than there had been during the Depression; this demographic swell "gave high school students new visibility."[49] While authorities in fields like education, sociology, and psychology examined teens for information about their values and lifestyles, manufacturers and cultural producers found it lucrative to market products directly to teenagers. Girls were constructed as consumers, more so than boys. During the 1920s the fashion industry had been the earliest to recognize the value of developing and marketing products specifically for teenage girls.[50] Teen marketing increased steadily over the following years; although the biggest surge did not arrive until after the war, the 1940s show a rapidly growing number of leisure goods—including records, snack foods, radios, jewelry, fashions, magazines, and myriad accessories and gadgets—marketed explicitly to teenagers, and girls in particular. Articles in influential magazines like *Life* disseminated information about girls' cultural practices as the main repository of teen subcultural styles. The same publications described male teens without specific subcultural markers, for, as Rachel Devlin puts it, "boyhood itself was defined against the kind of consumption which animated the 'bobby-soxer,'"[51] consumption that centered upon objects generally deemed trivial. Marking teenage culture as silly and inconsequential, such goods were overwhelmingly identified with girls, fostering a dismissive interpretation of girls in the public imagination.

As Lake's comment about "cuddle bunnies" overexcited by "free spending" implies, the rhetoric surrounding girls' sexual delinquency could overlap with concerns about their consumerism, since both seemed to suggest certain kinds of freedom that contradicted old maxims about girls' proper passivity and subjection to authority. Consumption, after all, involves engagement with the public sphere, especially when integrated into a youth culture based on peer-group activities. Women's public activity, in patriarchal cultures, has for centuries been considered a risk to their chastity, hence the familiar mandate that a woman's place is in the home (a safe interior space where her purity remains protected). This tradition can work in girls' favor, as we saw in chapter 1, when the connections between interiority and sacred space allow girls to develop a useful sense of inviolable personhood. But the association of femininity with interiority or privacy obviously has a repressive function as well; the words "streetwalker" and "tramp," meaning a prostitute, suggest how much a woman's respectability depends on her not perambulating publicly. When adolescent girls of the 1940s began circulating in groups that demonstrated a unified, publicly enacted, and slightly "unfeminine" peer culture, their critics associated them subtly with a degraded form of sexuality, a link made all the easier by the news media's accounts of victory girls.

One hint of that link appears in 1940s representations of girls' fan culture, which implied that movie consumption made girls too aggressive and even slightly insane, tapping into the old anxieties, reflected in the Payne Fund studies, that films could negatively affect youth's morality. Judy Graves fits this pattern somewhat; although *Junior Miss* raises no questions about Judy's chastity, it strongly suggests that movie consumption overstimulates her and leads her toward such inappropriate romance-related behavior as festooning the building's elevator with posters of a movie idol and manipulating adults' love lives. The links between movie consumption and transgressive behavior emerge more strongly in a 1943 film entirely about bobby-soxers' fandom for movie stars. Its plot and its publicity highlight both fans' incipient sexuality, coded as worshipful aggression, and the threats it poses. The film centers on a group of teenage autograph hounds who vigorously pursue their favorite actors and actresses, breaking rules when necessary (telling outrageous lies to gain access to hotel rooms) and, significantly, defying their fathers' injunctions to stay at home. In true bobby-soxer style, a subplot concerns the protagonist's mistaken fear that her father is having an affair, and the disasters that follow when she tries to fix the situation. As *Good Housekeeping* said in its review, "Virginia Weidler leads a precocious group of ardent young things who get their autographs no matter what! They also get their elders in no little trouble—which is no laughing matter to them—but a laughable situation for you!"[52] The link between "ardent" feelings, consumer culture, and aggressive peer-group behavior clearly spells "trouble" for "elders." The film's title, *The Youngest Profession*, puns on "the world's oldest profession," a familiar euphemism for prostitution. It is perhaps not coincidental that this film was released in the same year that saw the rise of the victory-girl panic.

In 1945 *Collier's* magazine published an essay titled "America's Kid Sister" which summarized the recent shifts in girls' roles in public culture. Author Amy Porter traces these shifts directly to the burgeoning teen consumer market:

> [O]nly in the last few years have these growing-pain girls been taken very seriously by their parents. They were the awkward age, the difficult kids you had to endure until they grew to reasonableness. . . . Now, overnight almost, the awkward age has disappeared. These girls are getting their own specially designed clothes, their own magazines, their own radio programs, their own big influential clubs, and the chance to speak up about everything they like and want and hope for. They are Somebody in the community, important not just because they are the future generation but for themselves.[53]

Although she notes the suddenness of this phenomenon, Porter's words reveal no disapproval or worry; she does not undercut her own statements that girls are now "Somebody" and "important . . . for themselves." But other commentators viewed the same cultural shift in a more critical light. An illuminating example appears in "Teen-Age Girls," the 1945 *March of Time* newsreel we encountered briefly in the introduction, which opened by stating, "Of all the phenomena of wartime life in the United States, one of the most fascinating and mysterious, and one of the most completely irrelevant, has been the emergence of the teenage girl as an American institution in her own right." Although the newsreel presents girls' status as consumers only in its positive aspect, it nonetheless subtly critiques girls' culture as ineffable and oppositional to adults' expectations; its condescending tone manages to seem celebratory of girls even while casting a critical eye on the rapid growth of their cultural influence.[54] The emphasis on girls as consumers—particularly a scene in which a noisy group crowds around a soda fountain, wolfing down decadent desserts—underscores girls' irrelevance by suggesting that they hedonistically gobble their way through inconsequential, "junk food" lives.

Contemporary teens who saw this newsreel, and read the related articles about teenagers in *Life* magazine, often recognized and disliked the Time-Life company's insulting view of them. *Scholastic*, a magazine for youth that circulated through schools, had the clever idea of asking its readers to express their opinion of the newsreel and the *Life* articles. It received so many impassioned replies that two issues were required to fit the best letters into the magazine's "Jam Session" column. The students were most angered by Time-Life's repeated assertions that teenage sub-culture inducted its members into a never-never land of frivolous fun, wholly cut off from the grim contemporary realities of war (a construc-tion of youth that also informed film and radio comedies). As one young woman put it, "What about our brothers, fathers, and close friends who went away to war? Many of them will never return and those who come back may be changed. I speak for many girls when I say that we think a great deal about the deeper and more important things in life: religion, economic and social problems. Perhaps we haven't solved any of them, but we're trying. Isn't that something?" Another wrote angrily, "Un-touched by war—when our friends and relatives went into the armed forces? Why did we wear our old clothes and collect scrap paper, fats, and usable clothing? Certainly not for glamour! Those daily letters—did we write only for *our* morale? Those bonds we bought with spending money—was our interest only financial and *personal*?"[55] These teens' let-ters, rife with wounded indignation, are among the very few clues we have today to suggest the gap between teens' experiences of their own lives in wartime and adult culture's construction of those lives in the entertainment and news media.

Indeed, even the newsreel's producers must not have found the teen-age girl wholly "irrelevant," since they spent time and money producing a film about her. Nor does the content of the newsreel, which describes girls' impact on various industries and fields of study, suggest irrelevance. The cultivated appearance of silly frivolity may have helped soften a fear of teens' socio-cultural impact, making youth practices look mild and harmless. It may also have comforted adults by suggesting that one could avoid the depressing rigors of wartime existence if sufficiently young. Through the temporary process of identification which entertainment allows, adults could project themselves into the carefree teen world they saw in popular culture. But anxiety over the "generation gap," as it would later be called, equally infuses this visual text; a fictitious scene of a girl's home life shows her bemused father reading a book titled *Do You Know Your Daughter?* as he struggles to understand the alien creature in the next room.

The fact that her father, not her mother, needs to read this book points to one of the central reasons why bobby-soxer culture disturbed even while it entertained: the emergence of teen-girl culture posed a particular challenge to conceptions of a patriarchally organized society by highlighting the "importance" of the teenager to contemporary American culture. The newsreel shows a teenage girl being interviewed by an august panel of scholars and professionals who seek information about modern youth. This scene participates in a larger cultural trend of treating teenage opinions as a legitimate subject of study, a perspective that implied a shift in social hierarchy; numerous texts on radio and in the print media focused on teens' opinions and a new awareness of teenage "rights." The *New York Times*, for example, published a "Teen-Age Bill of Rights" in 1945, the same year in which Time, Inc. produced the "Teen-Age Girls" newsreel. Compiled by sociologists and educators, the list includes the right "To Have Rules Explained, Not Imposed" and to "Question Ideas," indicating an evolution away from childrearing philosophies that favored strict adult control of the young. This seeming erosion of traditional social hierarchies also informs the interview scene in "Teen-Age Girls." In the recent past, the idea of professional experts' paying sober attention to the yammerings of a girl-child would have seemed patently absurd, yet the interview of this teen is presented as the scientific collection of important data. Girls' and teens' rising roles as experts in their own right, whose opinions were taken seriously by social scientists and industries, challenged grown men's monopoly as the "real" authorities whose opinions mattered.

Ironically, that interview scene could be read quite differently: it resembles the painting described in the introduction in which medical doctors dissect the corpse of a young woman to learn where the basis of her attraction lies. The collection of data from teenage girls ultimately served patriarchal and hegemonic purposes, allowing social authorities superior access to what made teen girls "tick," thus improving the surveillance techniques of panoptical institutions like social service agencies, schools, and the advertising industry. But the means to that end required an apparent celebration of adolescence which seemed to suggest that girls' indigenous cultural practices—their sloppy clothing, their aggressive and smart-alecky slang, their unabashed (and suggestively sexual) public shrieking over idols like Van Johnson and Frank Sinatra—were the sole engines driving girls' sudden social ubiquity. This false construction implied that social authorities were merely reacting to teens' burgeoning cultural presence, instead of helping to shape it, and it facilitated what would soon appear in the bobby-soxer entertainments: a public backlash against the "uppityness" of the very girls who were psychologically probed for the benefit of patriarchy and capital. At the same moment that the teenage girl became "an American institution in her own right," she also was constructed as a threat to other American institutions—including the health of the U.S. military, and the patriarchal hierarchies that traditionally structured private and public life. Addressing these threats, the bobby-soxer subgenre instantiates a pattern Jon Lewis noted in later teen films, offering plots that center on the apparent disruption but ultimate restoration of conservative, traditional codes of social order.[56] Indeed, tales about daughters provoke the reestablishment of patriarchal order even more powerfully than tales of sons often do, because of girls' doubled opposition to fathers in age and sex.

We have seen that contentious images of the father/daughter relationship derive partly from the synecdochic relationship between family and nation: when girls were perceived as threats to social and governmental institutions, popular culture showed them enraging their fathers. But these combative father/daughter juxtapositions also derive inspiration from shifts in the structure of domestic life, and in the role of the father in the nuclear family. In his history of American fatherhood, Robert Griswold notes changes that occurred during the early twentieth century when local and federal government agencies, and institutions such as schools, assumed many of the protective and disciplinary roles that had previously been performed privately by fathers. This development left fathers with little power beyond that which followed from their role as the breadwinner. In response, and in concert with the rising popularity of Freudian psychology, child-rearing experts circulated a new idea of fatherhood as a psychological, rather than authoritative, influence. Popular discourse in the interwar period encouraged fathers to adopt emotionally based roles in their homes as companions and models for their children. Oedipal theory averred that fathers play an especially important role in the successful emotional and sexual development of their children, insulating boys from overfeminization by their mothers and ensuring that girls learn the respect and appreciation for masculinity necessary for their future marriages. The new fatherhood stressed men's companionate role over their disciplinary role.[57]

In the eyes of some fathers, this new role seemed less satisfying than the former standard. In January 1940, shortly after the original "Junior Miss" story made its first impression on the *New Yorker*'s readers, noted author Fairfax Downey wrote "The Care and Feeding of Fathers" for the *American Girl,* official magazine of the Girl Scouts of America. Articulating a rueful reaction to the changes in American family dynamics, Downey laments his teenage daughter's manipulation of him to obtain her ends. "I am being Circumnavigated," Downey mourns; "I am being Got Around." Writing for an audience of young girls, Downey adopts an indulgently humorous tone, but there is no mistaking his point: "Surely no father who discovers himself being Circumnavigated welcomes it at first. Certainly I did not. It struck me as too revolutionary, too dire a menace to paternal prestige and dignity. Why, it was only two generations ago that we fathers were absolute dictators! . . . Undoubtedly it wasn't good for us fathers. But, one reflects wistfully, it must have been fun."[58]

Fun indeed. Like Jim Treloar, whose fractious daughter felt inspired by Nancy Drew's autonomy to defy his authoritarian gestures (see chapter 1), Downey implies that the frustrations of losing a power struggle with a child are especially acute when the child is female. Evoking the old rhetoric about women's wiles undermining masculine power, Downey likens his daughter's machinations to those of his wife, who has been "molding" him "for years"; now that his daughter has reached her teens, he must contend with two domestic vixens instead of one: "I don't doubt that you and your mother have ganged up on your father more than once. You girls stick together. Perhaps your father, like me, has sometimes felt inclined to go a-picketing, wearing a placard which reads, this household unfair to father." An illustration renders the scene even more pathetic: in addition to the plaintive placard, the father also holds an umbrella, for it is raining. Poor Dad must picket in a downpour, ousted by scheming females from the home that should have been his castle and his shelter from the storm. Offering a father's-eye view of the new social codes, the article elicits its young readers' pity in order to nudge their attention back to the conservative project of protecting a father's "prestige and dignity," offering him the proper "care and feeding."

It takes little effort to see texts like the play and film *Junior Miss* as cooperative tools in that same project. While the bobby-soxer genre dramatizes the worst possible humiliations and agonies for fathers, such texts compensate for the emasculation they represent by moving the father from the periphery of the story—where he often hovers in boy-centered comedies—to its center, jockeying for position with his rival, the teen girl. Adults, not youth, have their worldviews affirmed and (ultimately) strengthened in this genre; it is not surprising, then, to consider that adults were originally the primary consumers of the play *Junior Miss.*

But we know that children and teens did attend Broadway plays, and of course they formed an even larger consumer base for films. Like Fairfax Downey's father-saving message to young readers of *American Girl* magazine, the privilege given to patriarchal ideologies in the play and film *Junior Miss* functions as a socializing agent for daughters even while it offers compensatory commiseration for fathers. Bobby-soxer texts trained girls to view themselves, their peers, and their cultural practices through the eyes of older men, teaching them to internalize a construction of themselves as the Other.

Although the cultural assessment of teen girls as gobbling, greedy menaces had only begun to spread in 1941, we can see traces of it in the critics' responses to *Junior Miss.* Chodorov's and Fields's condescension toward Judy, Fuffy, and Lois was mirrored by the reviewers who acknowledged the bobby-soxer's consumerism as the root of her misbehavior. "Comedy Has as Its Central Character Girl of 13 with Movie Obsession," summarized the headline of one review, while another noted the "movie-fed minds" of the young girls.[59] In the second of his *New York Times* reviews, Brooks Atkinson discusses literal consumption—eating—in his ruminations about the realism of the play's portrayals. His title, "Girls Are People: Two Sisters Distort the Home Life of a Charming Family in 'Junior Miss,'" betrays his bias against the daughters. Atkinson uses the play as an opportunity for nostalgic reflection, assessing the realism of its portrayal of youth by comparing it to his own recollections. Contemporary girlhood also influences his decision about the play's accuracy, but he seems to have had a limited knowledge of that subject. In this instance, his data comes entirely from a letter written by a young girl. Asking rhetorically, "But are girls of [teen] age so giddy? Do they live in a world of vertigo?" Atkinson uses the unnamed girl's letter to answer himself affirmatively:

> Confidentially, they do. A morning or two after "Junior Miss" had left its first glow of good cheer across the town, this department happened to receive a terse note tapped out by a junior miss in a polite school upriver. Paragraph by paragraph it skipped from pain to ecstasy with no transitions—from tragedy on the one hand to gluttony on the other. "Please excuse the mistakes I am making in typing this for I have my hand all bandaged up due to a sprained thumb. So I only have partial use of my four fingers," the note confided, and then swept on to the climax: "My, but I'm full! We just finished Thanksgiving dinner of which we all had sixth and seventh servings. It was delicious." You bet it was![60]

Presumably, Atkinson chose to comment on this letter because its schoolgirl author reminded him of the characters in *Junior Miss.* Skewering her (oxy)moronic emotions and syntactic gaffes, Atkinson's mockery bespeaks a consciousness of grammatical precision more common in the 1940s than it is today. But even some 1941 readers might have wondered at his snide tone. Like a colonist introduced to the strange doings of natives, Atkinson examines this girl's letter as a commodity from which he can gain some profit, rather than respecting its intention. He thereby can laugh not only at her writing skills, but also at her "gluttonous" consumption—despite the fact that gluttony at Thanksgiving is a common tradition for Americans. Given this patronizing disdain for what Atkinson terms the "lightheadedness of growing girls," the article's title becomes ironic rather than declarative; he does not seem to believe that "Girls Are People," unwittingly putting his finger on the problem of teen girls' personhood in the media. His interpretation of this letter mirrors the tone of the play he reviews; news and entertainment texts cooperate to erode the personhood of the girls under discussion, suggesting how specific ideologies take on the appearance of "common sense" if repeated often enough by a wide enough selection of authorities.

Not all reviewers of *Junior Miss* were so snide, or so naïvely persuaded by the play's slapstick exaggerations. But while some lamented the overuse of comic stereotypes and the application of a formulaic plot to Benson's highly original fiction, none considered these flaws serious impediments to enjoying what they unanimously hailed as a marvelous comedy. The story *Junior Miss* sold about teenage girls was clearly a story many Americans were happy to buy. The book's and play's considerable success sparked more cross-media exploitation: within months Judy Graves and her family were the subject of a weekly radio serial with Shirley Temple herself in the title role (offering an ironic symmetry to Judy Graves's attempts, in the short story "Daddy Dear," to mimic Shirley Temple). *Junior Miss* had a complicated history on radio, for the initial series ran only for six months in 1942, although it was revived from 1948 to 1950. After a two-year hiatus, it returned from 1952 to 1954. Episodes of this series are scarce, and the few that exist do not come from the original 1942 run,[61] but we can speculate that Judy Graves may have been rendered more sympathetically on radio than on stage, especially in the first season, when Sally Benson herself wrote the scripts.[62] Significantly, the earliest radio version of *Junior Miss* met with the approval of actual teen girls; when *Calling All Girls* magazine did a survey of its young readers' cultural tastes in 1942, *Junior Miss* outranked—by a wide margin—all other contenders in the category "Favorite Radio Program."[63] The series *A Date with Judy* (which debuted before *Junior Miss*, ran much longer, and is considered one of the "greats" of teen radio comedy), ranked only in seventh place. Readily available today, episodes of *A Date with Judy* confirm that it, too, portrays teenagers as mildly ridiculous people. It's tempting to surmise that the different rankings of these two programs indicate that one viewed girls more "indigenously" than the other; but without access to Benson's scripts, we can only speculate that the sympathetic tone of her fiction extended to her radio writing.

Certainly the film version of *Junior Miss*, written and directed by George Seaton, employed no such tone. Following Chodorov's and Fields's play script closely, Seaton reproduced their "imperial" perspective and thus evoked a similar critical response. The *Commonweal* titled its review of the film "The Juniors Take Over," a slightly uneasy statement, while Bosley Crowther wrote a serio-comic warning to the readers of the *New York Times*. Knowing that far more children would see the film than had seen the play, Crowther predicted a hazardous side-effect of the film's release: "So let the parents who have young girls in their households beware for their health and sanity, for, as soon as this film gets circulation, there are going to be a lot of changes made in many homes. . . . [W]hen this adult admission of the child's power is widely revealed to youths, it is likely to start some conscious scheming in their dear heads. And heaven help us when they learn their own strength!" He concludes by judging *Junior Miss* "a happy picture—provided you feel it's worth the risk."[64] But the criticisms of girls in the various Junior Miss texts and in their reviews, condescending though they are, seem almost kind compared with what would soon follow. In 1941, when *Junior Miss* debuted on Broadway, the victory-girl moral panic had not yet taken off; by 1943, it was in full flight. And in 1943 a new girl character appeared, one who was destined to have even wider circulation and greater longevity than Judy Graves. This cycle, about a girl named Corliss Archer, took the stereotypes solidified by *Junior Miss* and added to them a paradoxical combination of fear and desire triggered by girls' powerful sexual appeal—the same paradox that faintly tinged the Nancy Drew movies, but to a far more explicit degree.

Sexy, Bitchy, and Ignorant: Meet Corliss Archer

Judy Graves is barely in her teens, but subsequent bobby-soxer tales tended to focus on girls of fifteen or more, old enough to pass for adult women in a darkened room. Because these girls are more developed, their representations in narrative cycles become more sexualized; the girls' quasi-maturity allows American institutions' patriarchal gaze at the teenager to collapse into the familiar male gaze at the figure of the sexually desirable female. Many bobby-soxer comedies focused on two repeated issues: the teenage girl's romantic/sexual interests and her parents' fear that she has lost her virginity. The sexual attractiveness of the teenage girl, and the libidinous possibilities it poses, become the primary objects of pleasure in the narratives, combined with the earlier comic theme of teen chaos. As the brief example of *Janie* has already suggested, the key to successfully rendering a teenage girl in these comedies lay in positioning her on the fine line between subjective and objective sexuality; her inherent sexual innocence disqualifies her as a legitimate threat, hollowing her of threatening agency and leaving viewers free to project titillating possibilities onto her.

But sexual innocence is merely the most literal method of rendering a heroine blank or hollow. More symbolic methods reach their apotheosis in the Corliss Archer cycle, which hollows out its heroine in many ways at once: her sexual fetishization by her author and other characters is more pronounced than that of any previous heroine; her immaturity and ignorance provide a focal point for numerous texts; and her author repeatedly positions her as lesser (in competence, ethics, and intellect) than other characters. Hitting all the diminishment buttons at once, Corliss Archer fast became the most widely circulated teen character of her day: she appeared in every single narrative medium of American culture—a feat no other teen hero/ine accomplished—and stayed in the public eye consistently from 1943 to 1956. Beginning as a series of short stories in *Good Housekeeping* (1943), *Meet Corliss Archer* was published as a book in 1944. A stage play, *Kiss and Tell*, opened on Broadway in March 1943 and ran until June 1945, with a total of 956 performances, far surpassing the runs of *What a Life*, *Junior Miss*, and *Janie*.[65] *Meet Corliss Archer* debuted on national radio in 1943, where it stayed for thirteen years—one year less than *The Aldrich Family*, but four years longer than its nearest girl-centered competitor, *A Date with Judy*.[66] In 1945 Columbia Pictures released *Kiss and Tell* as a film; a sequel, *A Kiss for Corliss*, was released by United Artists in 1949, a year after Corliss briefly appeared in her own comic book, produced by Fox Features Syndicate.[67] In the early 1950s *Meet Corliss Archer* resurfaced twice as a television comedy (1951–1952; 1954–1955).[68] Nor was her popularity limited to the United States: by 1949 an advertisement for *A Kiss for Corliss* claimed that this character had been "seen, heard or read about by more than 250,000,000 people in twenty-five countries and fourteen languages."[69]

To understand Corliss's immense popularity, we should begin by considering her creator, F. Hugh Herbert. Unlike other cycles' authors, Herbert wrote most of the Archer texts himself—fiction, play, numerous radio scripts, and first screenplay—and thus kept the cycle remarkably consistent not only within itself, but with the rest of his *oeuvre*. Herbert's writing career spanned four decades and included a variety of themes and genres, but he specialized in sexual/romantic comedies about very young women. Drawing inspiration from earlier strands of discourse, he wove them into a tight and powerfully cohesive set of tropes about female adolescence which became his trademark. He enjoyed a reputation as an expert on teen girls, even receiving requests to write dialogue for such characters in other writers' scripts, and his work firmly established a body of "knowledge" about teen girls that later writers found easy to recycle.[70] When we study Corliss Archer, then, we are studying not only the most successful entry in the 1940s' genre of the teen comedy, but also the most pronounced crystallization of a long-lived vision of adolescent femininity written by the era's most influential architect of teen-girl constructions.

In an author's note after one of his novels, Herbert explains, "The female adolescent in particular, with her refreshing mixture of childlike sweetness and feminine bitchiness, has always intrigued me."[71] Herbert defines "bitch" as a woman who uses sex to manipulate men. In the play *Kiss and Tell* Mr. Archer comments on Corliss's cold-hearted manipulation of her smitten boyfriend: "I'm beginning to suspect that our dear little daughter has a streak of bitchiness in her." When his wife objects to the vulgarity, he corrects himself sarcastically: "Ok, let's call it femininity then. Like that better?"[72] Archer's equation of femininity and "bitchiness" is merely the clearest of Herbert's numerous articulations of an age-specific misogyny: while his middle-aged women are often paragons of dignity and wisdom, femininity in his teenage characters usually manifests as irrational or cruel behavior. Meanwhile, his teenage boys—such as Corliss's boyfriend, Dexter—may be clumsy or awkward, but never exhibit any ethical flaws. Acceptable when separate, but dangerously explosive when combined, adolescence and femininity render Corliss "a strange and rather delightful mixture of child, woman, and she-devil."[73]

Herbert often romantically juxtaposes his teenage heroines with fathers or father-substitutes. His career paralleled the steady rise in popularity of Freudian psychology in America, and Herbert's erotically inflected father/daughter scenarios offered popular images that complemented the new ideas of Oedipus and Elektra complexes which were gaining public circulation and acceptance. In these scenarios the teenage girl becomes men's ultimate problem and simultaneously their ultimate delectation.[74] Nature obligingly assisted Herbert's career by providing him with two daughters; when Pamela and Diana Herbert reached their teens, their father used them as the inspiration for his Corliss Archer cycle.[75] One edition of *Meet Corliss Archer* explains the cycle's genesis on its dust jacket: "F. Hugh Herbert was driving down Hollywood Boulevard with his sixteen-year-old daughter when he stopped to give a lift to a personable young infantryman. His daughter's spontaneous 'charm act' not only devastated the soldier, it sent Herbert himself to his typewriter to record the incident for *Good Housekeeping* Magazine and posterity."[76]

That moment of conception encodes the cycle's subsequent focus on Corliss's sexual antics. In earlier bobby-soxer texts like *Junior Miss* or *The Youngest Profession*, girls' cultural consumption signifies a diffuse sort of sexuality; through movie fandom, girls act upon aggressive appetites. But Corliss dispenses with the middleman: as the narratives' primary threat, consumerism and pop culture are almost wholly replaced in this cycle by the girl's flirtations and erotic manipulations. While Herbert fetishizes Corliss's sexuality, holding it up as an object of display, he also scolds her for it. Her flirtations are aimed at inappropriate targets like older boys in uniform (a frequent topic of the cycle, which played on the victory-girl panic) and also, of course, at her own father. The paternal/filial relationship Herbert portrays resembles the one described in the 1940 *American Girl* essay by Fairfax Downey, who complained that his daughter "circumnavigated" him with feminine manipulations. Herbert's vocabulary underscores the quasi-sexual nature of Corliss's circumnavigation. In the book's inaugural story, Corliss attempts to wheedle money from her father after her mother has said no:

> Corliss walked over to her father, put slim arms around him, and strained him to her childishly.
> "Angel," she cooed, "make her say yes."
> Mr. Archer, who felt himself weakening, shoved her away, chuckling.
> "Save that smooch," he advised, "for that unhappy youth next door. It doesn't cut any ice with me."
> He brushed the soft dark hair out of her face and rubbed his knuckles against her smooth, cool young cheek. He knew that he lied in his teeth. It cut a lot of ice. Corliss could generally smooch him out of anything.[77]

Similar scenes resurface throughout the cycle, suggesting a ritualized mating dance between the soft-hearted father and the crafty, seductive daughter who "coos" at him and murmurs endearments in his ear. As Mr. Archer himself notes, this treatment would more appropriately be aimed at her boyfriend than at him. Corliss unfailingly flirts with her father only to gain a Machiavellian end; he receives her attentions with pleasure but knows their underlying motives, and he thus responds to her with a frequently callous and unpleasant sense of humor.

Rachel Devlin reads this embattled relationship as a response to contemporary concerns about the diminishment of paternal authority in American homes: "the social relevance, indeed the social control, of fathers was ingeniously recast by locating his power as inherent to his sexual identity as a man, rather than his prerogatives as a father."[78] The diminishment of fatherly power in the home did not pose as great a threat to American ideologies of masculinity as the Depression had, but it, too, prompted a compensatory reaction in popular narratives; no longer the undisputed masters of their homes, fathers could nonetheless retain "social control" as sexual beings—as consumers and controllers of adolescent female sexuality. In virtually every text of the cycle, Corliss Archer is treated with a combination of patronizing paternalism and suppressed lust by her father, her boyfriend, and especially her author, who uses Mr. Archer and Dexter to voice his own paradox of fascination with a bewitching girl together with a hostile desire to put her in her place.

Because Corliss deploys her charms as a weapon against inappropriate targets, the texts dramatize numerous punishments intended to subordinate her. Her boyfriend, Dexter, the youngest and hence least suave of the cycle's males, punishes her most crudely: when she manipulates and teases him in the story "Time on Her Hands" (the title reveals that torturing boys is her antidote to boredom), Dexter brandishes a hammer with which he threatens to beat her. Teenage Dexter is not yet a patriarch, but we know he is destined to become one because Herbert draws several parallels between Dexter and Mr. Archer. Both are susceptible to Corliss's charms and therefore, despite some of the tensions between fathers and boyfriends typical in the comic genre, both are united in the brotherhood of the oppressed. After witnessing a particularly egregious example of Corliss's mistreatment of Dexter, Mr. Archer (a lawyer, naturally) offers aid to his fellow sufferer: "Dexter—if you ever want to throttle her with your bare hands, I'll defend you free of charge."[79]

Dexter Franklin's role (the hapless, sensible boyfriend of an exasperating girl) was a stock figure in the teen cycles, where boyfriends and sidekicks tend to have unusual names. But unlike *Janie*'s "Scooper Nolan" or *A Date with Judy*'s "Oogie Pringle," Dexter Franklin's name is laden with significant associations. His first name in Latin means "right," which encodes a quality of moral superiority as well as spatial direction: our word "dexterity" indicates that the left/right binary privileges the right side, while the word for left—"sinister"—proves the same dichotomy from the negative side. Not surprisingly, Dexter is often more right than Corliss, for Herbert delineates him as logical, resourceful, and competent. These blessings augur successful manhood in American mythology, in part because they are legendarily associated with another Franklin—Benjamin, one of the United States' original patriarchs (a founding "father") and our über-icon of pragmatic competence. As dexter's opposite is sinister, so Dexter's opposite is Corliss, the selfish "bitch." Corliss's name means "careless" or "carefree," an apt description of Corliss Archer's character, especially when combined with her last name, which has some fairly obvious applications.[80] Corliss's guiding ethos is unbridled eros: her misguided actions follow from the passionate appetites that seize her in various moments, making her as capricious and wanton as the archer of classical mythology, Cupid, who often appears in popular culture as an agent of disruptive desire.

The binary oppositions Herbert establishes between Dexter/Corliss, right/wrong, and logic/desire require that Dexter—who, we are frequently told, will marry Corliss one day—reestablish the proper hierarchy of their relationship by punishing Corliss's misbehavior. Several of the texts refer to the couple's shared childhood, during which he would frequently "sock" her when she became too irritating. As Corliss reminds him, they have outgrown such raw violence, yet Dexter remains "consistently baffled by the strange anomaly whereby you could be absolutely crazy about a girl and at the same time experience a frequent and urgent desire to sock her in the nose"[81] (an anomaly that seems to have baffled American audiences, as well, given the bipolar tone of the media's discussions of teenage girls). Herbert concludes his collection of stories with an optimistic vision for the future of patriarchy: after torturing Dexter more horribly than usual, Corliss feels a pang of remorse. "'Oh Dexter,' she sighed, 'if *ever* I act like such a *heel* again—*please* biff me in the eye.'"[82] By naming a biff in the eye as the perfect corrective to her "bitchiness," Corliss complies with the replication of patriarchal privilege; she expects, and even wants, to be put in her place when she goes too far.

The patriarchal/paternalistic tone of these stories signals Herbert's own credentials as a pater, for he constantly emphasized his use of his own children as models for Corliss. The dedication of the book *Meet*

Corliss Archer reads, "Through these pages walk the most wonderful girls in the world—my daughters, Diana and Pamela—whose endearing struggles with adolescent problems have given me most of the material for this, their book." This sounds like a ringing endorsement of adolescence, as does Herbert's later comment that he imbued Corliss with his own daughters' "natural gaiety, bounce, and charm."[83] But a faint alarm is raised by his language; that he finds his children's troubles "endearing" is our first clue that Herbert is what Doherty would call an imperial narrator rather than an indigenous one. It is worth noting that Sally Benson also had a daughter, but explicitly told interviewers she did not use her child to inspire the character of Judy Graves.[84] Perhaps that refusal to conflate real and fictional daughters helped Benson to narrate Judy's misadventures without lapsing into the condescension that dominates all of the Archer stories, one of which briefly highlights the flaws in Corliss's imagination. Her parents watch, fascinated, as their silly daughter descends the staircase:

> Corliss, daintily poised on the balls of her feet, hands fluttering in pretty gestures, a lovely, unearthly smile on her lips, was making a slow, rhythmic, almost floating descent, completely unaware that she was being observed, but carefully watching her own reflection in a mirror in the living room. . . . For an instant the comfortable, familiar hall dissolved into a haze. She was descending the great marble stairs of the Embassy and the ballroom was filled with cheering throngs of men, all intoxicated by her beauty . . .
>
> "Good grief! What does she think she's doing?" Mr. Archer whispered behind the cover of his newspaper.
>
> Mrs. Archer shook her head wonderingly and made quite a clatter with the electric toaster.
>
> "Corliss, dear," she said equably, "when you've quite finished admiring yourself, we'll be charmed if you'll join us for breakfast."[85]

A comparison of this scene with Benson's previously quoted "Daddy Dear," which also depicted the gulf between an adolescent girl's romantic imaginings and the flat-footed realism of her parents, highlights the unkindness of Herbert's passage. Seen through her parents' eyes, Corliss's daydream becomes risibly solipsistic. Unlike Judy Graves, whose eager fantasies in the play and film *Junior Miss* center on saving her parents' marriage and rehabilitating her "wayward" uncle, Corliss's fantasies are rarely other-directed, but rather focus on her desire to be worshipped by "throngs of men" whom she "intoxicates." This passage intertwines Corliss's sexuality with vanity and immaturity, explaining why she uses it so inappropriately and must repeatedly be punished for it.

Herbert uses Corliss's linguistic errors, as well as her absurd fantasies, to encode her infantilism and make her a lightning rod for sexual innuendo. Corliss often utters malapropisms with erotic *double entendres*, as when she haughtily calls Dexter "il duce" (Mussolini's nickname) but mispronounces the word as "douche."[86] When she complains to her parents, "Honestly, I might just as well be living in a monastery, for all the excitement there ever is around this house," her father starts to make a dirty joke: "'Put you in a monastery,' he grinned, 'and you'd probably get all the excitement you—'" His wife abruptly silences him and corrects her daughter: "You mean convent, Corliss. Monasteries are for monks."[87] Readers can laugh at Corliss's verbal ignorance, while enjoying—as her father clearly does—the hostile image of her being crushed by a lustful stampede of celibate men. Corliss is the only character singled out for this form of degradation: the cycle's male youngsters make no verbal errors, let alone any with sexual connotations. In the hands of paterfamilias F. Hugh Herbert, all of Corliss's efforts to make authoritative pronouncements are undercut by blunders that humiliate and sexualize her—first "hollowing out" her intellect, and then symbolically penetrating her.

Even when not directly casting Corliss in a sexual light, her errors of logic or judgment almost unfailingly catalyze the events of her narratives, emphasizing her role as the abject. Many episodes of the *Meet Corliss Archer* radio series turn on some catastrophe caused by either Corliss's ignorance or her frank lack of ethics. In "Corliss Archer—Authoress," after overhearing her father narrate the plot of a melodramatic romance, Corliss commits an act of plagiarism by putting the garish tale into her own words and submitting it to a fiction contest. But the story was actually written, as a secret hobby, by one of Archer's clients, a Mr. Prendergast; to protect his client's confidentiality, Archer pretended to have made up the lurid tale himself when laughingly repeating it to his family. When Corliss wins the contest and the story is published in the town's newspaper, a wounded Prendergast confronts the Archers and complains, "What I resent so bitterly—apart from the betrayal of my confidence—is the fact that many people will read this—this concoction of your daughter's—and I'll be ridiculed." Archer hastens to reassure him: "Just to keep the records straight . . . the story was published under my daughter's name. If anyone's ridiculed, it'll be Corliss."[88] This calms and cheers the flustered Prendergast, providing the relief for the plot's central tension; if ridicule must be in the offing, its only acceptable target is the teenage girl, despite the fact that the first ethical failing—the repeating of a secret—had been her father's.

This episode's absurdly expedient conclusion (a movie studio options the story for a film, whereupon Prendergast becomes wealthy and forgives Corliss completely), like the equally absurd conclusion of *Junior Miss*, occurs as an indirect result of the teen heroine's actions but without her deliberate orchestration. She thus can claim no legitimate credit for the happy accident that leaves everyone satisfied. Her only deliberate actions—the overhearing and plagiarizing of a story—are foolish and harmful, and can only be ameliorated by the promise of her humiliation. Many episodes of this series similarly rely on ridiculing Corliss to provide the main direction for their plots; the hollowing out of her intellect and judgment becomes the very basis for the cycle's action.

Corliss is further hollowed out when she mis-performs maturity, putting on airs to seem more sophisticated. This image of teenage femininity had forebears in earlier teen-centered stories, but usually ones with male protagonists; in texts like Tarkington's *Seventeen* and the Andy Hardy film series, mincing girls with "sophisticated" affectations are drawn as headaches for the down-to-earth, sensible heroes. Herbert adapted this figure for a girl-centered cycle but did not change her semiotics; as with the maddening girlfriends in boy-centered films, Corliss's pseudo-sophistication serves only to elevate others around her, preventing her from being the heroine of her own story. Dexter complains in the film *Kiss and Tell*, "Holy cow, why do you have to put on a corny act all the time?" while her parents, elder brother, and even housekeeper scold her affectations constantly. Meanwhile young Raymond—Corliss's twelve-year-old neighbor—provides a superior example of early maturity: he is an unsmiling, eerily precocious capitalist with a fondness for black coffee. Raymond's precocity inspires laughter because of its uncanny accuracy, while Corliss precisely reverses this joke: although older than Raymond, she cannot perform maturity persuasively, and merely looks absurd.

Earnest patriotism, Corliss's one saving grace, allows her some elevation as a figure of idealism, but she cannot act upon even this noble quality successfully. In the short story "Blood Is Thicker Than Tulips," fifteen-year-old Corliss pursues a war job: "I want to be a welder," she declares, and cuts school to apply at munitions factories where the minimum age for employment is eighteen. Because she mimics maturity so poorly, no one believes Corliss when she lies about her age. She returns home dejected, and her author underscores the defeat by showing that her objectives did not deserve success: her patriotism manifested only through deceit (cutting school, lying about her age) and she has spent the day running around town unchaperoned, without permission, chasing a gender-transgressive job ("Welding's for men," as Dexter says). Her late arrival home provokes Mr. Archer's violent anger: "For two pins . . . I'd turn you over my knee, big as you are, and whale the daylights out of you!"[89] When he learns of her noble intentions he softens, and readers, too, can view Corliss temporarily through a dewy-eyed appreciation of youth's high ideals. But the fact remains that she failed what she attempted because her goals and methods were inappropriate. Drawing upon the trope of youth as "the bright promise of tomorrow," this story simultaneously sees teenage girls as incompetent, transgressive, and troublesome.

The popularity of Herbert's stories suggests that their audience enjoyed this insulting vision of girlhood; significantly, and not surprisingly, that audience seems to have comprised only adults. Unlike *Junior Miss*, the book *Meet Corliss Archer* was not reprinted by a children's publisher and never became a staple of adolescents' libraries, facts which suggest a certain gap between the desires of girl consumers and the vision of girlhood embodied in Corliss. Since Herbert scripted so much of the Archer cycle, all media incarnations of this character may have offered only mixed pleasures, from youths' perspective. We have no data to indicate children's or teens' reactions to the Corliss Archer films, or to the long-lived *Meet Corliss Archer* radio series; debuting only in 1943, it was not yet available when *Calling All Girls* magazine conducted its 1942 survey of readers' tastes that showed *Junior Miss* to be the favorite radio program. But that survey provides other data indicating that girls' views of the world differed substantially from those ascribed to them by writers like F. Hugh Herbert. Conducted only shortly after the bombing of Pearl Harbor plunged the United States into World War II, the survey—filled out by thousands of the magazine's mostly teenage readers—reveals consistent preferences for narratives about strong, capable women and girls, with a particular emphasis on stories set against the backdrop of war: the top three positions in the "Favorite Book" category went to the Nancy Drew Mysteries, *Little Women*, and *Gone with the Wind*, the latter two of which are set during the Civil War, while the girls' most favored movie was the contemporary wartime drama *Mrs. Miniver*. Their favorite film actress was Bette Davis, known for playing strong and competent women, closely followed by Greer Garson, noble heroine of *Mrs. Miniver*.[90]

The suggestion inherent in these choices that homefront girls took inspiration from rousing tales of female heroism is borne out by girls' letters to the same magazine. In 1944 Jean Grossman, who had long been writing *Calling All Girls*'s advice column under the pen name Alice Barr Grayson, published *Do You Know Your Daughter?* which summarized the knowledge she had gleaned from years of reading girls' letters.[91] Grayson states definitively, "If there is one Ariadne's thread that can be followed in all the maze of varied adolescent problems in the thousands of letters to *Calling All Girls*, it is the yearning to be a somebody."[92] She quotes, as one example, the letter of a fourteen-year-old somewhat like Corliss Archer—anxious to contribute to the war effort, and frustrated by the lack of means to do so:

> I have four cousins and two uncles in the Services of our nation. . . . The other night I had a dream that they were killed in action. Now of course that was a silly dream but it could so easily happen and it got me thinking that I wasn't doing very much for the war effort. Of course I buy war stamps regularly and this summer I am helping harvest the crops (such as berries, beans, etc.). . . . I think that many girls think the same as I do.[93]

Letters like this, and girls' stated preferences for strong, effective female role models, bespeak an earnestness, a sincere desire to have a beneficial impact on the world in a time of crisis. Ironically, these were the very traits which underlay the ridicule of girls in the bobby-soxer genre. Judy Graves, too, has a sincere yen to set the world right, meddling in adults' lives because she is certain she can "help"; Janie Conway defends her rowdy party for soldiers as a patriotic contribution to the war effort; Corliss Archer struggles comically to get employment in munitions factories. More generally, Corliss's numerous efforts to be noticed and admired ("worshipped by throngs of men") suggest that she wants very much to be seen as "a somebody."

In other words, the producers of these entertainments almost got it right; the qualities they saw in teenage girls (earnestness, patriotism, a desire to feel important) were true in some ways. But by stripping those qualities of their sincere intention and using them instead as the basis of jokes—foregrounding an imperial, rather than indigenous, interpretation of girlhood—they reflected reality while badly distorting it, like a funhouse mirror. Real girls may have noticed those distortions (as the angry teens' letters to *Scholastic* would suggest), but did not necessarily refrain from consuming the products that insulted them. The *Calling All Girls* readers survey shows numerous teen-centered texts occupying privileged positions in the hierarchies of favorite entertainment narratives, many of which, like the Andy Hardy film series and the radio comedy *A Date with Judy*, tended to portray girls through stereotypes of frivolity or fluffy-headedness. Girls' avid consumption of teen characters in popular culture suggests that they considered a distorted reflection better than none at all. The teen comedies, laden though they were with mild insults to girls' intelligence and dignity, at least presented girls as the center of something. That status apparently provided real pleasures to young female consumers who yearned so keenly "to be a somebody," even while the same texts arguably offered even greater pleasures to adults who preferred to deny the "somebody-ness"—the personhood—of teenagers.

In the case of Corliss Archer, the most intense dissolution of personhood occurs in the play and film scripts, through the use of Corliss's body as a site for sexual humor and male anxiety. We have seen that girls often become more sexualized or more diminished when translated from fiction to theatrical or filmic texts; Herbert's stage play and film *Kiss and Tell* continues this trend, for it sexualizes Corliss more overtly than do the short stories or the radio series. The event that starts the action is, again, a denigrating joke that reinterprets girls' wartime altruism. Volunteering at a charity bazaar for the Red Cross, Corliss (played by Shirley Temple) and her friend Mildred attempt to sell hand towels to the soldiers in attendance, but soon discover the greater profitability of selling kisses. Playing directly upon the victory-girl controversy, this scene exploits the titillation of teen-girl sexuality but keeps it safely contained in a public booth in daylight. Even this relatively minor sexuality enrages the girls' families when they discover their smooching daughters at the head of a long line of grinning GIs; each family accuses the other's daughter of corrupting its own. Formerly close friends, the families feud vigorously and draw other neighbors into their row. The fracas increases when Corliss is later spotted emerging from an obstetrician's office, giving rise to a rumor that she is pregnant. In fact, she has merely accompanied a pregnant friend who secretly married weeks earlier, and who has sworn Corliss to silence, leaving her unable to defend her own reputation. Corliss's sexuality catalyzes a negative form of the consensus noted earlier in wartime films: while strife reigns between family and neighbors, the divided community can all agree, at least, on the identity of their common enemy. Because Corliss's supposed crime includes not just premarital sex, but illegitimate pregnancy, she thus threatens several social orders at once: the peace of the sanctified American home and the stability of the neighborhood at large (both of which imply the national democracy), and even the bedrock of patriarchy itself, legitimately produced heirs.

As in other cycles, the interests of patriarchal society appear symbolically in the interests of the Father, for Corliss's misbehavior has particularly pointed implications for Mr. Archer. In defending his daughter against slander, Mr. Archer fights one of his neighbors and comes home bruised and bloody; the family rallies around him to tend to his wounds and soothe his rage. Not only has he been physically injured, but the lawyer is now embroiled in a lawsuit himself, for he and his fellow pugilist sue each other for damages. As in *Junior Miss*, all the father's suffering can be traced to his daughter's immoderate pursuit of pleasure and ill-considered schemes. A similar scene appears in the sequel *A Kiss for Corliss*, when Corliss's flirtation with a middle-aged Casanova leads her father into another fist-fight. Interestingly, both films—which were made by different studios—were publicized with strikingly similar advertisements. Lobby cards for both depict the family gathered around a bruised Mr. Archer, suggesting that teen girls' damage to their fathers was deemed a strong selling point by both film studios.[94]

This assaultive relation to fatherhood earns Corliss strong assaults in return; her defining trait is to catalyze extreme passions, be they affectionate or hostile. One story in *Good Housekeeping* asked in its subheading, "What's to be done with the enchanting Corliss? Should we strangle her, or smother her with kisses?"[95] A binary of exaggerated love or anger are the only possibilities imaginable. Both responses are physical, "grabby," and disrespectful of boundaries; the teen girl is someone we lay hands on, for good or ill. (Nor are the good and ill really opposites: smothering is just as deadly as strangling.) Furthermore, the pregnancy plot of *Kiss and Tell* constructs Corliss not only as "to-be-looked-at," but as "to-be-penetrated": the characters, the author, and the audience spend the play's duration imaginatively dwelling between Corliss's legs, cogitating on her hymen, the prime mover of the plot. Even the films' advertising combined lust and rage: the two most-repeated images on posters and ads were a close-up of Corliss kissing a soldier and one of her stretched across the lap of her father, who stares intently at her buttocks as he brandishes a hairbrush (providing a visual reinforcement of his desire to "whale the daylights" out of her). But "whaling," in this image, expresses more than anger; Mr. Archer's intense gaze at his daughter's buttocks suggests a desire to control and consume her sexuality—especially since sex is the crime for which he punishes her, and Shirley Temple was

Sweet sixteen . . . and never been kissed? ? ?

45/218

Figures 5 and 6. In these publicity images for *Kiss and Tell*, Corliss Archer commits the crime of kissing soldiers and receives the punishment of her father's spanking. *Kiss and Tell* © 1945 Columbia Pictures Corp.

famously endowed with a round, pert bottom. Corliss's unperturbed facial expression and the "cheesecakey" posing of her separated legs, in high-heeled shoes, lend a further erotic subtext to the image. Her passivity connotes her acceptance of Dad's actions, harking back to her request that Dexter, her future husband, "biff [her] in the eye" when she needs it. Significantly, no such spanking occurs in the film; the studio concocted this image solely for the advertisements, suggesting its recognition of the image's appeal to a wide audience.

Not surprisingly, the critics' responses to *Kiss and Tell*, on both stage and screen, reified the cycle's binary of anger and desire. One reviewer of the play described Corliss as a girl "whose adolescent behavior leaves the family about as jittery as it would feel with a time bomb in the cellar, and no clock to go by," while *Variety* described Corliss on film as a "teen-

"Honestly, you'd think I was a child. All I did was kiss and tell!"

aged brat who does more than her share to upset several households,"[96] even though, technically, Corliss causes very little of the conflict, most of which stems from the mean-spirited gossip of her neighbors. The text's hostile tone seems to have made a deeper impression than the facts of its plot. Meanwhile, other reviews reflect how strongly the film, in particular, subtly encouraged a pedophilic response to Corliss's body. Casting Shirley Temple as Corliss exacerbated this nuance, for the recency of her tenure as the world's most beloved baby gave an added piquancy to her role as a supposedly promiscuous teen. In his review for the *New York Times* Bosley Crowther forestalls discussing the film until the third paragraph, first recalling Temple's childhood and the media hype surrounding her chrysalis moment—her "first" kiss—in *Miss Annie Rooney* (1942): "It seems only yesterday that Shirley Temple got her first screen kiss. . . . But with such momentous significance was that osculation endowed that it was blazoned to the public with mingled delight and awe. America's favorite moppet had reached the kissable age. . . . Oh, boy, what a whale of a difference just [three] years make! And what a remarkable transformation the current Miss Temple represents!"[97] Crowther writes as though he were salivating over his typewriter keys, but noted author James Agee, reviewing the film for the *Nation*, took a darker view of its sexual implications; he notes sourly that the audience "may tickle itself with the thought" of young Shirley's pregnancy, and that viewers are "pimpishly helped out by the camera, which develops an almost pathological interest in the girl's hind quarters."[98]

Corliss Archer represents the apotheosis of the diminishment and fetishization of teen girls in the bobby-soxer genre. Because she is most thoroughly sexualized, she suffers the most egregious lack of full personhood; her boundaries are entirely penetrable. Old enough for troubling sexuality, young enough for discipline, she invites a complex response combining desire and anger. No wonder American audiences, caught in their own paradoxes of desire for and dread of teenage girls, clamored for Corliss and the other teen-girl characters of the day. This subgenre's eroticized and hostile relationship between teen girls and patriarchs, and the steadily increasing emphasis on girls' sexuality, address adult concerns about the power of patriarchy at the moment when the teen girl emerged as an American "institution in her own right," as the *March of Time* newsreel put it. This emergence threatened some of society's traditional boundaries and hierarchies (the proper centrality of adult men; the traditional prescriptions of fatherly roles; the health and strength of the American military) even while supporting others (providing government and industry with a new subject of surveillance; contributing to the economy by opening up a new market; and symbolizing the "average" American home as a unifying national construct). As the image of Mr. Archer's spanking Corliss implies, sexualized teen heroines who succumb to the power of patriarchy allow producers and consumers alike an imaginative space in which to express their conflicted responses to the challenges posed by female youth.

Perhaps the strongest and most consistent example of the paradoxical bobby-soxer tropes, the Corliss Archer cycle was also one of the last. As World War II came to a close, the particular nexus of social and cultural conditions that had enabled these conflicted images of girls gave way to new concerns that, in turn, prompted a different interpretation of the girl's role in her family, and in her society at large. Between 1945 and 1949, bobby-soxers gradually faded as a subject of representation.

The Last Days of the Bobby-Soxer

After having played both Judy Graves and Corliss Archer, Shirley Temple finally cemented her latter-day reputation as Hollywood's ultimate bobby-soxer when she starred in the only film to use the term in its title: *The Bachelor and the Bobby-Soxer* (1947). The most polished of the genre, *Bachelor* featured an all-star cast (Myrna Loy, Cary Grant, and Rudy Vallee) and earned an Academy Award for its screenwriter, a young Sidney Sheldon.[99] It employs all the standard tropes of the genre: a teenage girl who is rendered without personhood as an object of others' fears and desires; a legal representative as a guardian (her older sister, a judge, as well as an uncle who is a court psychiatrist); and fears about her chastity as a central comic device. Also typical, its plot centers on the bobby-soxer's inappropriate romantic pursuit of an older man. The combined box-office draw of Temple, Loy, and Grant, together with Sheldon's witty script, made *Bachelor* a success even as the genre it typified—and the youth culture it described—were on the decline. The set of cultural styles that first defined the bobby-soxer had begun in the late 1930s with the rise of swing music, and had thrived in the early and mid-1940s. By 1947, however, these styles were becoming passé; just as the phrase "sub-deb" had ceased to be a common signifier of teenage girls after the Depression, so the "bobby-soxer" was mentioned less and less frequently after the war. Among comic narratives, *Bachelor* was the last great showcase for the figure of the bobby-soxer; thereafter she appeared only in minor films, or else as a secondary character in major films primarily about other people.

In 1949 the bobby-soxer celebrated her final year of mass cultural exposure, appearing in at least three mainstream comedies: *A Kiss for Corliss*, *Dear Wife*, and *Father Was a Fullback*, all of which indicate that rigor mortis was creeping into the genre. *A Kiss for Corliss* made an unlikely sequel; released fully four years after *Kiss and Tell*, it was also produced by a different studio and written by a different screenwriter. Although it used the same director as the first film and reprised Shirley Temple in the starring role, the sequel lacked the spark of *Kiss and Tell*, in part because it repeated the first film's plot rather too closely. Mr. Archer's fears about Corliss's virginity drive the action, while she conducts another of her inappropriate flirtations, this time with an aging, divorced womanizer played by David Niven. A failure at the box office, the film is distinctive only for being Temple's last; she retired from acting after its release. *Dear Wife* was also a cycle text, the sequel to a film (based on a stage play) called *Dear Ruth* (1947), which updated the Cyrano de Bergerac theme of the proxy who writes love letters on behalf of someone else. Unbeknownst to Ruth, a young woman living at home with her family, her teenage sister, Miriam, uses Ruth's name while corresponding with a soldier overseas; after the resolution of the predictable mix-ups, Ruth and the soldier marry. *Dear Wife* presented the young couple's further adventures, leaving kid sister Miriam in a distinctly secondary role. Had the film been made a few years earlier, it would have been titled *Miriam* and would have placed the teen firmly at the center instead of on the sidelines.[100]

The decline of the bobby-soxer is even more strongly exemplified in *Father Was a Fullback*, the title of which not only omits the bobby-soxer, but also omits signifiers of the female-oriented domestic comedy genre; if audiences assumed the movie was about grown men and football, they would not have been far wrong. Several aspects of this film make it a significant bridge between the bobby-soxer genre and two other filmic trends on the ascendant in the late 1940s: college comedies and family comedies that centered more upon the tribulations of a father than on the hijinks of adolescents. College films, while never disappearing from Hollywood after their heyday of the 1920s, surged after the war as college enrollments swelled; campus frolics, in comedies and musicals, thrived between the late 1940s and early 1950s. At the same time, the teen-centered comedies subtly metamorphosed into the father-focused domestic comedies that we recognize more often, today, from our memories of early television: a portrayal of the family as a unit organized around a well-meaning but slightly bumbling father, who upstages his children as the text's true center.[101] In *Father Was a Fullback*, one of the protagonist's main concerns is his mournful teen daughter's lack of popularity, but the more pressing conflict involves his employment: as the coach of a steadily losing college football team, George Cooper fears the imminent loss of his job. In a classic bobby-soxer plot, the teenage daughter, Connie, seems to hasten her father's dismissal when she publishes a scandalous and wholly fictitious magazine story about working as a nightclub "bubble dancer." Despite Coach Cooper's incompetence, it is his daughter's sudden sexual notoriety that finally makes the university threaten to fire him.

In focusing on the father's perspectives and worries, *Father Was a Fullback* repeats the narrative tone that shaped *Junior Miss*. But it goes a step further in privileging father over daughter: George Cooper has many scenes with his wife, his football team, his neighbor, and his colleagues. In earlier bobby-soxer films, even when a paternal view shaped the text, fathers appeared in few scenes without their daughters; the teen girl herself was the main on-screen figure. *Fullback* further privileges the parents over the children through its casting. Betty Lynn, a minor actress with only a few previous movie roles, plays teenage Connie Cooper, while her parents are played by established stars Maureen O'Hara and Fred MacMurray. Similarly, *Dear Wife* cast an experienced but second-string actress named Mona Freeman as the bobby-soxer, while the more prominent character (the soldier-turned-brother-in-law) is played by William Holden, a major leading man of the 1940s and 1950s.[102] By contrast, when Shirley Temple made *Kiss and Tell* four years earlier, she had been the biggest star in the cast, surrounded by actors who usually worked as second leads at best.

In 1949, then, we can see signs that the bobby-soxer genre waned as other trends waxed. Rehashed, shopworn scripts and diminishing prominence for the girl character (both in narrative role and in casting) accompanied the decline of the 1940s teen comedy and the gradual rise of the 1950s domestic comedy, with its added emphasis on fathers. Cultural trends are rarely so accommodating as to rise and fall within the neat parameters of a decade, but the bobby-soxer subgenre of teen comedy nearly did: rising in concert with the end of the Depression and America's entrance into World War II, the trend ended almost precisely in 1949 in response to changes in the cultural landscape. The postwar development of suburbia and the concomitant rise of television cooperated to drain away a large portion of the filmgoing audience, with the result that many formerly profitable filmic trends, like the adult-serving teen comedies, no longer reaped reliable profits. With revenue dwindling, studio chiefs may have seen no reason to extend the bobby-soxer trend in its original form. Moreover, the image of adolescence in society began to change as the end of the war led to the famed family boom of the 1950s, with its early marriages and high birth rates, its emphasis on picket fences and backyard barbecues, and its preoccupation with domestic life as the harmonious ideal of personal satisfaction. These ideological constructs, explored further in the following chapter, redefined the role of the daughter in her family, subordinating her antics into a wholehearted acceptance of patriarchal imperatives and almost entirely erasing images of female adolescence as oppositional or rebellious.

4

The Postwar Fall and Rise of Teen Girls

 The conventional wisdom about the history of teenagers holds that teens fully came into their own during the 1950s. In many ways this is true; the 1950s further capitalized on the youth market that had grown over the previous years, and many cultural products aimed at teenagers flooded the marketplace. The birth of rock 'n' roll music started a vigorous and widely visible strand of national youth culture. Popular narrative forms, from the movie industry to the dawning television industry, targeted teenagers either with teenage protagonists or with themes considered particularly appealing to youth, as in the notorious "exploitation films" like *I Was a Teenage Werewolf* and the television program *American Bandstand*. But what has not been so well preserved in Americans' cultural memory is that many of these teen-oriented developments happened only in the latter half of the decade; between 1950 and 1955, images of teens, and girls in particular, dwindled significantly from their 1940s standard. Teens appeared less prominently in films; on radio and television, some of the 1940s teen-centered cycles continued, but no new successful teen cycles emerged. Teens of both sexes in postwar radio and television comedies were often rather bland creatures, subordinated within ensemble casts that gave parents equal time, and represented without any of the extremes of good or bad that characterized them in 1940s plays and films. In both method and frequency of representation, teen girls significantly fade as prominent characters in the early to mid-1950s. After 1957, the teen-girl genre was reinvigorated by the characters of Tammy and Gidget and thrived in the following years, up through the mid-1960s.

This chapter begins by discussing how and why the image of the teenage girl dissipated and fragmented after the war, increasingly replaced in popular narratives by older ingénues, before exploring her return to prominence in the late 1950s and early 1960s. The 1950s brought a new "crisis of masculinity" and, as it had in the Depression, this perceived crisis led to a spate of non-threatening ingénues in popular culture. On television and radio some remained teens; in film, ingénues were most often out of high school, old enough to marry. This alteration reflected the social values of postwar society, with its emphasis on marriage and the home as the defining components of a happy American life. The discourse of family development, ironically, was both a factor in creating the masculine crisis and a means for healing its sting. As we saw in the previous chapter, Rachel Devlin has noted the dawning concern in the 1940s over the potentially weakening effects of the mid-century conceptions of fatherhood on traditional masculinity, and others have made related arguments; Barbara Ehrenreich perceptively interprets the successful launch of *Playboy* magazine in 1953 as a reflection of men's discomfort with the suffocating milieu of suburbia, playpens, and casseroles.[1] In popular entertainment of the postwar period, the replacement of the teen comedy by the domestic comedy pushed dads into the center of the tales. Some men may have found home life emasculating, but its representation in popular narratives partly compensated by making Dad the character who really mattered.

In the early 1960s, as the growing "space race" and the optimism surrounding John F. Kennedy's presidency began to dissolve anxieties about a masculinity crisis, the first wave of the massive baby-boomer generation entered high school. Girls of that generation received numerous direct messages about aspiration and achievement from their culture; public discourse in multiple venues encouraged girls to plan for careers (to a limited extent) and to be active in civic issues. As it had in the 1940s, the 1960s' combination of a resurgence in national masculine vigor, a larger-than-usual generation of youth, and expanding definitions of girls' social agency allowed images of aggressive teenage girls to blossom once again in popular narratives. Teen girls' portrayals in this era often include greater measures of apparent personhood than we find in earlier texts; yet, as in the 1940s, such narratives often admonish girls for their aggression and dramatize how patriarchal authority must put such girls "back in their place."

Because no new, successful teen-girl cycles emerged before the late 1950s, this chapter begins with a survey of what there was instead: a

trend in girls' representations toward domestic containment in the immediate postwar period, contrasted to the contemporaneous portrayals
of rebellious young males. The second section charts the rise of the baby-
boomer generation and its considerable impact on America's cultural
landscape in order to demonstrate why American patriarchs resented the
increasing influence of adolescents, crafting constructions of youth that
punished them for perceived transgressions. *The Patty Duke Show* and the
popular Gidget narrative cycle, analyzed in the final section, demonstrate
the application of these constructions; both Patty and Gidget are paradoxical characters, modeling increased agency and power for girls while
still being subject, subtly, to an enforced recontainment which neutralizes
their power.

The Ingénue and Postwar Gender Ideology

"Where have all the young girls gone? Gone to young men, every
one." When Pete Seeger penned this line in the mid-1950s as part of his
anti-war anthem "Where Have All the Flowers Gone?" he might as well
have been describing the American film industry. Starting gradually after
the war and with increasing frequency after 1950, popular culture tended
to focus on girls simultaneously older and less rebellious than the bobby-
soxers of the 1940s. These two traits cooperated to show girls at the
marriageable age, with a desire to become wholesome wives and mothers.
This shift corresponded to the postwar cult of domesticity and the concomitant pressure on women to leave the workforce and return to the
home, what Wini Breines has called "a policy of containment."[2] As servicemen returned and restarted their civilian lives, young American cou-
ples initiated a surge in marriages and first home purchases, a trend in
nest building that continued to grow throughout the 1950s. Born during
the Depression and coming of age during the war years, young adults
of the postwar period embraced the promises of middle-class family life
as the guarantors of security and happiness; they "married at a higher
rate and at a younger age than did their European counterparts,"[3] and
many young women married while still in their teens.[4]

Mainstream culture celebrated traditional family life and its strictly
separated gender roles. Images of girlhood in periodicals, advertisements,
and popular narratives focused heavily on romance and the eventual goal
of marriage, emphasizing beauty, fashion, and "boy catching." Girls' culture had included beauty and romance for many years, of course, but

these topics greatly intensified after the war. In just one example, *Calling All Girls*, which debuted in 1941 as the first mass-market magazine for teens, spent the duration of the war intermingling advice about fashion and beauty with articles about civic duties, global awareness, and career preparation, as well as an ongoing comic strip about a girl pilot. After the war, however, the coverage of professional or civic topics decreased markedly as feminized identity rituals—beauty, consumerism, and boy hunting—began to dominate the magazine. In 1949 *Calling All Girls* changed its name to *Senior Prom*, reflecting its new orientation more accurately and portending the obsession with high school culture that typified images of white teens in the 1950s.

As in earlier years, images of hyperfemininity reflected trepidations about American masculinity. In the 1950s, older concerns about men's loss of authority in the home were exacerbated by changes in the nature of the workplace. Popular books like *The Organization Man* and *The Man in the Grey Flannel Suit* questioned the conformity required for men to succeed in corporate culture, suspicious of its threat to the rugged individualism that mythically defines American masculinity. Breines sees masculine anxieties as the impetus for the "emphatically differentiated" gender norms of the 1950s that "exaggerated traditional femininity, sexual and domestic."[5] Popular consciousness frowned upon a woman's acting too aggressive, too powerful, or too independent when men's ability to exercise those qualities seemed in jeopardy. Moreover, traditional gender divisions augmented Americans' sense of patriotism during the Cold War, since women's ideal roles as wives and mothers constituted one of the noteworthy differences between American and Soviet culture, as Americans imagined them. Elaine Tyler May notes that "American women, unlike their 'purposeful' and unfeminine Russian counterparts . . . cultivated their looks and their physical charms, to become sexually attractive housewives and consumers under the American capitalist system."[6]

The ideological conditions of which May and Breines speak had a clear influence on the 1950s portrayals of girls as marriageable, innocent, hyperfeminine, and non-threatening, a trend augured by some girl-centered comedies of the late 1940s. In 1948 Jane Powell starred as the titular heroine of *A Date with Judy*, a musical comedy based upon the popular radio serial. Powell plays Judy Foster, a teenager wrongly convinced of her father's infidelity (a plot similar to those of *Junior Miss* and *The Youngest Profession*). But although she creates a misunderstanding, the

plot avoids extremities of conflict or chaos; the tale unfolds as an optimistic narrative of wholesome youth and only minor family discord, a
sunny, cheerful context that typified mid-century musical comedies.

A Date with Judy was one of the last films of the period to place a
teenage girl—played by an actual teenager—in the center of the narrative. Increasingly over the postwar years, the heroines became older girls
in their twenties bent upon finding a husband, as in *Every Girl Should Be
Married* (also 1948). Cary Grant plays a middle-aged doctor zealously
pursued by a much younger girl (Betsy Drake), a role quite similar to
one he played a year earlier in *The Bachelor and the Bobby-Soxer*. What
had been a teenager with an irrational crush in 1947 became a girl of
about twenty with an equally irrational crush in 1948. But unlike *Bachelor*,
Every Girl Should Be Married gives its stamp of approval to its heroine
because she follows the ideological mandate of the title. Although her
single-minded pursuit of Grant (which looks rather like stalking, to modern eyes) and her ill-considered antics cause serious problems for several
older men—as had the antics of bobby-soxers—the film constructs
Drake's lunatic aggression as charming rather than frightening, because
it ultimately aims to establish a traditional, conservative female identity
for Drake's character.

A similar trajectory shapes the 1950 film *Father of the Bride*, in which
Elizabeth Taylor plays a twenty-year-old who lives with her parents, does
not work or attend college, and plans her wedding. The perspective of
her father, played by Spencer Tracy, literally frames the narrative. As
the title indicates, this is Dad's movie; Tracy begins and ends the film
with direct address to the camera, and his voice-over narration throughout directs the audience to accept his version of events. No other character exercises this kind of authority, which considerably surpasses the
privilege given to fatherly perspectives in *Junior Miss* and *Kiss and Tell*.
Tracy's comments to the audience express the inconvenience and expense
he suffers because of his daughter's impending nuptials. As in the earlier
bobby-soxer comedies, a daughter's sexual maturity is portrayed as a
source of trouble to her father, but the "trouble" here appears fundamentally harmless—again, its aim is the patriarchal ideal.

Within a few years, however, the feverish husband-hunter of *Every
Girl Should Be Married* and the frustrating daughter of *Father of the Bride*
gave way to a more harmonious image of female purity and containment.
The crop of young actresses who dominated the genres of musicals and
domestic/romantic comedies—like Jane Powell, Doris Day, June Allyson,
Debbie Reynolds, and Shirley Jones—projected cheerful, clean-scrubbed

images and usually played characters whose spunky dynamism overlaid a fundamentally tame, or tamable, nature. All but Powell were over twenty when their film careers ignited, yet all mimic the purity, goodness, and non-threatening aggression of the 1930s "Miss Fix-It" teen heroines. Indeed, several 1950s girl-centered films were remakes of 1930s predecessors. Doris Day's *Young at Heart* (1954) is a moderately close revision of *Four Daughters* (1938). Jane Powell's *Three Daring Daughters* (1948) borrows heavily from Deanna Durbin's *Three Smart Girls* (1936), and the striking similarity in titles was probably an intentional ploy to attract viewers who fondly remembered Durbin's films. Powell, whose soprano voice was featured in all her films (as Durbin's had been), later starred in *Nancy Goes to Rio* (1950), a faithful remake of Durbin's *It's a Date* (1940).[7]

The nearly exclusive filmic portrayal of girls as harmless ingénues who protect patriarchal values also influenced 1950s television. The 1954–1955 *Meet Corliss Archer* television series revamped its heroine as less of a vamp; without her "female perversity," she becomes almost unrecognizable from her 1940s incarnations. Corliss and Dexter talk frequently about their future marriage, and the program juxtaposes their little problems as a couple with the senior Archers' little problems as a couple, implying that teens and adults share the same aspirations of conformity to the middle-class ideals of home and family. Moreover, the paternal dominance embedded in such ideals structures this series and others like it, in which teenage daughters often occupy only secondary positions, giving way to their parents. Lynn Spigel has noted early television critics' complaints that fathers in domestic comedies appeared ineffectual and unmasculine.[8] But although contemporaries may have feared a loss of masculine authority in American homes, in fact most such programs are unabashedly father-centered and reinforce patriarchal ideals. *Meet Corliss Archer* usually focuses on the series' male characters, Mr. Archer and Dexter, even though the program is named for the teen girl. The announcer, who offers comical commentary between scenes, sometimes addresses viewers specifically as adult males: "you" should never attempt to understand women, for the futile effort would drive "you" mad; such comments pepper several episodes. This flagrant interpellation of viewers as patriarchs partially counterbalances Mr. Archer's portrayal as a mild bumbler, for he enjoys the supreme authority as a narrative position; the stories are custom-built for his worldview. Not surprisingly, the program's producers explicitly stated that their show was "aimed at a middle-aged audience."[9]

In postwar texts, then, portrayals of girls and young women underwent several changes. Cultural emphases on marriage and domestic life
moved high school teens out of the narrative center, replacing them with
girls old enough for marriage, while the roles themselves shifted away
from the hellions of the 1940s with a resurgence of wholesome innocence
and dedication to traditional female roles. These shifts reflected the
growing societal concerns about the threats to masculinity in American
domestic and professional life. This diminishment of the figure of the
girl can also be seen in the context of portrayals of youth at large, including boys, in the same period.

Images of Youth, 1950–1957

During the early 1950s high-school-aged teens, as such, commanded
national attention in one of two ways: either as consumers or as "rebels."
The teen consumer market continued to grow steadily after the war,
thanks largely to the efforts of one Eugene Gilbert, a market researcher
who spent the 1940s and 1950s energetically proving to American manufacturers that teenagers constituted a booming market. With his system
of polls, his syndicated newspaper columns, and his corporate accounts
with an ever-growing roster of clients seeking to tap teenage dollars,
Eugene Gilbert kept the image of the American teen as a consumer fresh
in adult culture's consciousness steadily from the late 1940s to the
1960s.[10]

If teens' burgeoning consumerism allied them with their parents as
supporters of the capitalist economy, their construction as rebels differentiated them sharply from approved adult norms. In 1951, J. D. Salinger's novel *The Catcher in the Rye* made a deep cultural impact by portraying its sixteen-year-old hero as a sensitive outcast who deplores the
"phoniness" of society and resists indoctrination into adulthood. This
androcentric portrait of surly alienation echoed the delinquency rhetoric
of teens as hostile to social conventions. It is perhaps no coincidence that
the image of the disaffected male teen emerged in a period characterized
by disaffected male adults. Delinquent boys acted out the raw aggression
that domesticity and corporate life were said to be draining from adult
men. The very active, pervasive delinquency rhetoric of the 1950s thus
gave adult males a cathartic opportunity to project their own desires for
rebellion onto others, while still protecting the privilege they enjoyed as
lawful conformers to dominant ideologies. The crisis of masculinity,
then, contributed to the diminishment of the figure of the girl not just

in her actual portrayals, but also in her representational displacement in favor of male teens. Popular culture overwhelmingly coded adolescence as male in the early 1950s, and those males were more often angry than playful or charming, as Andy Hardy and Henry Aldrich had been.[11]

Most American teens were, of course, not delinquent; as James Gilbert argues, the widespread delinquency rhetoric reflected changes, not so much in teen behavior, but in the practices of federal institutions (Congress, the Children's Bureau, and the FBI) which, by increasing their efforts to record and disseminate delinquency statistics, fostered a panic discourse somewhat disproportionate to reality.[12] But the image of youthful delinquency was extremely popular, as demonstrated by the successful release of the film *The Wild One* in December 1953. Marlon Brando plays Johnny, the leader of a motorcycle gang and the first rebel without a cause (asked what he is rebelling against, Johnny replies laconically, "Whaddaya got?").[13] In 1954 the social preoccupation with delinquency and the entertainment trend toward harmless ingénues were bizarrely grafted together in *Susan Slept Here*, in which Debbie Reynolds plays the oxymoronic role of a cute, perky "delinquent." The film centers on a middle-aged screenwriter who struggles with a script about juvenile delinquency, the new fad. To help inspire him, his pals on the police force bring him a genuine juvenile delinquent to interview. The improbable tale concludes, naturally, with the delinquent and the screenwriter falling in love. The casting of wholesome, twenty-two-year-old Debbie Reynolds as a teenage delinquent made as much sense as the later casting of white, non-singing Natalie Wood as an operatic Puerto Rican in *West Side Story* (1961), and both casting decisions reveal the same Hollywood logic: a desire to represent an embodiment of cultural Otherness without challenging contemporary ideologies. *Susan Slept Here* thus exploits the topicality of a popular moral panic, but sanitizes it by subordinating it to the romance-and-marriage plot, with a "delinquent" heroine as harmless as a mouse.

In 1955 Hollywood began to portray actual teenagers more often, and the images of rebellion and disaffection became more serious. This shift was heralded by two films released that year, *Blackboard Jungle* and *Rebel without a Cause*. Also by 1955, rock 'n' roll music had emerged as a youth-oriented style that represented a "rebellion" against the musical standards of white adults. These events were watersheds through which the teenager became, once again, a massive preoccupation for Americans, particularly in the guise of the rebellious male.[14] After this sea change, teenagers returned to Hollywood in two distinct ways: as high-school-aged characters in mainstream films, and as the target audience for a slew of exploitation films that constituted Hollywood's response to demographic data suggesting that the industry had underestimated the adolescent portion of its audiences.[15] Desperate to attract customers in a period of financial losses, studios used exploitation themes and marketing tactics to lure teenagers. This produced a large crop of films, both from major Hollywood studios and from smaller companies that specialized in exploitation themes.

The exploitation genre of "teenpics," as Doherty calls them, centered on crime, rock 'n' roll, science fiction, and horror. These films were often low-budget affairs that dispensed with some of the traditional codes of mainstream narratives: in teenpics, characters with little or no interiority dash through flimsy, sensationalist plots, and the production values are often notably poor, as even the big studios tended to use second-rate actors, writers, and directors on such projects. What made these films financially successful was that their style particularly suited an audience predominantly made up of youngsters. For the big studios, this represented a paradigm shift from the earlier years of Hollywood, when conventional wisdom held that films had to appeal to the widest audience possible. Between the mid-1950s and the late 1960s, the teen exploitation genre thrived with such titles as *Teen-Age Crime Wave, Drag Strip Riot, Rock Pretty Baby, Teen-Agers from Outer Space,* and *Teenage Bad Girl.* As this last title indicates, the exploitation genre rarely featured girls in prominent roles unless they were somehow "bad": rioting in reform schools, or rioting in sorority houses, or rioting somewhere else. The rock 'n' roll films offer some exceptions to this pattern, but "teenpics" mostly had no place for wholesome, average girls, except as minor characters or victims of monsters. The exploitation genre was explicitly and deliberately aimed at boys. American International Pictures, a successful exploitation studio, adhered to a lucrative formula: "a girl will watch anything a boy will watch," though "a boy will not watch anything a girl will watch"; similarly, "a younger child will watch anything an older child will watch," while the reverse was not true. Thus, films were aimed ideally at "nineteen-year-old males" in order to attract teen girls and younger adolescents.[16]

The cultural obsession with delinquency and rebellion overlooked the fact that most actual American teens were not delinquents. As Doherty notes, "At a time when good wholesome middle-class families were proliferating like crabgrass, the market for like-minded movies had been only dormant, not dead."[17] That market began to get its due in 1957, when Universal Studios released *Tammy and the Bachelor*, a variation on the Cinderella story which gave Debbie Reynolds, now twenty-five, another opportunity to play a seventeen-year-old. Based on Cid Ricketts Sumner's popular novel *Tammy out of Time*, about a sweet innocent who lives in a Southern bayou with her grandfather and a pet goat named Nan, this film participates in the 1950s ideology of presenting heroines as pure-bodied, pure-hearted "Miss Fix-Its." Strong-willed and outspoken, Tammy nonetheless remains a simple ingénue with a quaint, folksy vocabulary and salt-of-the-earth values; in the course of the film she saves a life and rescues a family of fading Southern aristocrats from bankruptcy. *Tammy and the Bachelor* became a surprise box-office hit, proving that there was, once again, a market for teenage girls as central characters. This point was also proven, in the same year, when European émigré Frederick Kohner wrote *Gidget*, a novel loosely based on his daughter's adventures in the surfing subculture at Malibu Beach; it became an immediate best-seller and launched a multimedia cycle. The first mainstream novel to treat the still-marginal sport of surfing, *Gidget* initiated the surf-and-sun craze of early 1960s youth culture, including the popular series of beach films produced by American International Pictures.[18]

Over the course of the next several years, the baby-boomer generation made a significant impact on American society, and led to another full-blown obsession with teens in popular culture. If girls' representations during the 1950s tended to resemble those of the 1930s, representations during the 1960s tended to resemble those of the 1940s: once again, a demographic surge created a larger crop of teenagers, to whom society reacted with a mixture of pleasure and anxiety for precisely the same fundamental reasons: teens' increased consumer power, and girl-teens' sexual energy and appeal. Thus, when teenage girls returned to the center of American entertainment, they were represented very much as bobby-soxers had been: girls who are charming and buoyant, whose incompetence, disturbing sexuality, and mild insanity make their efforts at agency appear dangerous while ultimately proving harmless.

Adorable Barbarians at the Gate

Adult culture of the postwar period both embraced and decried the increases in teenagers' cultural influence, opportunities, and freedoms, so that teen-girl texts of the 1960s construct their heroines within a discourse of "putting her back in her place." This section explains what prompted that containment—why cultural patriarchs of the late 1950s and early 1960s felt provoked, once again, to use popular narratives as a place to forcibly diminish the figure of the teenage girl, even while seeming to celebrate her. As had happened before, this narrative gesture responded to a perceived threat to patriarchal orders from adolescent sexuality and consumerism.

The mild tone of alarm and displeasure that characterized 1940s discussions of teens became more pronounced, less humorous, and more aggressive after the mid-1950s. Adult observers expressed concerns that teens seemed to be "taking over" American life, particularly in their sudden influence over the entertainment industry. Between the mid-1950s and the mid-1960s, teenagers seemed to be the star of virtually every show—not just in the prolific exploitation genre, but also in mainstream dramatic films, like *Peyton Place* (1957), *A Summer Place* (1959), and *Blue Denim* (1959), all of which dealt frankly with the "shocking" subject of teenage sexuality in plotlines about rape, premarital sex, and pregnancy. Nabokov's *Lolita* (1955), although a more highbrow text, reached mainstream consciousness because its story was so alarming (the mutual seduction of a twelve-year-old girl and her middle-aged stepfather) that it sparked a public controversy, ensuring widespread publicity.

The dark, complex, and sexual portrayals of adolescence emerging from these novels and films point to a shift in popular perceptions of genre and representation: the late 1950s were the first time in which high-school-aged teens became the central protagonists of dramas that highlighted contemporary teen concerns. As we have seen, the 1930s and 1940s had made teens the central hero/ines of comedies, while teens in dramas tended to be secondary characters or to be removed from contemporary adolescent discourse. Teenagers, the comic genre implied, belonged in the "carefree," lighthearted atmosphere of the comfortable middle-class home, or the happy peer culture of the high school. The conventions of dramas, by contrast, employ different tropes: their characters often have three-dimensional psychological interiority, displaying complicated reactions to complicated situations. The protagonists of a drama or melodrama are literally "taken seriously." When Hollywood studios placed teens in a teen-specific context at the center of dramatic mainstream films, they implied that teenage issues were *worthy* of the same serious representation that was formerly given more often to adult life.

Also significant was the rendering of teenagers in the context of social and sexual problems. Eager to lure audiences away from their newly ubiquitous television sets, filmmakers attempted to offer pleasures unavailable on television, either because of technical limitations or because of the television industry's strict rules against potentially controversial topics. As television maintained a policy of squeaky-clean content, Hollywood competed by making increasing assaults against the decades-old Production Code that had forbidden sexual language or situations. F. Hugh Herbert's comedy *The Moon Is Blue* (1953), based on a stage play, struck the first blow by uttering the word "virgin." From this humble beginning, great changes emerged in films by the end of the decade. In one example, *A Summer Place* (1959) deals frankly with the repressive sexual codes of the 1950s. Sandra Dee and Troy Donohue, two of the biggest teen idols of their day, fall in love and have sex. Dee becomes pregnant, and the couple must confront harrowing struggles with parents, busybodies, and punitive social codes before finally obtaining their parents' permission to marry and establish a happy ending for themselves. While films like this portrayed teens as three-dimensional people, more realistic than their stick-figure counterparts in most of the exploitation genre, they nonetheless echoed the exploitation films' construction of adolescence as a time of rebellion and ill-considered hedonism. The mainstream dramatic films starring teens, then, could trouble adult sensibilities on two counts: they made teenagers appear as important human beings rather than "wacky kids," and they reinforced a hoary and highly problematic construction of youth as "trouble."

Teens' cultural influence affected other media as well. Television networks offered several programs aimed at youth, either with teen protagonists or with gimmicks, settings, or plots that had particular youth appeal.[19] Youth's tastes increasingly dominated the music industry as well, most notably through the rise of rock 'n' roll music and the steadily high levels of merchandising that accompanied the teen-idol phenomenon. Television and music combined in the enormously popular teen dance show *American Bandstand*. Initially airing only as a local Philadelphia program in 1952, in 1957 the program was syndicated nationwide and became an immediate hit.[20] *Bandstand* allowed teens to see their favorite musical acts perform, an infrequent opportunity in the days before music videos. But more importantly, perhaps, the show fostered a united point of identity for teens around the country, exhibiting the clothing and dancing styles of distant peers. The popularity of this program and its cast of dancers gave it a high degree of visibility, even among adults.[21] Many of the *Bandstand* regulars became popular celebrities in their own right, appearing on the covers of magazines like *'Teen*, another item recently added to the teenage marketplace.

The late 1950s saw a boom in the production of teen-specific magazines. *Dig* debuted in 1955, one the first periodicals to focus on rock 'n' roll and rhythm and blues. With regular columns written by disc jockeys, *Dig* also featured articles about high school life and teen interests, written in an irreverent tone. The first issue proudly announced its separation from adult standards by joking that "the PTA will probably ban us for having unscrupulous people on our staff." Over the following several years, a growing crop of periodicals focused on teen-oriented popular culture and fads, especially *'Teen, Movie Teen Illustrated*, and *16*, all of which debuted in 1957, the same year that *Bandstand* became nationally syndicated. Meanwhile, the consumer marketplace teemed with gadgets and trinkets adorned with the names and faces of the teen idols represented in the magazines and on television.

Although teen consumerism obviously helped the American economy, and thus was embraced and encouraged by countless businesses, it also posed some ideological challenges. The proliferation of for-teens cultural products prompted some adults to lament the apparently shrinking field of adult entertainment. In 1959 William K. Zinsser, erstwhile drama and movie critic for the *New York Herald Tribune*, complained that when he and his wife were in the mood to see a movie, the only fare available in their small town was Elvis Presley's *King Creole:* "[It] made me wish that some day the theater would get around to showing a movie that adults could also enjoy. *High School Confidential* had been there the previous week, and it in turn had followed various other exercises in horror and assault as practiced by the younger set, such as *I Was a Teen-Age Frankenstein.*"[22] Zinsser was not alone; as cultural producers increasingly catered to youth, many older Americans felt pushed aside—an unpleasant sensation which, predictably, led to a good deal of grousing. Some of their grousing stemmed less from any real cultural privation than from the outright effrontery of it all; many wondered how culture had deteriorated to such a state that the children were running the world. Grace and Fred Hechinger's 1963 polemic, *Teenage Tyranny*, states the problem frankly on the first page of its introduction:

> Teen-age . . . is nothing to be ashamed of. Nor is it a badge of special distinction worthy of a continuous birthday party. And while teen-agers should be afforded mitigating circumstances for some of their actions and views, on the basis of natural immaturity, they should neither be placed in an aquarium tank for purposes of exhibition and analysis nor be put on pedestals to be extolled for that admittedly enviable condition—youth. . . . American civilization tends to stand in such awe of its teen-age segment that it is in danger of becoming a teen-age

society, with permanently teen-age standards of thought, culture and goals. As a result, American society is growing down rather than growing up.[23]

Similarly, the July 1965 issue of *Esquire*, "the magazine for men," asked anxiously on its cover, "Does today's teen-ager influence the adult world?" Inside, the entire issue was devoted to a study of teenage fads and to the various industries that cater to teens. An editorial page, "The Last Word," revealed the editors'—and many of the readers'—opinions about all this adolescent brouhaha. Describing "teen-agerism" as "a virulent disease," it listed the symptoms as they manifested in a hypothetical teen: "He behaves as if he had arrived somewhere, as if he had already achieved his own sort of perfection, celebrating what he is (very little), instead of worrying about what he may become (anything)." To many adults, the teenage craze was offensive because it suggested that adolescence was a valuable condition in and of itself. This contradicted the logics of biology and traditional culture, which interpreted adolescence as something to be outgrown on the path to permanent adulthood, a more valid existential condition. Overappreciation for adolescence, the writer argued, could lead youngsters to draw incorrect conclusions, and hence damage their future ability to perpetuate the status quo of adult-centered ideology: "The danger is . . . that having become a matter of interest you will come to think of yourselves as therefore interesting, which is not quite the same thing. You have not created a valuable sub-civilization merely by being too young to vote." Three months later, this tone of condescension and mild disgust was repeated by Joseph Roddy, a curmudgeonly television critic for *Look* magazine, who blamed youth-oriented test-marketing techniques for what he considered the miserable inanity of the fall season's new programs.[24]

Ironically, the real problem that plagued Zinsser, Roddy, and *Esquire*'s staff was caused by adults, not youth: the overabundance of low-quality cultural products for teens was caused by executives who relentlessly, and not always discerningly, hunted teenage dollars as quickly and efficiently as possible. Many teens were happy to partake of this array of products—good, bad, or otherwise—but they were not the ones responsible for producing and marketing them on such a vast scale. Nonetheless, those who observed the avalanche of teen culture with a skeptical eye tended to blame teens themselves. The backlash against youth seems particularly unfair when we consider that many of those who complained about teen-agers' influence also profited from it—as did *Esquire*, by devoting an entire issue to the subject. Within the general discourse of anti-teenage backlash, girls received a particularly intense form of scrutiny and comment, partly for the same reason that bobby-soxers had been scrutinized in the 1940s: girls, more than boys, supported the industry of teen-oriented consumer goods. As Moya Luckett notes,

> Girls spent more than boys (who saved for large ticket items like cars), shopping regularly for clothes, records, makeup, books and magazines. Suddenly their tastes and activities really mattered, acquiring an economic importance that resonated outside the confines of their bedrooms. These increases in teenage spending were accompanied by close and often critical media investigations into youth trends [which] suggested that there was some essentially "feminine" quality to teenage life at this time.[25]

As it had in the 1940s, the image of consumerism melded with increased fears about teens' sexual behavior. There were no victory girls in the 1950s and early 1960s, but there were other social phenomena which associated girls, once again, with increased sexuality and increased circulation outside the home.

Expanding Possibilities for Girls

Women's and girls' sexuality, and their professional prospects, received heightened cultural attention in a variety of media during the postwar period. As mentioned above, the youth-centered dramas of the age routinely placed their young heroines in sexual situations, frequently ones involving the scandalous topics of premarital sex, pregnancy, and rape. The films *Peyton Place* (1957) and *Lolita* (1962), each adapted from highly sensational novels, portrayed stepfather-stepdaughter incest, and *Lolita*, in particular, managed to suggest that its adolescent star was in fact the primary seducer; contemporary audiences, polled upon leaving theaters, almost unanimously expressed pity for the poor, addlebrained Humbert Humbert, led astray by the wiles of his predatory stepdaughter.[26] Girls' sexual subjectivity also began to be expressed in popular music with "girl groups" like the Shirelles and the Supremes, who gave young women a voice for expressing romantic or sexual desires and concerns that found no outlet in other public venues.[27] In 1960, the FDA's approval of the birth control pill raised concerns about a supposedly imminent tidal wave of teenage sexual delinquency, although, as Douglas notes, the actual facts were far less dramatic than alarmists implied; the only substantial statistical increase in sexual activity occurred among young women of college age in committed relationships.[28] But there were no indications that casual sex was rampant, or that girls of high school age were markedly increasing their sexual activities. Nonetheless, as they always had where "delinquency" was concerned, the media offered a diet of worst-case scenarios rather than a balanced representation of the truth. Thus, throughout this period, stories about the "sexual delinquency" of teens continued to pepper adults' periodicals, and continued to create the impression that teenagers were, by definition, a sexual problem.[29]

Continuing fears about unbridled sexual hedonism among young women were complemented by issues particular to this historical period, which offered increasing possibilities for girls to enjoy public agency either through careers or through civic engagement. Although career opportunities remained mostly limited to secretarial or similarly assistant-level work, a growing consciousness assumed that it was normal and even proper for a middle-class white girl to earn a college degree and then to earn her own living—at least until she became a full-time wife and mother. Girls' magazines of the early 1960s presented articles on both professional preparation and domesticity, encouraging girls to plan their educations and careers, even while the traditional emphasis on fashion, beauty, and dating remained dominant. This emphasis on achievement sprang partly from the American reaction to the Soviets' 1957 launch of Sputnik, which resulted in changes to the American educational agenda. Distressed that Russia had beaten the United States in the "space race," American policy makers implemented changes in the educational curriculum to add emphasis on topics like science and math. President Kennedy himself said that "we should make every effort to see that the intellectual talents of every boy and girl are developed to the maximum."[30] Included in this national agenda, girls sat beside their male classmates and absorbed the message that they shared the intellectual responsibility to secure the superiority of their nation.

The injunction to reach one's maximum potential was an impractical and confusing message for girls, given the lack of an infrastructure to support it: most American industries had little interest in hiring women, and, as we have seen, the dominant cultural discourse used notions of "unfeminine" Russian females to encourage traditional gender roles among American women. As Susan Douglas recalls these contradictions, "No one said, 'Just boys—just you boys study hard.' This was on everyone's heads, girls too, and we were not let off the hook. . . . [W]e had to get A's as well, to fend off the red peril and save our country and ourselves. Now, on the other hand, no one painted seductive pictures of us girls growing up to become engineers."[31] These incongruities could be keenly felt by girls with professional ambitions. In July 1964, one frustrated girl vented her feelings in a letter to *Dig* magazine: "The next time I hear someone say 'a woman's place is in the home,' I am going to scream. And I imagine I'll be doing a lot of screaming since I hear this remark constantly." Confessing her desire to become a research chemist, the anonymous girl pinpoints the double standard behind the American dream:

> A man is able to devote part of his time to work and part to his family and still be a successful father. A woman can do the same thing if she only wants to. [Working mothers] shouldn't be looked down on. They should be looked up to. Five hundred years from today, historians will marvel that people in the twentieth century were foolhardy enough to believe that women were inferior to men, that some races were inferior to others, and that bigger and better bombs were the answer to anything.[32]

Clearly, not all girls happily conformed to the cultural ideals of full-time domesticity for women; the postwar rhetoric about achievement inspired girls as well as boys—even while society continued to scold girls who took such ideas too seriously.

The implied encouragement for female achievement, vague and contradictory though it seemed, thrived in girls' fiction as well. Starting during the war, the new genre of the "junior novel" (what today is called the Young Adult or Teen novel) often included plots involving careers. Almost without exception, those careers were imagined in the traditional feminine venues: fashion, the arts, nursing, child care, and so forth. Moreover, romance remained a dominant focus even in career stories; in the usual formula, the heroine's job brought her into proximity to a male superior with whom she could fall in love. Along with the newer genre of the junior novel, the established series-book genre, too, showed an increased attention to girls' professional prospects. Stalwart Nancy Drew—who sleuthed for fun, but never profit—continued to dominate the series-book field, but the wartime and postwar periods initiated a spate of series with heroines who earned their livings. Among the most popular were the Cherry Ames series (1943–1968), about a nurse; the Connie Blair series (1948–1958), about a "career girl" in the advertising industry; and the Vicki Barr series (1947–1964), about an airplane stewardess. While these series privilege adventure over romance, they nonetheless conform largely to patriarchal values: the heroines are less authoritative than the men around them, and do not controvert any of the stereotypes of approved femininity. But professional settings proved exciting and inspirational to many readers, and career-girl novels were even used as textbooks in some schools. In 1953 Anne Edwards, a high school teacher, recommended the use of career-oriented fiction like *Paintbox Summer*, *Peggy Covers the News*, and *Shirley Clayton, Secretary* as texts for a "commercial" English class, one in which the students were not college-bound. As Edwards says of her ninth-grade students: "Here were thirty-two girls soon to try to find a place for themselves in the business world. . . . Yet, how poorly equipped they were, and how unaware of the competition facing them!"[33] Edwards addressed this problem by using career fiction and career-themed articles from magazines like *Seventeen*, *Charm*, and *Mademoiselle* to teach her students "how to act in an office."

Girls' culture also encouraged them to think about non-paying forms of public achievement. President Kennedy's establishment of the Peace Corps inspired young Americans to think globally; themes of passionate volunteerism and commitment to social causes began to infuse teen culture regularly for the first time since World War II. Numerous articles in the ever-growing body of teen-girl magazines, throughout the 1960s, exhorted readers to pursue educations, careers, and local and national volunteer opportunities. The July 1962 issue of *Teenagers Ingenue* magazine, celebrating a patriotic theme in honor of Independence Day, offered quotations from several of President Kennedy's speeches in which he encouraged youth to envision themselves as active participants in their nation's future and in the welfare of the world. The same issue of the magazine asked readers to join "Teen-Agers CARE," a youth-specific branch of CARE, the international relief organization. Girls who reached their adolescence in this period received a steady stream of encouragement to imagine themselves as an effective, important presence in the world, both as professionals and as agents for social change. These messages complemented the growing changes in adult women's lives, too, as the second-wave feminist movement began to develop; Betty Friedan published *The Feminine Mystique* in 1963, a landmark book that questioned the limitations of women's traditional roles as wives and mothers, and the National Organization for Women was founded in 1966. During the period between the late 1950s and the mid-1960s, then, American females, young and old, were using growing opportunities and cultural developments to imagine a larger and more important role for themselves in American society, without necessarily sacrificing the femininity that earned them the approval of their culture.

Discourses about femininity, adolescence, and achievement informed the structure and content of girl-centered narrative texts. *The Patty Duke*

Show (1963–1966) and *Gidget* (1965–1966), two of the most prominent girl-centered television series of the day, combined two contradictory and mutually complicating impulses: to capitalize on the marketing bonanza represented by baby-boomer girls, and simultaneously to reassure parents and other cultural patriarchs that girls' growing freedoms and opportunities need not disrupt traditional social stratifications. While *The Patty Duke Show* and *Gidget* appealed strongly to adolescent girls by offering representations of the increased agency that attached to young women in this period, they simultaneously figured the results of that power as pyrrhic victories; in fact, both of these programs consistently reinscribe their energetic and clever heroines in positions of near-total powerlessness and ridicule. These paradoxical comedies reiterate the narrative strategies used in films like *Junior Miss* and *Kiss and Tell*, with the result that they ultimately make the same points as those films: first, that teenage "agency" results only in chaos, and second, that adolescent female sexuality is a force rightly contained by paternal authority. In these constructions of female adolescence, *The Patty Duke Show* and *Gidget* emphasize that girls' lives, consciousnesses, and sexuality were not only the agents driving the rampant baby-boom consumerism, but were in fact the items *to be consumed* by a patriarchal society fraught with conflict in its attitudes toward its daughters.

Patty Duke and Teen TV

As we saw in the earlier part of this chapter, 1950s images of youthful femininity in both film and television subordinated girls fairly consistently to their fathers and other male characters. In the 1960s, this subordination markedly decreased and was partly counterbalanced by a growing number of portrayals that placed girls at the center of attention and presented them as lively, interesting, and active. This change occurred in concert with the fading of the 1950s "crisis of masculinity." The post-Sputnik national interest in the space race had a good deal to do with this change, for it gave Americans a new outlet for fantasies of masculine capability. As the famous opening of the television series *Star Trek* stated, space was "the final frontier," and it conjured all the ideals of masculine power and conquest that historically attended American frontier narratives. This quintessentially American masculine metaphor made an even more significant appearance in one of President Kennedy's speeches; in 1960 he told the delegates at the Democratic National Convention, "We stand today on the edge of a new frontier—the frontier of the 1960s."[34] Kennedy made space exploration an explicit part of his presidential agenda, and he himself helped to reignite a national sense of masculine competence; young, vigorous, a war hero and a renowned womanizer, Kennedy embodied many American fantasies of masculinity. As it had during World War II, the perceived restoration of American masculinity allowed for a change in representations of girls from ingénues to more aggressive and publicly engaged girls. But, as we shall see, girls' aggression could be *represented* without being consistently *sanctioned*; 1960s girl narratives showed their heroines aggressing, but often punished them for it.

The revived teen-girl image on television marked a shift away from patriarchal narrative dominance, particularly in the programming of ABC, the network that most consistently developed teen-friendly series in the early 1960s. Their first truly successful teen-girl series was *The Patty Duke Show*, which enjoyed such popularity that it launched a mini-cycle of its own, inspiring a short series of Patty Duke books. This situation comedy was one of the earliest to attempt to place a teenager's perspective at the center of the series' logic. Part of the motivation to elevate the importance of the teen girl, in this instance, was that Patty Duke herself was already a renowned symbol of teen achievement: after becoming the youngest actress ever to win an Oscar, for her role as Helen Keller in *The Miracle Worker* (1962), Duke set another record with her eponymous TV program as the first teen to have a series named for her. True to the promise of the title, the program focused almost exclusively on the exploits of its dual heroines, both played by Duke: Patty Lane, a New Yorker, and her "identical cousin" from Scotland, Cathy. But although this program attempted to orient itself around the subjectivity of a teen girl, in fact its narrative assumptions reflected the consciousness of its creator and chief scriptwriter, Sidney Sheldon, far more than that of its star.

Sheldon had already established a reputation as a weaver of teen tales for adults; in 1947 he had won a screenwriting Oscar for *The Bachelor and the Bobby Soxer*, a film with significant impact on *The Patty Duke Show*. The resemblance of 1960s teen-girl characters to those of the 1940s was, in this instance, not at all a coincidence. *The Bachelor and the Bobby Soxer* centers on a "wacky" but lovable high school girl, Susan Turner, who lives with her elder sister Margaret, a judge. Male authority is provided by Uncle Matt, a psychiatrist. As in so much of the bobby-soxer genre, Susan's domestic authority figures are also figures of cultural authority, adding weight to their criticisms of teen behavior. Judge Turner scolds

Susan for her slang, her laziness, her hyperbolic emotions, and her careless use of the telephone. After seeing a debonair guest speaker at her
school, Susan sets about making herself more "mature" to appeal to him,
snubbing her teenage boyfriend and giving an absurdly hyperbolic performance of "adult" behavior (a routine that must have felt familiar to
Shirley Temple, after having done the same as Corliss Archer). Eventually, the inappropriate crush is resolved when the older man, at the
judge's prompting, pretends to cooperate with Susan's obsession by dating her and forcing her to recognize the prohibitive gap in their ages.
Finally convinced that they are mismatched, Susan returns to her teenage
boyfriend, believing that he "needs" her more.

When Sheldon created *The Patty Duke Show* sixteen years later, he
did not bother revising his fantasies about adolescent femininity, but
dusted off his Oscar-winning screenplay and simply recycled it. Like
Bachelor, the inaugural episode of *The Patty Duke Show*, titled "The
French Teacher," opens one weekday morning at home as Patty is dryly
scolded by her domestic and cultural authority figure, a father who is a
newspaper editor. Mr. Lane scolds Patty for the same reasons Judge
Turner scolded bobby-soxer Susan: slang, laziness, and inappropriate use
of the telephone. At school Patty gets a crush on her new French teacher,
and the rest of the plot follows suit: she makes an elaborate performance
of "maturity," snubs her classmate boyfriend, and recovers from the absurd crush only after her father and her teacher conspire to teach her a
lesson by ostensibly giving her what she wants—a date with her dream-
boat—and letting her learn the folly of it, so she can return to the boyfriend of her own age. If any observers happened to notice that Sheldon
had frankly plagiarized himself, they do not seem to have said so in the
public record. The recycling of this plot escaped detection, which perhaps suggests how naturalized the stereotypes of adolescent girlhood had
become; wholly integrated into Americans' consciousness of "how it has
always been," these tropes lost the specificity that would allow anyone
to consider their reappearance as a repetition of an individual text.

This episode set the tone for the remainder of the series; indeed,
Patty's portrayal remained extremely consistent, for Sheldon, by his own
claims, wrote all the episodes himself.[35] The traits Sheldon portrays are
those which he deems constitutive of the "typical" teenage girl and are,
in nearly every instance, held up for ridicule. After Patty slangily asks
her father to sign her report card, Mr. Lane replies, "I presume that in
some unknown tongue that's a request for my signature," suggesting that
teenagers speak a different, and inferior, language. The report card itself

is perfect, which arouses her father's suspicion; closer examination proves that Patty attempted to trick him by producing the grades of her more intellectual cousin Cathy. Patty's real report card reveals a string of Cs and a D in French. Mr. Lane sarcastically names the activities she practices with more diligence: "If you were graded in boys and telephone, you'd be at the top of your class." Patty validates this deprecating remark by arguing that she has no use for French, or other subjects, because they will not help her get a husband. When Mr. Lane complains that bookish Cathy isn't sufficiently "rubbing off" on Patty, his wife laughingly reminds him of girls' priorities: "Haven't you heard, darling? Girls are influenced by *boys*." Both Patty and her mother thus validate the view that romance matters more to American teen girls than self-improvement or pride in achievement.

In less than five minutes, the show presents nearly all the facets of its titular heroine that will appear for the next three years: the American teenager (as opposed to European Cathy) is a slangy trickster who hates to work, loves to chatter, and navigates her life by the North Star of the opposite sex. This teenager's easy distraction from the "appropriate" channels for her energy impedes her inherent potential; teenage life and teenage concerns are thus opposed hierarchically to the more "legitimate" concerns of parents. As the lyrics of the series' theme song tell us, "While Cathy adores the minuet, the Ballets Russes, and crêpes Suzette, our Patty loves to rock 'n' roll—a hot dog makes her lose control." Throughout the series, "our" American girl, Patty, is the more consistent focus of attention than European Cathy, and Patty is thus the series' privileged representation of adolescence. The program's central heroine, then, is presented as lovable partly because of her uniquely American teen cultural practices, which involve lowbrow tastes and the easy loss of "control"—precisely the same teen traits that adult culture was constantly criticizing in the news media. Just as in the 1940s films (including the one that Sheldon wrote), the point is to celebrate and scold the American teen girl for similar reasons.

Those reasons are represented in each episode through Patty's energetic and creative schemes, which Susan Douglas describes as "zany antics."[36] These antics made Patty an appealing and popular character among her contemporary young audiences, for they represent her as an effective agent. Earlier teen-girl comedies had also relied upon plotlines driven by the teenager's crazy schemes, but *The Patty Duke Show* increases and underscores the representation of the teenage girl as a resourceful and determined person with big ideas—as when, in a 1964 episode, she decides to join the Peace Corps. The episode concludes, predictably, with enforced containment: her parents convince her not to go to Africa because she's needed more at home. But for the majority of the episode, viewers get to see Patty throwing herself energetically into learning about African language, art, and dance, in preparation for her noble adventure. This portrayal offered particular pleasures to girls of that generation, raised as they had been on rhetoric about the ambitions and potential of American youth, and the simultaneous, contradictory messages that marriage and motherhood were the proper goals of women.

Douglas has argued that characters like Patty Lane (and Gidget, who appeared in the time slot immediately following *The Patty Duke Show* in the 1965 season) appealed to girls because they seemed to offer a way out of the contradictions between social agency and femininity: "It was usually 'perkiness'—assertiveness masquerading as cuteness—that provided the middle ground [Patty and Gidget] needed to get their way and get male approval, two goals that were often mutually exclusive."[37] But this perkiness was a double-edged sword: while it offered teen girls a vision of admirable agency, and thus could serve an empowering function, it was simultaneously constructed within the teen-girl conventions that militated against taking girls seriously. In almost every instance, Patty's and Gidget's schemes—like all teen schemes—are ultimately revealed to be untenable, absurd, and potentially destructive of social hierarchies. Patty's and Gidget's admirable antics, then, provided girl viewers with pleasurable opportunities to fantasize about various adventures while also admonishing them, "don't try this at home."

A significant part of Patty's perkiness, for example, is the frequency with which she adopts disguises to achieve temporary goals. In "The French Teacher," the disguises are figurative rather than literal, as Patty dons several female personae culled from popular stereotypes: at various moments she becomes the romantic heroine ennobled by love, the future homemaker of America who cooks and bakes to please her man, the star student who studies hard and answers every question correctly, and the moral influence whose love can keep a man on the right path. Patty performs each of these roles hyperbolically, providing the episode's humor by revealing the overreactive silliness that supposedly typifies teenage girls. The results of these awkward behavioral "disguises" are nearly all positive, as we see Patty apply herself toward goals that she ultimately reaches: her grades sharply improve, she acquires new culinary skills, and she learns to see herself as a competent achiever. But does she? Most of the goals she achieves do not last; even her crush dissolves quickly, suggesting that girls' desires are fickle and not worthy of steady pursuit. The methods Patty employs to obtain her desires—temporary, exaggerated acts motivated by inappropriate emotions—undercut her achievement, for she never realizes the value of hard work for her own self-esteem or her own progress in life. Instead the show reinforces the idea that, as Mrs. Lane said, "girls are influenced by *boys*." At its most benign, Patty's role-playing gains her only temporary adventures, but no permanent benefits.

Patty's agency more often surfaces in the form of business schemes, one factor which differentiates this program from the bobby-soxer films in which girls' schemes almost always focused on romantic or domestic endeavors. Several episodes reveal Patty's keen grasp of capitalism as she embarks on various moneymaking ventures. But here, too, she does not achieve any lasting goals. Two episodes with this theme ran in consecutive weeks in 1964, "Horoscope" and "The Tycoons." In "Horoscope," Patty consults an astrology book that happens to prove correct a few times; persuaded that she has a reliable tool for predicting the future, she opens shop in her bedroom, charging her friends fifty cents apiece and ignoring the warnings from her sensible cousin and her disapproving father. Patty is eventually shut down by a police detective investigating reports of an illegal fortune-telling operation. This detective, an adult male representative of the state, enters not just Patty's home, but also her very bedroom, in order to put her back in her place. To teach Patty a further lesson, Cathy takes the proceeds Patty has earned and offers them to the policeman for charity. Patty's scheme is scotched by the law, and by her law-abiding Scotch cousin.

The following week "The Tycoons" aired, in which Patty goes into business marketing dresses created by Cathy. Again she makes some strides in achieving her goals, but eventually the roof caves in: at the climax of the episode an agent from the Internal Revenue Service appears at her door to say that she owes an enormous sum of money, and is in trouble for not having the proper export licenses. Her father must extricate his foolish daughter from the mess, at the cost of hiring "two lawyers, an accountant and a business manager." The teenage girl's entrepreneurial escapades are not only silly, but financially deleterious to the entire family. Once Patty's disruptive energy has been contained, however, the show can afford to offer her a modicum of consolation. When she laments her "failure," her mother cheers her by saying, "You tried, Patty. You had an idea and you followed it through. I'm proud of you." Her father adds, "You almost accomplished a very rare feat. For a minute or two there, I thought you were really going to start a business without experience, assets, or capital. It could have set a dangerous precedent." Dangerous indeed: if Patty's overblown ideas ever truly succeeded, they might suggest to America's teen viewers that even further social influence was available to them, a patriarch's nightmare in this age of perceived "teenage tyranny." Few images of authoritative containment could surpass the sight of policemen and IRS agents entering a girl's private space and threatening her with legal action. At the same time, the episode shows viewers that girls were *important* enough to warrant such high-level surveillance and containment, proving—albeit more negatively than positively—that girls could have an impact on adult affairs. The episode also offers better opportunities to fantasize about professional agency than are offered by the 1940s bobby-soxer tales like *Junior Miss*, in which the girl's only connection to "business" is the indirect and unintentional impact she has upon her father's employment.

The Patty Duke Show further demonstrates the containment of subversive teenage potential by sublimating sex into temporary romance. While the popular press continued to print nervous pieces about teenage girls' explosive sexuality, Patty's love life constitutes a recurrent focus of this sitcom. Although the conventions of comic narrative and the television industry militated against the portrayal of sexual relationships, several episodes treat Patty's dates, doomed crushes, or misunderstandings of men's intentions. As in the 1940s texts, the teen girl often chooses inappropriate targets for her romantic infatuation: in "Operation Tonsillitis" Patty falls in love with the doctor (former teen idol Troy Donohue) who is to remove her tonsils, and mistakenly thinks he loves her, too, when she overhears him speaking words intended to describe his boat ("she has trim lines"). Along with her failing business schemes, Patty's sanitized, sometimes misguided, and always temporary relationships mitigate the truly threatening possibilities of teen-girl "agency" in all its guises. As we saw with the 1940s texts, which many girls eagerly consumed in spite of their insulting messages, girl viewers could embrace a character partly because they enjoyed seeing *any* representation—even an imperfect one—of adolescent female agency. The fact that Patty fails what she attempts more often than she succeeds is softened by the knowledge, as Douglas reminds us, that true agency in this period was perceived as boys' territory, and therefore that any girl who succeeded too much would threaten boys to the extent of losing her popularity among them—an undesirable fate. Patty's failures, then, make her a safe role model; they allow her to catalyze and scheme, while still enjoying the popularity with males that make her a successful female.

These same messages resurfaced in the program *Gidget*, which debuted two years after *The Patty Duke Show* on the same network, and aired on the same night. The *Gidget* television series follows its predecessor's lead in manifesting its heroine's agency through featherweight schemes that either fail or are rendered harmless, so as to diminish the threats they pose. One critic has analyzed an episode in which Gidget defends a local hamburger shack, a beloved teen "hangout," against her father, a member of a civic committee that wants the shack razed to make way for a museum. High culture and teen culture battle for turf, as they were doing in society at large in the mid-1960s. Eventually both parties agree that the new museum will include a room for the hamburger shack: "The laughable compromise was of course absurdly convenient. But [it] summarily neutralized all organized opposition and counterhegemonic ideologies represented by Gidget and her constituency."[38] Similarly, in "All the Best Diseases Are Taken," Gidget organizes a demonstration against a theater that charges high prices. The episode exploits the topical 1960s incidence of youthful "protest" while trivializing it, suggesting that political demonstrations benefit teens less than those oriented toward self-interested consumerism—no accident, surely, since the power of teen consumerism was precisely what the network counted on when developing the *Gidget* series.

But one difference between *Gidget* and *The Patty Duke Show* is that Patty attempts public projects (related to school or jobs) as often as private ones, while Gidget operates more consistently in a domestic context of family and romance. This context allows Gidget to appear enterprising while keeping her more rigidly focused on the patriarchal projects of heterosexual union and its attendant rules of feminine display. Gidget gives her best friend a make-over ("My Ever Faithful Friend"), boosts the self-confidence of an awkward boy ("Ego-A-Go-Go"), and initiates a campaign to make boys more considerate dates ("Chivalry Isn't Dead"). In each scenario Gidget's untenable, hyperbolic *modus operandi* goes awry. Her attempts to beautify her friend LaRue are meant to enhance LaRue's self-esteem; the unsightly results, however, have the opposite effect, and LaRue cheers up only after Gidget's father comforts her by praising the appeal of naturalness. The episode renders Gidget with affection—she is a loving friend, albeit a misguided one—but the happy ending has nothing to do with her "agency," and everything to do with Daddy's wisdom.

Other episodes grant partial success, rather than failure, to Gidget's efforts. But comic conventions require that some disaster occur before the
tidy conclusion, and those disasters usually derive from Gidget's incompetence, which is linked to her age. Like *The Patty Duke Show*, *Gidget*
views youth through the interpretive lens of adulthood so that—even
while offering a better representation of teen-girl subjectivity than had
appeared earlier—these programs find teen girls laughable creatures.

The tones of the laughter generated by Patty and by Gidget are markedly different, because *Gidget* sexualizes and diminishes its heroine more
than *The Patty Duke Show* does. Indeed, the narrative cycle surrounding
Gidget resurrects many of the sexual constructions of adolescent femininity employed by F. Hugh Herbert in his Corliss Archer tales, in which
the teen girl's eroticized relationship with her father becomes the site for
both celebrating and containing her sexuality. Such scenarios could offer
pleasurable possibilities for girl viewers; as Douglas says, comparing this
program to *The Patty Duke Show*, "Gidget was more appealing. Not only
were [actress] Sally Field's hairdos and clothes cuter, but also the show
featured the great Electra fantasy: Mom gone and a kind, handsome,
well-to-do, and indulgent Dad all to yourself."[39] *Gidget* thus offered girls
some of the same pleasures as did the Nancy Drew books, as we saw in
chapter 1. This television series took a plot element attractive to girls
(having a wonderful daddy all to oneself) and rendered it more exploi-
tatively than empathetically. The same Freudian awareness that had allowed Corliss Archer's Oedipal themes in the 1940s had, by the 1960s,
grown and been compounded by the intervening years' increased images
of sexual themes in popular culture. The result, in the Gidget cycle, is a
portrayal of girlhood that maximizes the stereotypes of teen girls as crazy
and potentially destructive, but redeemed through diminishment and sexual subordination to the father.

Gidget's Origins and Development

Gidget was the center of a mass-media cycle that surpassed even Corliss Archer's impressive circulation and endurance. Kohner's novel appealed not only to the 1950s' cultural obsession with teenagers but also
to the particular appetite, within that obsession, for a glimpse of "authenticity" in the unique styles and fads of youth. Surfing was a little-
known sport in the United States when *Gidget* was published. Its portrayal of surfers' distinct "slanguage" and its descriptions of how to
perform the sport itself (both of which Kohner learned from his daugh-

ter) made the novel a novelty. Written in only six weeks, it became an immediately popular cross-media commodity; within eighteen months, the first film (*Gidget*, 1959) was in theaters. Starring Sandra Dee, perhaps her era's most definitive representative of idealized adolescent femininity, *Gidget* was an instant hit. It spawned two sequels, *Gidget Goes Hawaiian* (1961, starring Deborah Walley) and *Gidget Goes to Rome* (1963, starring Cindy Carol). By the time "the Gidge" premiered on television, she was firmly established as a fixture of popular culture, and remained so long after: following the initial series there was a string of television movies (1969's *Gidget Grows Up*, 1972's *Gidget Gets Married*, and 1985's *Gidget's Summer Reunion*, which in turn spawned a second regular series, *The New Gidget* [1986–1988]). As of this writing, dozens of websites celebrate some facet of the Gidget phenomenon, and the films and part of the first television series have been released on commercial video, ensuring that the character retains some name recognition nearly fifty years after her debut—an astonishing lifespan. Among the baby-boomer generation, Gidget was arguably the reigning exemplar of the twentieth-century teenage girl.

Like other teen-girl narratives of the late 1950s and early 1960s, the Gidget tales not only appealed to children and teens, but also reflected and addressed adult culture's concerns about teen delinquency/sexuality and consumerism, both of which arose from fundamentally the same fear: how much decision-making power should a society grant its children, and what other kinds of freedom might follow? *The Patty Duke Show* answered that fear primarily through plots about failed business schemes, and secondarily through a sublimation of sex into temporary, harmless, and ultimately untenable crushes. *Gidget* precisely reverses this formula, offering a few visions of Gidget's failures in capitalist economy, and multiple expressions of her sexuality, which is constructed without fail, in all the cycle's texts, as a domestically contained force: either Gidget's suitors behave like fathers, or else her father behaves like a suitor. These are the representational methods used by the producers of the Gidget texts to address the patriarchal concerns that haunted cultural conversations about youth, femininity, and other perceived threats to the dominance of mature white men.

The Gidget cycle fetishizes its heroine's sexuality as a means of asserting patriarchal control over her; she is held up as an object of sexual scrutiny to delight the patriarchal eye and soothe its fears, even while she offers girl viewers the same pleasures that Patty Lane offered. The Gidget narrative cycle provides an excellent case study of how a fad enormously popular among girls can, paradoxically, encode opportunities to fantasize about agency while subtly offering instruction in the logics of subordination. The remainder of this chapter charts the development of this construction of adolescent girlhood across the span of Gidget texts, with particular attention to the television series.

The first and most important point to be made about the Gidget character is that we have evidence of her popularity among young girls, something we do not have for Corliss Archer. That popularity allows us to know that Gidget's attractions for girls were real and suggests the extent to which her coded prescriptions of sexual subordination were absorbed by young female consumers. Angela McRobbie has used Gramsci's theory of hegemony to analyze the prescriptive potential of popular culture; she finds in girls' magazines, for example, "an explicit attempt to win consent to the dominant order" of patriarchal sexual ideology, for they occupy "the sphere of the personal or private, what Gramsci calls 'Civil Society.' . . . Hegemony is sought uncoercively on this terrain, which is relatively free of direct State interference. Consequently it is seen as an arena of 'freedom,' of 'free choice,' and of 'free time,'" which facilitates consumers' digestion of the attendant ideologies.[40] These arguments apply equally to narrative texts, similarly consumed within paradigms of leisure and pleasure.

Gidget's impact on girls can be measured by the character's incredible longevity and diversity of representation across media forms, as well as by the direct comments of adult women who consumed Gidget as children or teens. The four actresses who played Gidget on film or television before 1966 were consistent figures in a wide variety of celebrity magazines aimed wholly or in large part at teenage girls; every new Gidget incarnation was accompanied by a saturation of Gidget coverage in numerous girl-oriented publications, all of which discussed the actress in question as an emulable role model. The standard rhetoric of such publications painted female teen stars as "average girls just like you," detailing their activities, their beauty regimens, and their "tips" to girls in a construction that combined accessibility of identification with an instructive tone.

The project of selling Gidget to teen magazine-readers involved constructing her as non-threatening. *TV Picture Life* in December 1965 ran a story called "Meet TV's Newest Darling: Gidget." The illustrations show Sally Field vamping with a string of pearls and a cigarette holder, mimicking a 1920s flapper and laughing to show that even *she* cannot take herself seriously when dressed like that. Other photos show her playing with her hair, making funny faces, and sticking her tongue out. The accompanying article discusses her thwarted desire to be a *femme fatale:* "If Sally Field could have one wish in the world, she'd want to be a sexpot." But sexpots are potentially dangerous; a woman who owns her sexuality can deploy it against men, as the "she-devil" Corliss Archer had done. Sally Field may or may not have wished to be sexy in her own life, but as Gidget, her appeal depended on demonstrating a "perky" femininity that allowed observers to consume her sexuality, while leaving her with an aura of ineptitude and innocence—the same preference for objective over subjective sexuality that informed the bobby-soxer texts.

TV Guide, too, emphasized Gidget's innocence in its cover story for May 28, 1966: "There are these two THINGS about Sally Field, who plays Gidget on ABC. She's actually LITTLE and FUNNY and makes these FACES. But she is AWFULLY old. She'll be 20 in NOVEMBER!"[41] The author's use of capitals adds to the tone of silly teenage hyperbole that characterizes the rest of the article. Clearly, being little and making funny faces were considered central traits of adolescent female identity. This style of coverage, which blanketed such magazines as *'Teen, Calling All Girls, Movie Teen Illustrated, TV Picture Life,* and countless others, worked hard to make young female readers project themselves into the identities of the teen-girl actresses the magazines portrayed. These periodicals' millions of readers seemed to eagerly welcome this coverage and the fantasies of identification it allowed.

The growth of the for-teen and for-children commodities market also allowed *Gidget*'s producers, as well as those of *The Patty Duke Show*, to license toys with the girls' likenesses: not just comic books (which Corliss Archer also had), but also board games, coloring books, and paper dolls. Clearly aimed at younger girls than the ones who read *'Teen* or *Seventeen,* these toys indicate that Patty's and Gidget's audience included girls in the same age group, between child and teenager, that constituted the primary audiences of the 1940s teen-film characters (girls between the upper grades of elementary school and the lower grades of high school). It is interesting to note that, in the case of *Gidget,* the merchandising accompanied the television series more than the films, perhaps reflecting producers' knowledge that television reached much wider audiences, and offered increased possibilities for mass-marketing a character.

It may seem ironic, then, that the initial *Gidget* series endured only for a single season (1965–1966), as such short lifespans are usually interpreted to mean that a series failed. Actress Sally Field shed light on the fortunes of this series when she appeared on *The Tonight Show* on March

28, 2002. Reminiscing about Field's role in *Gidget*, host Jay Leno erroneously claimed that the program had been a "hit"; Field corrected him by saying that *Gidget* achieved strong ratings only in the summer following its single season on the air, by which time the network had already canceled it. At its debut, *Gidget* was scheduled on ABC opposite CBS's new sitcom *The Beverly Hillbillies*, which ranked in the top ten of the Nielsen ratings and which had more general appeal to adults, including fathers, than *Gidget*.[42] Only in the summer, when reruns were aired, would American daughters have a better likelihood of commanding the television set during prime time. *Gidget*'s becoming a "hit" during the summer, then, suggests that it did indeed meet the desires of its target audience. Some of that audience even fought to keep *Gidget* on the air; upon the series' cancellation in 1966, the producers received numerous protests from girls who launched "save Gidget" campaigns of letters and petitions, but the network would not change its mind.[43]

Field's comments about summer ratings lead us to a relevant question: the degree to which daughters controlled the television sets in their homes. David Morley's studies of television-watching patterns among families confirm that "[m]asculine power is evident in a number of the families as the ultimate determinant on occasions of conflict over viewing choices"; ironically, fathers' insistence on controlling the family's viewing habits might bespeak "a sense that their domestic power is ultimately a fragile and insecure thing."[44] Morley's subjects were British families in the 1980s, but his observations apply to the American postwar period as well. We have seen that the mid-twentieth century's discourses of domesticity, and the increasing social influence of women and children, threatened established prerogatives of masculinity. But of course, the very fact that so many families in Morley's study consented to the father's domination of the television proves the breadwinner's continued position of privilege in the home.

Sally Field's anecdote suggests that *Gidget* and similar texts were popular with young girls because they offered a vision of young female power to young females who had little. Appearances to the contrary, consumer power is not the same as real power. The millions of baby-boomer girls who supposedly had so much influence over society that the media complained about it nonetheless could not keep a program they liked on the air if it contradicted the viewing desires of the domestic patriarch. Though teen consumers could make a success of a film or a musical group, they could not do the same, to the same degree, with a television program. Movies and music were consumed in cinemas and concert halls, venues where youth gather without adults. But television was consumed in the home, where fathers—their anxieties to the contrary—still enjoyed more prerogatives of authority and decision making than the rest of the family. What all the media brouhaha about "teen power" managed to overlook (not surprisingly, since most of it was written by and for an adult male perspective) was that daughters had little real authority, even in the one arena most strongly coded as theirs: the home. Just as *The Patty Duke Show* did, *Gidget* offered two paradoxical pleasures, simultaneously, to adolescent girls living in patriarchy: first, it represented an ideal reality by showing its teen heroine subordinated to a father authoritative yet perfectly loving and indulgent; secondly, it offered some (partial and compromised) images of a girl's potential for independence and achievement.

The initial popularity of the Gidget cycle in the late 1950s, when it emphasized surfing more than in later years, suggests some of the heroine's proto-feminist appeal. The mere fact that the story was true (or rather, selectively based on truth) made a significant point: a short and skinny fifteen-year-old girl named Kathy Kohner really did infiltrate an exclusive enclave of male athletes in their twenties and adopt the tools, skills, and activities that had previously marked "male turf." The nickname Gidget (combining "girl" and "midget"), given to her by the male surfers, codes the unlikelihood of her accomplishment; her sex and her diminutive size would seem to militate against her mastery of a dangerous, male-dominated sport. To girls of the 1950s, surrounded by rhetorics of domesticity and by images of sugary ingénues, this athletic, competitive image of girlhood must have been a joy to see.

Of course, both the 1957 novel and the 1959 film of *Gidget* more than compensated for Gidget's gestures toward aggression and autonomy; as we shall see, both texts heavily employ patriarchal narrative tropes and Oedipal themes to recontain their heroine. But, as had often happened before, girl audiences proved that even a partial and mediated representation of autonomy could inspire: in the growth of American surfing that followed the release of the film *Gidget*, females—although never equaling the number of males—gradually became common participants in the surfing culture, whereas Kathy Kohner had faced a lonelier challenge in an initially hostile environment. Surf expert Deanne Stillman, in her introduction to the 2001 reissue of the novel, describes it as "a long-lost *Catcher in the Rye* for girls," because it shows a girl "defying social convention." Still "legendary" among surfers, the real-life Gidget was ranked by *Surfer Magazine* "as number seven of the twenty-five most important surfers of the [twentieth] century, one of two women to make the cut."[45]

In addition to her athletic prowess, the character of Gidget could appeal to teen girls because of the "perkiness" Susan Douglas described—the ability to demonstrate competent agency without sacrificing the femininity that guarantees popularity among boys. Upon the death in 2001 of actress Deborah Walley, star of 1961's *Gidget Goes Hawaiian,* broadcast journalist Anne Taylor Fleming eulogized her by recalling, "I ached to be Gidget at twelve." Her comments explain Walley's appeal: "She was it: the bouncy, flirty baby doll in those early bikini movies, *Gidget Goes Hawaiian* and *Beach Blanket Bingo,* the girl you wanted to be. . . . She was what girls were supposed to be back there in the early 1960s: uncomplicated, petite, sweet but with a hint of sexiness. Could we close our eyes, please, and wake up in her swimsuit, with her perfect bangs and thick ponytail? Could you have just one true Gidget moment?"[46] Fleming's memories of her twelve-year-old yearnings echo those of Susan Douglas, who admits that "one of my highest ambitions was to be just like Gidget, popular, cute, and perky."[47] Whether admiring her surfing acumen or her "bouncy, flirty baby-doll" popularity, teen and preteen girls saw an image of empowerment in Gidget which made her seem "the girl you wanted to be," in Fleming's phrase.

Significantly, however, Gidget—a semi-factual fantasy written by a father about his daughter—was also the girl that *daddies* wanted her to be; the television series was deliberately crafted to appeal to the whole family, not just young girls, and the studio's demographic research for the pilot episode revealed that adults responded to the program favorably. In their summary of the audience test results, ABC found that "[t]he majority of adult viewers enjoyed GIDGET because it was 'Good and wholesome entertainment,' 'Good and clean,' 'Wholesome comedy' that was 'Good for all the family' and 'Full of fun.'"[48] Because she is a teen girl approved by adults, Gidget's construction across all media texts is heavily inflected with paternal fantasies and fears. We have seen the tendency among American cultural producers to construct adolescent femininity as a "chrysalis moment," a liminal crossroads between two categories of identity, and the mystique this liminality can grant to the figure of the "budding" teenage girl. Her sexual development is simultaneously a source of pleasure and fear to social and domestic patriarchs; they exercise the first emotion while exorcising the second, scrutinizing and analyzing the Otherness of the teen girl as scientists would scrutinize a specimen on a laboratory slab. The following section documents how the rhetoric of authenticity in the Gidget cycle combines with the texts' emphasis on father/daughter sexual tension to construct adolescent femininity as the fetishized object of the scientist-patriarch's "penetrating" gaze.

Authenticity, Penetration, and Appropriation

The most salient fact about Gidget in her literary, filmic, and televised incarnations is her status as "a daddy's girl," a daughter who dotes on, and is doted on by, her loving father. The methods used to link Gidget with her father differed radically between the literary and visual texts, however. In literature, Frederick Kohner created an "authentic" family by using his own family—not just the lone figure of Kathy/Gidget—as his model. The Hofer family, like the Kohners, consisted of two parents who had emigrated from Europe and two first-generation American daughters; Kathy Kohner and her literary counterpart, Franzie (Gidget) Hofer, were the younger daughters. In all eight of the Gidget novels Kohner wrote between 1957 and 1968, the series' central familial relationship is that between Franzie and her father; the mother and elder sister barely appear. Kohner himself, who held a Ph.D. from the University of Vienna, lectured in the film departments at USC and UCLA in addition to his long career as a screenwriter, and he made his alter ego a college professor, too—thereby replicating, coincidentally, the established model of making a teen character's father a figure of social authority as well as domestic authority.[49] The close relationship that Dr. Hofer shares with his teenage daughter is, thus, based partly on a mutual intellectualism. Franzie refers glibly in these novels to Sartre, Proust, and Franz Kafka, for whom her father named her.[50] She opines about the "soggy" operettas of Johann Strauss, saying she prefers Brahms, and she understands German, although she admits that the Viennese dialect is beyond her.[51] The girl portrayed in these books is an obviously first-generation American sharing her father's ethnic and ideological traditions.

In the typical tradition of translating literary characters to the visual media of film and television, all of Gidget's Otherness was erased in favor of promoting an "average" American image. The films and television series Anglicized the family's name to Lawrence and Franzie became Francie. Some of the visual texts retained her father's status as an intellectual, but none of them portrays Francie as remotely interested in highbrow culture. Like the dichotomy between Patty Lane and her Scottish

Figure 7. The first text in the cycle to jettison its heroine's mother, the *Gidget* television series highlighted and intensified the father-daughter relationship. Harry Ackerman Collection, negative number 30683, American Heritage Center, University of Wyoming.

cousin Cathy, the dichotomy between the literary and visual Gidgets reveals a construction of American teenagers as interested only in popular culture and peer culture. Nonetheless, even without the shared love of Proust, father and daughter remain closely linked in all Gidget texts, sometimes to such an extent that the boundaries between her identity and his begin to blur. This blurring occurs, in part, because the very inception of the character in Kohner's mind occurred through an appropriation of teen-girl subjectivity. In order to write this character—and, equally important, to publicize her—Frederick Kohner received his daughter's permission to appropriate her secrets, studying her activities, reading parts of her journal, and listening to her phone conversations to learn her peer group's slang.

Tellingly, concepts of secrecy have been instrumental to the construction of girls in popular culture, particularly in the period in which Kohner wrote *Gidget*. By the 1950s, the traditional associations between teenage girls and precious interiority had solidified to the extent that the most widely recognizable signifiers of adolescent femininity in American entertainment were objects that demarcate private zones: bedrooms, telephones, and diaries. These symbols remain potently linked to adolescent femininity even today, despite the fact that boys use the same objects as well. Tropes of privacy construct teen girls as people with delicious secrets hidden in precious spaces, which are often exposed in teen-girl narratives; films, for example, will typically expose these spaces in lingering shots of girls in their bedrooms, sometimes partially undressed; talking on the telephone, usually to an excessive degree; and writing in their diaries, often reading aloud (or thinking aloud, in voice-over) as they do so. Although objects like diaries had actually been in use by teenage girls for many decades, they did not become widespread, systematic cultural signifiers of teen girlhood until World War II, part of the general trend of adult culture's solidifying the stereotypes of "youth." The use of diaries, bedrooms, and telephones in teen-girl narratives positions producers and consumers alike as probing voyeurs who wish to "get inside" these darling girls.

The entire history of the Gidget phenomenon, including its publicity and public response, rests on these issues of appropriation and exploitation. The novel's basis in Kathy Kohner's experiences in the surfing subculture led critics to hail its use of authentic "teen-age lingo" and to praise the accuracy of the reports it brought to middle (and middle-aged) America from the frontlines of adolescent self-discovery.[52] Kohner and his daughter-muse appeared in national magazines, where both spoke

joyfully about the translation of her life into his art; *Life* magazine publicized *Gidget* the month of its release, by printing photographs that
showed Kohner eavesdropping on his daughter's phone conversations.[53]
But in her foreword to the 2001 edition of *Gidget*, Kathy Kohner Zuckerman reveals that the idea had originally been her own:

> One day I told my dad that I wanted to write a story about my summer days at
> Malibu: about my friends who lived in a shack at the beach, about the major
> crush I had on one of the surfers, about how I was teased, about how hard it was
> to catch a wave—to paddle the long board out—and how persistent I was at
> wanting to learn to surf and to be accepted by the "crew." . . . My father, Fred-
> erick Kohner, was a Hollywood screenwriter at the time. He became absorbed
> and amused with my tales of the beach. He told me he would write the story for
> me.[54]

Thus the first paternal appropriation of filial subjectivity etched itself
onto the Gidget legend with the full support of the *fille* herself.

But one of Kathy Kohner's contemporaries recognized, at least in
hindsight, that this appropriation had problematic implications. Billy Al
Bengston, one of Kathy's fellow surfers and a partial model for the character of Moondoggie, said that the novel was not authentic, but rather
"her father's fantasy. Can you imagine? Just stealing a child's life like
that?"[55] Additionally, Kohner chose to write seven of the eight novels in
Gidget's own first-person voice (only the aptly titled *Cher Papa* is narrated by her father). This narrative decision co-opts Gidget's identity in
order to connote authenticity, which Kohner heightens with a confes-
sional mode of address, as in these opening lines from the first novel:
"I'm writing this down because I once heard that when you're getting
older you're liable to forget things and I'd sure be the most miserable
woman in this world if I ever forgot what happened this summer. It's
probably a lousy story and can't hold up a candle to those French novels
from Sexville, but it has one advantage: it's a true story on my word of
honor."[56] The unpunctuated, hyperbolic, and slightly ungrammatical
style conveys "teenageness," but if true authenticity were Kohner's goal
he would have encouraged or assisted his daughter in writing the book
she initially imagined. By co-opting the position of author, Kohner could
ensure that the "teen" prose served a patriarchal purpose: successful conformity to the entertainment industry's images of adolescent femininity,
principally the construction of teen girls' lives as "secrets" to be exposed.
This inaugural sentence promises the voyeuristic pleasures of reading a
girl's memoirs or diary, offering a peek into her private life.

The second sentence, in addition to its promise of "truth," raises the specter of appropriation: the phrase "French novels from Sexville" alludes to *Bonjour Tristesse* (by eighteen-year-old Françoise Sagan), a novel about a romantically inflected relationship between a father and his teen daughter which caused a minor sensation when published in the United States two years before *Gidget*. The *Los Angeles Times* called Gidget "a fifteen-year-old American answer to Françoise Sagan,"[57] but in doing so, it overlooked two important differences between these precocious girls: Sagan was a real teen, not a hybrid of reality and fiction, and—more to the point—she wrote her own book. The heroine of *Gidget* is less a real person than a ventriloquist's dummy through which the father speaks.

Despite her disclaimer, Gidget's story holds a very respectable candle to the "novels from Sexville." Besides surfing, the narrative cycle's most consistent theme is Gidget's sexuality and the anxieties it engenders in the adult male doctors in her life (her father, a professor, and her brother-in-law, a psychologist). Claims of authenticity further crack here under the weight of Kohner's résumé. In his early Hollywood years he had collaborated on the screenplays of some Deanna Durbin films in the 1930s and 1940s, including *It's a Date* (1940), in which Durbin falls in love with a man destined to become her stepfather by the film's end. Kohner well knew the tropes dictating that a teen girl's imminent sexuality is her most interesting feature, and that its opposite term is an older man or father figure. In *Gidget*, accordingly, he combines the facts of his daughter's experiences with a wholly fictional romantic subplot about Gidget and the older surfers whose expertise she worships; Kathy Kohner herself has said that, despite the silent crush to which she alluded, there was no romance between her and any of the male surfers.

Like F. Hugh Herbert, who exploited Corliss Archer's sexuality while reassuring consumers of her innocence, Kohner establishes Gidget's virginity while making her highly sexed; she mentions her sexual fantasies and dreams in several novels. Her sexuality is even used as a marketing tool: the cover of *The Affairs of Gidget* shows its heroine wearing only a large shirt and revealing a lot of leg as she sits surrounded by stuffed animals. The image codes and exploits the sexual liminality of girls between childhood and womanhood, and the caption reads, "Let me clue you in, fans. Under-sized girls have over-sized drives."[58] Those drives surface in the first novel, when Gidget—small of frame and flat of chest—mourns her status as a sexless mascot among the surfers she idolizes, who prefer older girls with "big knockers": "Bosom talk brings out the worst in me. I'm so self-conscious on account of my meager output and in desperation had turned to some ointment which is supposed to work when you rub it in for three weeks. I did rub and went on rubbing for six weeks but nothing happened."[59]

Kohner later changed his mind about the size of his fictional daughter's bosom; once in college, Gidget compares herself favorably to her roommate Mimsy: "We both were what you might call well developed. . . . But while I'm round, peachy and fully packed, Mimsy, though no flatsville, mind you, is just a bit short-changed."[60] Gidget's age (well past the pubescent growth spurt) and her lilliputian stature make the sudden inflation of her bra size bizarre—apparently, hope springs eternal in Gidget's breast(s). This narrative strategy of training consumers' gazes upon Gidget's sexual anatomy was one of the few details to bridge all media: the first film and the pilot television episode both show a forlorn Gidget engaged in vigorous bust-enhancing exercises. As in so much of this genre, the Gidget cycle inscribes sexual appeal to an authoritative male gaze as the pinnacle of a teen girl's *raisons d'être*. If budding sexuality itself eludes a father's control, this substitutive form of scopophilia keeps at least its construction subject to patriarchal interpretation.

"Dear Diary, Et Al.," the television series' pilot episode, clearly articulates this appropriative dynamic. As the title indicates, the plot's central object is Gidget's diary, and its central event is the revelation of that diary's contents to the wider audience of her family and the episode's viewers. This plot device, which capitalizes on the violation of girls' boundaries and the exposure of their secrets, had been used several times before in teen narratives, notably in the sequel to Herbert's *Kiss and Tell*, 1949's *A Kiss for Corliss*. The film centers on Corliss Archer's fabrication of a romance in her diary in order to manipulate her boyfriend, who she knows will read it; complications arise when the diary falls into her parents' hands, who believe the *prima facie* evidence and panic about the state of her virginity. This "false threat of sex" plot (which, of course, had also informed the first Corliss Archer film) became one of the most popular tropes in teen-girl narratives of the postwar era. *Gidget Goes Hawaiian* (1961) uses a similar plot, although it substitutes a conversational miscommunication for the device of the exposed diary. In the inaugural episode of the television series, the diary returns: Gidget writes about a passionate kiss with Moondoggie which made her "sink into nothingness." Her elder married sister, Anne, is a busybody; she reads Gidget's diary, misinterprets the telltale passage as an admission of intercourse, and rushes to tell their father. Dr. Lawrence confronts Gidget about her "morals," but does not reveal Anne's snooping; Gidget then weeps in her bedroom over what she assumes to be her father's violation of her privacy.

At the same time, however, she disavows her own outrage. Through voice-over, a technique that again promises authenticity, we hear Gidget's "private" thoughts: "I'd hate to think he wouldn't mind if I ever did anything as jerky as that" (i.e., have sex). Whose authenticity is this? Gidget seems to care more about protecting the objective symbol of her privacy (her diary) than she does about the real privacy of her sex life, which she feels her father has a right to monitor. Even her concerns about her diary, however, are soon negated. After Dr. Lawrence has been cleared of blame and received Gidget's forgiveness, Gidget allays his fears about her chastity by voluntarily showing him that the disturbing diary entry was a fabrication, post-dated for the next day: "When things get dull, I make up a little," she explains cheerfully. "*Tomorrow* I sink into nothingness, and then Friday I start living a life of regret." Because Daddy (and the audience) want to know the contents of her diary, she obliges their curiosity first by falsifying events to craft a "better" story, revealing the scriptwriters' awareness that audiences considered a teen girl's sex life her most interesting feature, and, secondly, by voluntarily exposing the words she had previously wanted to hide. These gestures ally Gidget with those who would consume her. The episode tells teen-girl viewers that good girls are those who comply with their own exploitation, freely granting domestic and institutional patriarchs full access to fetishized zones of privacy.

Most of this episode unfolds in Gidget's bedroom, where she performs her breast exercises, her diary writing, and her eventual reconciliation with her father. The series very rarely shows Dr. Lawrence's bedroom because his privacy is not a fetish object, and thus does not warrant display. By contrast, nearly every episode prominently features Gidget's room, frequently with her father in it. The gaze of Gidget's father is mirrored in the gazes of the camera and the audience; all constitute the "Et Al." of the episode's title. This series' numerous scopophilic pleasures symbolically penetrate all of Gidget's privacies: her love life, her bedroom, her diary, her brassiere, and even her vagina, site of the worrisome hymen that her family fears she has lost. Paternalism and sexual voyeurism can easily collapse into each other: Kohner "studies" his daughter in order to commodify her as a fictional character, and in order to commodify that character successfully, Kohner and other textual producers sexualize her according to accepted discursive rules about teenage girls. Literal, fictional, and institutional fathers contain the filial sexuality they narrate, neutralizing its threats and maximizing the pleasures it offers to the adult male perspective. This process becomes more explicit when the texts symbolically conflate the subject positions of father and lover, placing the teen girl in parallel relational positions to each.

Gidget's Heart Belongs to Daddy

Several texts in the Gidget cycle encode a quasi-romantic relationship between Gidget and her father, and a quasi-paternal relationship between Gidget and her boyfriends. This construction of the teen girl's relationships echoes that of the Corliss Archer cycle, in which Mr. Archer and Dexter were often linked as mirror figures. Not merely a fabrication by Oedipally obsessed father-authors, this assumption about men's relations to women reflects some real-life social practices. In the traditional wedding ceremony, for example, fathers "give away" their daughters in a gesture that implies, "I used to be charged with the care and feeding of this creature—now you are." One patriarch hands her off to another, ensuring that her heart will belong to a "daddy" forever. The Gidget cycle perfectly enacts this conflation of the roles of parent and lover, and augments it through the narratives' repeated dependence on Gidget's tininess; as a petite and flat-chested female she resembles a child, and that childlike appearance is presented as one of the features that make her most sexually appealing. F. Hugh Herbert knew the value of tininess, too; in his 1954 novel *I'd Rather Be Kissed* (which, tellingly, is framed as the diary of a fifteen-year-old girl), his protagonist ruminates, "I have discovered that, for some reason, men like girls to be sort of small."[61] Kohner's Gidget cycle makes that "some reason" fairly clear: a girl's tininess allows her suitors to feel authoritative.

If Gidget's body is small, her actual abilities are even smaller. More than the novels or films, the *Gidget* television series traffics in a style of sexual display that depends on not only its heroine's physical tininess, but also her physical incompetence—a trait newly minted in the television incarnation, which again signifies childishness. As in the films, the television series' beach themes allow actress Sally Field to be costumed in bikinis and short skirts (the "cuter" clothes that, according to Douglas, made Gidget even more popular than Patty Duke among girl viewers). But just as Corliss Archer simultaneously signifies her immaturity and her sexiness by speaking malapropisms with *double entendres*, so television-Gidget signifies immaturity and sexiness through her cutely costumed but impossibly klutzy body—a rather bizarre trait for a girl who is supposedly an accomplished athlete. Her awkwardness provides much of the series' incidental humor, sometimes with sexual undertones. In one episode, "In and Out with the In-Laws," Gidget spills a soda on herself while in a restaurant and must swap clothes with an older, more developed girl whose shirt persistently slides off Gidget's shoulders, threatening to expose her breasts. In "I Love You, I Love You, I Love You—I Think," Gidget trips while running out of school and falls face-down into a pond, landing with lily pads resting on her upturned, "perky" buttocks, while her classmates laugh. By linking her sexual anatomy with her clumsiness, *Gidget* constructs its heroine's body through tropes of youth (incompetence) and femininity (sexual attractiveness) to "put her in her place," effectively compromising her agency. Although only the television series so ridiculed Gidget, the articulation of her as a diminutive and sexualized object of an authoritative male gaze inflects the entire narrative cycle.

We saw in the previous chapter that the postwar growth in circulation of Freudian theory informed plays and films like *Kiss and Tell*; Freud's influence continued to grow during the 1950s and 1960s, as psychoanalysis became increasingly popular among middle-class Americans, and Oedipal themes resurface in numerous Gidget texts. In the film *Gidget Goes to Rome* (1963), Gidget becomes smitten with the older man whom her father, his friend, has asked to chaperone her; her love object thus stands *in loco parentis*. In the first *Gidget* film (1959), the final joke is that Moondoggie, the seemingly maverick surfer whom Gidget has pursued in rebellion against her bourgeois parents, turns out to be the very same boy with whom her father has tried to unite her all along (he is the son of a family friend and, when not surfing, is an upwardly mobile college student with a normal name: Jeff Matthews). The values of the daddy, the boyfriend, and dominant ideology are presented as one and the same: a *telos* of middle-class respectability and patriarchal family structure. Gidget threatens to reject these values when she embraces the socially marginal beach culture, a liminal and therefore dangerous territory between earth and sea, between social propriety and natural wildness. But patriarchal values reestablish their rightful dominance through Gidget's full cooperation. As Allison Whitney says, "By following her father's instructions to go on a traditional arranged date, Gidget effectively gets what she wanted all along—a date with Moondoggie. Therefore, the message of *Gidget* is that one can avoid [trouble] by relinquishing control of one's life to paternal regulations and distancing oneself from the symbolic disruptions of the beach boundary zone Daddy fears."[62] The plot of the first film thus uses the figure of the boyfriend to recontain its heroine within patriarchally acceptable ideologies.

The film's theme song further suggests that the image and ideology of Daddy lurk behind even Gidget's younger admirers. Rather than use a song representing female subjectivity, the producers chose instead to employ The Four Preps, an all-male vocal group, to rhapsodize about Gidget's appeal to older boys who fetishize her tiny body and childlike sexuality: "Although she's not king-size, her finger is ring-size . . . / It very well may be, she's just a baby / Speaking romantically; / If that's her bad feature, I'll be the teacher." In addition to framing Gidget through tropes of traditional romance and marriage, the song implies that her sexual appeal depends on her "baby" appearance. The suitor's superior maturity and his assumed right to interpret and assess Gidget cast him as her authority figure, implying that a boyfriend is authorized to act like a father. Gidget's very name codes a similar message: in addition to connoting her "midget"-like stature it obviously resembles "gadget," exacerbating her status as something less than a real person. Apparently boys, too, like to play with baby-dolls. The ideology that casts men as women's protectors and providers blurs the line between parent and husband, and intensifies in a narrative whose heroine is equal parts woman, child, and dummy/doll.

The close bond between Gidget and her father returns forcefully in the television series. Like the film's theme song, that of the television program constructs both singer and listener as desiring males. The accompanying visual sequence makes clear the dyad between father and daughter; it ignores the series' other regular characters, showing images of only Gidget and Dr. Lawrence. This skews the ostensible meaning of the song's lyrics: "Wait till you see my Gidget—you'll want her for your valentine. . . . / But stay away! Gidget is spoken for. / You're gonna find that Gidget is mine." Lawrence's status as the only man on screen raises the pointed question of whose "valentine" Gidget is. The words "stay away" accompany a shot of him sternly wagging his finger, as though to chase off competitors for his daughter's love; in the final scene he plants a kiss on Gidget's smiling face.

The series further heightens Gidget's close ties to her father by killing off her mother, a drastic departure from earlier texts in the cycle. Gidget and her father thus become the only occupants of their home and the privileged objects of each other's affections. The maternal voice transfers to an inappropriate substitute: Anne, the married sister whose efforts to "protect" Gidget (by revealing the scandalous contents of her diary, for example) mask the jealousies of a less-favored sibling in a contest for Daddy's love. The scripts explicitly acknowledge these Oedipal themes, but only to disavow them; the problem of Gidget's sexual development surfaces in the speeches of Anne's husband, John, an overearnest psychology student whom Gidget and her father freely mock. In "Is It Love, or Symbiosis?" co-written by Frederick Kohner himself, John angrily upbraids Dr. Lawrence for his unhealthy attachment to his younger daughter:

> *John:* I think that as long as you've got Gidget, you'll never remarry. And then in about twenty years we'll have the classic spectacle of an elderly parent and a dried-up spinster daughter—still fixing your meals and rubbing your back. That's symbiosis!
> *Dr. Lawrence:* That's baloney!

Clearly the superior authority figure (for, as Gidget reminds us in multiple episodes, he is the best dad in the world), Lawrence represents the series' central perspective, leaving John to appear as an absurd worrier whose "baloney" ideas warrant dismissal.

But how effective are these dismissals? "Independence—Gidget Style" similarly mocks John's fears, but validates them moments later. This episode reflects and combines two contemporary phenomena: not only the erotic subtext of the father/daughter relationship (which, by this time, had been graphically represented to American audiences in the 1962 film *Lolita*), but also the 1960s social shifts, described earlier, which led to increased representations of girls as job seekers, job holders, and future career women. "Independence—Gidget Style" centers on Gidget's attempts at (limited) financial independence but contains those efforts within an Oedipally determined plotline. Gidget seeks a part-time job, not to earn money for herself, but to finance an expensive gift for her beloved dad's birthday. She applies for work at the Tomcat Club after overhearing an older girl discussing her job as a hostess there. But "the Tomcat Club" is a veiled allusion to Hugh Hefner's chain of Playboy Clubs and, like Playboy Bunnies, Tomcat Kitties wear sexually revealing costumes. Once again, Gidget's youth and physical tininess become her defining features: too young, at fifteen, to work in a men's club, she is also unfit for this job because—as she herself dejectedly admits—her own skimpy *décolletage* cannot compete with those of the more buxom applicants. Not one to give up, Gidget applies for work at a new club for teenagers. This time she is hired—but she performs her job so badly (forgetting orders and spilling food on the customers) that she is almost immediately fired, and can afford only a meager pipe-lighter for her father. He appreciates the gift fully, especially because his elder daughter, Anne, has forgotten his birthday. The episode thus contrasts the good daughter with the bad daughter, and clarifies how its producers envision success for a girl: her incompetence and inability to hold a job do not matter as long as she performs devotion to her Daddy. The title becomes a dark joke: "Independence—Gidget Style" means no independence at all, a comforting message to cultural patriarchs at the dawn of second-wave feminism.

Before the happy conclusion, however, the usual scene of familial chaos must occur and, once again, the agent of the chaos is the "bad" daughter, positioning the sisters as competitors for Daddy's approval. Snooping again, Anne finds the discarded application for the Tomcat Club in Gidget's bedroom and sounds the alarm with her father and her husband. Dr. Lawrence, whose adoration of Gidget is expressed and validated in every episode, refuses to believe the implications: "That's ridiculous. Couldn't possibly be. She's only fifteen-and-a-half years old." John grimly replies, "Lolita was twelve," directly naming the text that casts its long shadow over the Gidget cycle. Determined to prove Gidget's innocence, Lawrence goes to the Tomcat Club and inspects the hostesses, mistaking one of them, whom he sees from behind, for his daughter. Realizing his error, he mumbles an apology and turns to another hostess—only to suffer a brief hallucination in which the woman actually turns into Gidget, who, dressed in a Kitty costume, gives Dad a shy smile and a wink. "No!" he gasps, as the image dissolves.

Because it is just an illusion prompted by John's risible panic, the scene at the Tomcat Club can pair father and daughter in a profoundly suggestive moment while disavowing its erotic implications. But the sexual tensions between father and daughter were, in fact, a consistent element of the series; in episodes like "Daddy Come Home" and "We Got Each Other," the series' writers reinscribe Gidget's and Dr. Lawrence's persistent concerns about external threats to their privileged positions in each other's lives. Gidget worries about her father's dates, and he keeps an eye on her chastity, proving repeatedly that primary ownership of the Gidget-gadget devolves to Daddy, and vice versa. For all his supposed absurdity, John is the only one who seems to know a Lolita complex when he sees one.

Unlike Lolita, however, who exercises aggression and manipulation in Nabokov's novel and in Stanley Kubrick's film, Gidget remains the only person in her world who has no access to her own sexuality; it is a "look, but don't touch" commodity, displayed to exorcise others' desires and fears, but not to serve Gidget. With Moondoggie conveniently away at college, television-Gidget can form other attachments; but while she frequently develops crushes, they are often inappropriate (as when she falls for a new teacher), and short-lived. The only steady man in her life is Dr. Lawrence, leaving her in a permanent state of purity and filial devotion. And, as Lawrence knows after his trip to the Tomcat Club, patriarchs need not even worry about their own muted erotic desires toward their daughters; in domestic comedies, after all, such concerns are "baloney." Dad can indulge his scopophilia without compunction, for it's just good, clean fun. It is also, as Douglas suggests, one of the very reasons why adolescent girls enjoyed this series, for it provided a pleasurable fantasy of having the doting, adoring daddy "all to oneself." These pleasures allowed Gidget's teen girl consumers to unwittingly absorb a construction of their sexuality as a daddy-serving commodity, along with the more positive fantasy they consciously consumed.

The Oedipal sexuality that informs the Gidget cycle is one tool used by cultural authorities to put girls "back in their place" during the teen-saturated cultural landscape of the late 1950s and early 1960s. Other narratives, like *The Patty Duke Show*, do not employ such overtly sexual themes, but similarly portray their heroines as too immature, irrational, or incompetent to enjoy the full benefits of personhood—even while touting and celebrating those girls' (limited) agency as schemers and dreamers, and thus offering unique pleasures to teen girl viewers. Although energetic and creative, girls like Patty and Gidget are also hyperbolic, foolish, functionally incompetent, and inadequately authorized to claim dignity or autonomy for themselves, which leaves them vulnerable to the probing efforts of patriarchal representatives to define, exploit, and contain them.

Teen-girl narratives of this era won avid audiences by celebrating "authentic" teen experience and the "perky" agency that Douglas describes. But as McRobbie argues, popular culture's circulation in the sphere of leisure masks the coercion behind its ideologies, making them easier for consumers to swallow. In other words, as Julie Andrews trilled in *Mary Poppins* one year before *Gidget*'s television debut, "A spoonful of sugar helps the medicine go down." Gidget's sugary ability to energize or inspire teen-girl viewers disguised the taste of a rather bitter medicine: a model of adolescent femininity conflating ineptitude, sexual appeal, and filial subjugation. Taken as prescribed, this medicine could allow girl consumers to dream about increased agency without sacrificing the submissive femininity that earned them their culture's approval. This happy outcome, not coincidentally, equally served the needs of American domestic and institutional patriarchs who feared the loss of their prerogatives, privileges, and control over "teenage tyranny."

Epilogue

 Between 1930 and 1965, the dominant portrayals of the teenage girl in popular narratives coalesced around two interrelated issues: the degree of her adherence to patriarchally approved models of youthful femininity, and her effect upon her domestic and institutional "fathers." These representations did not delineate the girl with the benefits of personhood, but rather diminished her in a variety of narrative devices to present her more as the recipient of others' actions, desires, or fears. As the figure of the teenage girl commanded more public attention over the second third of the twentieth century, the possibilities she offered as a consumer and as a sex object combined to arouse paradoxical responses from her adult, male-centered culture. Her spending power made her a valuable asset to the American economy, while also prompting angry complaints about teens' too-great influence on culture. Her combination of a mature body and a childlike mind incited erotic responses to her, playing on fantasies of the sexiness of emptiness while still offering the comforting counter-message that her sexuality was not in danger of escaping paternal/patriarchal control. In every instance, the teen girl was imagined and represented in mass-culture narratives through the perspective of adult males. The father figure was her defining opposite, and all her representations hinged upon his own self-image: in periods defined by a widespread "crisis of masculinity," girls' images were diminished in proportion. In periods of greater masculine vigor, teen-girl characters became more aggressive, but were also slapped down more aggressively in their narratives by fathers and patriarchal institutions.

In these representations, interiority and private space served two contradictory functions: as a symbol of inner personhood, in texts specifically
crafted for girls (like the Nancy Drew book series), the associations between girls and precious interiority could inspire a developing sense of
inviolable personhood in young readers, and could thus assist some in
developing a nascent sense of agency. But in mass-culture texts, produced
for a more general audience and without the explicitly inspirational goals
of some producers who exclusively addressed children, the traditional
associations between girlhood and private interiority became refigured
solely in the literal, sexual aspect of interiority, as a symbol for the precious interior of a girl's body; as such, interiority figures as a prompt for
voyeurism, often coded through plots and verbal or visual techniques that
penetrate girls' spatial and sexual boundaries. Although offering girl consumers some visions of "agency" in portrayals of girls as active adven-
turers, these narratives' instances of agency are defined so narrowly, and
portrayed so ambivalently, that they heavily compromise any message of
personhood that young consumers might have gleaned. Almost invariably, mass-culture comic narratives about teen girls have served girls less
reliably than they have served adults, reflecting and supporting an "imperial" patriarchal perspective that assesses female adolescents as commodities to serve the needs of adult-centered social and economic sys-
tems. Often, that servitude takes form through plots that construct the
teenage girl as a sexual delectation or problem for an adult male, a father
or father-substitute. These representational patterns remained remarkably consistent for the first three decades of teenage girls' cultural visibility; one can readily find them in scores of girl-centered narratives from
this period.

But over the following years the uniformity of this presentation began
to crumble as competing ideas and images, prompted by the social
changes of the 1960s, expanded and complicated Americans' notions of
adolescent femininity. After 1966 popular culture continued to portray
girls with virtually all the same signifiers that pertained in earlier periods,
but rarely so unvaryingly and cohesively; rather, in our modern cultural
state of affairs, we can see strands of the teen-girl stereotypes intermin-
gled with competing threads that complicate, without unraveling, the
earlier fabric of representation. Changes in perceptions of girls' roles
have made several modifications to popular images of girlhood while still
preserving the fundamental ubiquity of a daddy-serving worldview in
popular culture.

The consistent image of girlhood that prevailed before the mid-1960s began to fade over the course of the decade. By the time *Gidget* left the television airwaves in 1966, the American public had already begun to shift its focus away from the figure of the teenage girl and onto her older sisters: young women of college age. The political student protests of the 1960s, coupled with the rise of the separatist "hippie" culture among young adults on and off college campuses, lent a slightly older face to the category of youth in the popular imaginary. Even the quintessential teen-girl comedy plot, in which a father frets over his daughter's chastity, was often transferred in 1960s comedies to girls in their very late teens who have reached legal adulthood—as when coed Sandra Dee distresses her attorney father, James Stewart, in *Take Her, She's Mine* (1963), or when Cristina Ferrare's campus antics torment her professor father, David Niven, in *The Impossible Years* (1968). These films faithfully replicate the patterns of the earlier, younger teen-girl texts. But that basic plot of chastity anxiety quickly receded, too, regardless of the girl's age. Teen sexuality became more accepted as the rise of second-wave feminism and the "sexual revolution" of the 1960s and 1970s ameliorated many of the taboos that had surrounded representations of girls and sex in earlier years. Indeed, sexual initiation figures as a prominent plot in many teen-centered tales after the 1960s; regardless of whether those texts take a celebratory or a cautionary tone, they acknowledge the centrality of sex in teens' lives, presenting desire as a just-so fact, without such frequent suggestions of terror or disaster as those that hover over pre-1960s narratives.

Simultaneously, the real threats of youth's political unrest and social activism in the 1960s displaced the symbolic threat of the loss of a girl's virginity as culture's worst nightmare. The delinquency panics had always hinged on fears of what would happen if aggressive youth "took over" society; in the late 1960s those fears seemed to come true in the form of student protests, prompting a backlash sometimes vicious and brutal, as when National Guardsmen opened fire on protesting college students at Kent State in 1970. Comedies about silly teen girls and the state of their hymens could no longer function as dominant reference points of social anxiety. As Scheiner notes, "Delinquents stopped being a marketable commodity" after the early 1960s,[1] and representations of teen-girl antics dwindled commensurately. Rachel Devlin further observes that "the figure of the teenage girl and her acts of consumption had ceased to be the important cultural and ideological reference points they once were,"[2] as the idea of teen consumerism and teens' social influence became increasingly assimilated into cultural norms, no longer requiring as much "explanation" or anxiety in popular narratives. Teenagers as such ceased to be a major focus of popular storytelling; consequently, the mid-1960s was the last time, for a long time, that the teen girl was portrayed with such uniformity of presentation.

Timothy Shary has noted "the dearth of teen stars and teen films in the 1970s" and the subsequent renaissance of these commodities in the 1980s. He attributes this resurgence of teen films to the rise of multiplex theaters in shopping malls, an "icon of youth independence" where Hollywood made a direct address to teens who congregated without adults.[3] Since the 1980s teen characters have continued to thrive, and a survey of modern teen films and television programs indicates how much teens' roles have widened; they appear now as staples not just in comedies (the pre-1960s norm) but increasingly in dramas of domestic life that privilege the perspective of the beleaguered teen more than that of the beleaguered parent. John Hughes's films of the 1980s exemplify this development, as does the internationally popular television drama/soap opera *Beverly Hills 90210* (1990–2000) and its many subsequent imitators. Teenage characters, including girls, routinely have their subjectivities represented more centrally now, and more seriously, than in earlier periods. Even comedies now foreground teen interiority more directly: whereas 1944's *Janie* and 1948's *A Date with Judy* both opened with an adult male narrator's voice setting the stage for the viewers and establishing a framework of interpretation, 2000's *Bring It On* opens onto the subconscious mind of Torrance, the protagonist, as we're plunged directly into her nightmare about becoming the captain of her high school cheerleading squad.[4] Although still written and directed by adults (and often, therefore, not representing teen experience any more "authentically" than earlier models), contemporary teen tales nonetheless address an audience that assumes the existence and validity of a teenager's own view of her life.

The portrayals of girls' physical aggression, athleticism, and violence have particularly changed. Some of this change follows such general cultural trends as the post-1970s craze for physical fitness and increased violence in the media at large, but the increase in girls' and women's physical aggression owes something to the influence of feminism and its general message of women's strength and capability. For school-aged girls and young women, the passage of Title IX in 1972—a federal law guaranteeing gender equality in school programs, including sports—has fostered a perception that young girls not only can, but should, exhibit muscular strength and athletic prowess. One cultural venue for expressions of female aggression appears in teen horror films; unlike their forebears, the 1950s exploitation films which often marginalized girls, modern teen horror films have frequently featured a powerful female who successfully vanquishes the madman slasher—a character Carol Clover has famously called "the final girl."[5] All genres have begun portraying physically fit or aggressive girls more often, but the terms in which this strength has been portrayed combine progressive ideas with a retrograde fetishization of girls' sexuality, for the happy byproduct of strength and fitness is a "hot" body. As *Buffy the Vampire Slayer* on television (1997–2003), Sarah Michelle Gellar kicked serious demon butt—in skintight slacks, miniskirts, and high heels. Her fashions, changing constantly throughout each episode, function almost as a co-star of the series. Moreover, Buffy's awe-inspiring strength rarely appeared as much in her intellect or her affect as in her body; her intense emotional vulnerability and her lack of intellectual acumen (notwithstanding a sudden, bizarre reference to high SAT scores at one convenient moment) resuscitate the oldest stereotypes of teen femininity. The addition of physical aggression and strength makes a significant alteration to the usual image of girlhood, but the continuation of many other stereotypes—sexiness, fashion-consciousness, emotional fragility—mitigates that alteration, making Buffy more palatable to the American consensus on teen female identity.[6]

Nor has the new emphasis on girls' physical action taken hold very widely; popular narratives will often make a quick, superficial reference to a girl's participation in sports, but rarely does one find a text that focuses specifically on a teen girl's athletic endeavors (one recent exception, *Bend It Like Beckham* [2002], was not a U.S. production and was not widely distributed in U.S. markets). In *Blue Crush* (2002), an American studio film about young female athletes, the heroines are slightly older than high school age. The film's breathtaking, daredevil photography accurately portrays surfing as a sport that can easily kill its practitioners, and thus emphasizes its heroines' endurance and bravery—a refreshing change from the ludicrous surfing scenes of the old Gidget movies, in which characters bobbed gamely on a stationary surface in front of a rear-screen projection of the ocean. But even while *Blue Crush* tells its viewers that girls are serious athletes who can take a pounding and keep going, it nonetheless encodes examples of patriarchal assumptions about girls: a substantial Cinderella subplot concerns the working-class heroine's love affair with a wealthy young man. Traditional romance remains a fundamentally necessary ingredient in stories about young women.

Predictably, the lead actresses of *Blue Crush* spend most of the film costumed in bikinis, a convenient "realism" that protects the privilege of a male gaze, as we can see more clearly when comparing the DVD edition's two commentary tracks: one by director John Stockwell, and one by the lead actresses (Kate Bosworth, Michelle Rodriguez, and Sanoe Lake). While Stockwell calls attention to the beauty of the actresses' faces and bodies, primarily Bosworth's, the actresses' comments reveal their occasional discomfort at how their bodies were filmed and treated during shooting. Over a scene that shows some "friendly" wrestling between the girls and a group of local male surfers, Rodriguez remarks, "This scene really pissed me off 'cause, like, Stockwell told [a male actor] to grab my ass. And I was angry. I almost fought that guy right there." As Bosworth crosses before the camera in one shot that prominently displays her bikini-clad bottom, Stockwell observes: "You can see Kate's in great shape. She developed a real surfer's body over the course of pre-production." Bosworth herself has a less appreciative response to the shot: "OK, my butt crosses the screen and I—look! God! It's like right in the middle of the screen! It's so horrible watching it, I'm like, 'oh *man*.'" Lake offers comfort by mentioning her own exposed bottom: "Oh, like *my* butt's not hanging out in that one shot in the beginning." When Bosworth later takes a shower, the camera shows her nude from the back. Stockwell tells viewers the shot originally extended further down to reveal more of her buttocks, but that it was trimmed because it "engendered controversy." He adds, "One thing that's wonderful is that the film plays so well with young girls who don't feel that it's exploitative. These girls really do surf in bikinis; we didn't have to sort of push that." To this blithe assertion of how well the film avoids exploitation (already made ironic by its delivery over a shot of a naked woman) we can contrast the comments of Rodriguez and Bosworth on the same scene: Rodriguez notes, "That must have felt weird." "Yeah," Bosworth says quietly.

The leering gaze of older men at the bodies of young women and girls has, of course, remained a constant factor in mainstream portrayals of teen heroines, even resurfacing in the father/daughter plots familiar from earlier eras. While such plots have been less ubiquitous recently than in the mid-twentieth century, they are enough of a cultural stereotype to reemerge in films like *She's Out of Control* (1989) and more recently in television series like the aptly titled *8 Simple Rules for Dating My Teenage Daughter* (2002–present), attesting to the continuation of the tensions between teen-girl sexuality and paternal control. The 2003 film *What a Girl Wants* reinscribes the conflation of a father's and lover's roles that characterized the Gidget cycle: Amanda Bynes enacts twin scenarios of shopping and fashionable dressing up, once with her boyfriend and once with her newly discovered father, both of whom express pleasure at the visual spectacle she presents; at the film's end, she is paired in succession with each of these two men during a romantic slow-dance.

Over the last twenty years, some filmic portrayals of sexual tensions between teen girls and father figures have surpassed the relative timidity of Kubrick's 1962 version of *Lolita*, which, at the time, had seemed so shocking; Adrian Lyne's 1997 remake features a younger-looking Lolita and more graphic scenes of sex play with her stepfather, while in the low-budget thriller *Wicked* (1998), Julia Stiles's teenage character actually has intercourse with her own father. Teenage Drew Barrymore seduces middle-aged Tom Skerrit, the father of the surrogate family with whom she lives, in *Poison Ivy* (1992). And in the plot of *Blame It on Rio* (1984), two middle-aged fathers, long-time friends named Matthew and Victor, take their respective teenage daughters, Nicole and Jennifer, on a vacation. Victor's daughter, Jennifer, has harbored a crush on Matthew for years and finally seduces him on this trip; he makes an easy target for her energies, since he reminisces fondly about his appreciation of her bare buttocks when she was an infant. When Victor begins to suspect that his daughter has a lover, he innocently asks Matthew to question the girl for him; the subsequent dialogue between these mismatched paramours reveals the endurance of a time-honored theme:

> *Matthew:* I'm supposed to find out who your lover is, before it drives your father crazy.
> *Jennifer:* Poor Daddy.
> *Matthew:* Yours, or Nicole's?
> *Jennifer:* Mine.
> *Matthew:* Oh, *that* poor daddy. You can't swing a dead cat around here without hitting a poor daddy.

Remarkably, this comedy about a libidinous adulterer who breaks trust with his best friend and exploits the overzealous emotions of a girl half his age, whom he has known since her birth, seems mostly concerned with securing our sympathy for *him*—"poor daddies" claim a right to our compassion when bedeviled by vexing teenage girls. These films draw upon F. Hugh Herbert's legacy, for they often treat the teenage girl as the primary schemer while the "poor daddy" is supposedly helpless.

In the 1990s, a popular cultural trend offered the illusion of "girl power" in contexts which actually signaled little more than a girl's active participation in her own sexual exploitation. "Girl power" began with the British pop group The Spice Girls, and the phrase consistently attached to other icons of teen-girl pop music. Singers like Britney Spears, Mandy Moore, and Christina Aguilera revived the image of the sex-tease virgin, the baby-doll. The *Boston Globe* called these artists "Lolitas with a Beat" in 2000, and noted that "[b]ehind the gloss that preteen girls love are the sexy lyrics that older men write."[7] Dancing in revealing costumes, these teen-girl pop stars sang lyrics with explicitly sexual meanings, written for them by the middle-aged, male entrepreneurs of the pop music industry. These cannily planned images ensured the singers' fame beyond their most direct fan base; as journalist Mark Binelli put it, girls like Spears and Aguilera "recognized that music videos involving school uniforms and/or nude body stockings would exponentially increase fatherly, big-brotherly and creepy-uncle-y tolerance for music that's pretty much unlistenable if you're not a thirteen-year-old girl."[8]

Tellingly, the males Binelli names are older than the girl; even the brother is a "big brother." Binelli emphasizes the crucial importance of that age difference by noting that these sexy girls are former child stars—specifically ones who worked for Disney, the ultimate purveyor of child fantasy in American popular culture: "There comes a time in the life of every teenage girl who works for the Disney Corp. when that girl realizes she has suddenly—how shall we phrase this?—'broadened her appeal.' For Annette Funicello, back on the original *Mickey Mouse Club*, that point came when boys began to notice the tightness of her regulation Mouseketeer sweaters."[9] Aguilera and Spears, too, labored for Disney as young children on a later version of the *Mickey Mouse Club*. Not surprisingly, these "Lolitas" have a strong appeal to daddies. Many critics have noted the presence of adult men in Spears's fan base, a fact humorously referenced in a commercial she made for Pepsi-Cola in 2000 in which a succession of slack-jawed admirers watch her perform on their television screens; last in the string of observers is Robert Dole. An elderly war veteran, Republican politician, and spokesman for Viagra (a treatment for erectile dysfunction), Dole perfectly embodies American patriarchy. Both he and the panting dog by his side watch Spears's bouncing body on their television with fixed gazes. Unable to contain himself, the dog finally barks. Dole smiles and murmurs, "Down, boy"—whether to his pet or to his pharmaceutically invigorated penis is left to our imaginations.

In 2004 another Disney alumna, Lindsay Lohan, found herself at the center of a public controversy about her breasts, which many commentators surmised were artificial precisely because of their prior knowledge of Lohan as a flat-chested child star; the opportunity for comparing before-and-after views intensifies a sexual gaze on young women's bodies. As Lohan told *Entertainment Weekly*, "I just got my chest in the past year, and I couldn't be happier because I used to be the flattest person ever, stuffing my bras. It scares me that older men would think about that, but hey, if they're going to write about anything, write about my boobs rather than making other stuff up."[10] Lohan reveals the complex construction of adolescent femininity: knowing full well that women are judged by breast size, she yearns as a youngster for big breasts. Yet when they arrive, her pleasure in them is tempered by the extremity of the reaction they provoke, specifically among one segment of the population: it now "scares" her that "older men would think about that," though she accepts the lecherous gaze as inevitable; at least it will validate the reality of her body, which she finds preferable to false rumors about plastic surgery. Joining the ranks of those titillated older men, Mark Binelli, Lohan's interviewer, begins his article by directly naming the issue in the first sentence: "Lindsay Lohan has been eighteen for just under a week when she tells me her breasts are real. I did not ask (gentlemen never do), though my reporting (discreet visual fact-checking, a goodbye hug) seems to confirm her statement."[11] Lohan initiates the topic, yet Binelli's coy references to his "reporting" reveal his own curiosity. The blossoming into womanhood—the delicious chrysalis moment—gains its intensity from the public's active memory of the woman as a child. Her status as a "pretty baby" still matters tremendously, as much now as it did when Shirley Temple, Bonita Granville, and other child stars of the 1930s had their "first kisses" touted in enthusiastic publicity campaigns. We have moved past the cultural moment when kissing signified maturity; now it is the possibility of plastic surgery that gives us the occasion to scrutinize the developing female body. In these lubricious assessments, the girl's child-star persona plays a crucial role. Our memories activate and reanimate her former self, even while her current teenage self strives mightily to prove that she has grown up. Her development into a woman is simultaneously fetishized and oddly negated by the evocation of our memories of her as a tot, and our pleasure in her current incarnation relies on this overlay of past on present for its power.

The "pretty baby" phenomenon also informs contemporary teen heroines through techniques of diminishment and incapacity. While such immediately visible details as plot points and lines of dialogue seem, today, to grant girl characters more power than their hapless forebears, teen girls are nonetheless still required to exhibit some form of vulnerability, clumsiness, or emotional or mental weakness before they can stake a full claim to audiences' affections. As neglected or orphaned daughters yearning for their absent fathers, Anne Hathaway in 2001's *The Princess Diaries* and Amanda Bynes in *What a Girl Wants* perform a manipulatively "heartbreaking" little-girl-ism, all wounded eyes and pouty lips as they cradle images of, or gifts from, the idolized papas whose absence haunts them. In *What a Girl Wants*, especially, the yearning for the implicit father/daughter romance harks back to the soapy 1930s dramas in which orphaned Shirley Temple perfected the sad-eyed pout. In the 1940s, Corliss Archer found herself mocked and scolded by boys her own age and younger, who enjoyed a greater degree of sympathy and approval from their author than she did. In 2003, Lizzie McGuire finds herself in a similar position in *The Lizzie McGuire Movie*. Although her younger brother does not receive more narrative privilege than she (he is portrayed as a nasty pest), he nonetheless frames our introduction to the heroine: the film opens with his ingenious use of technology—a hidden camera mounted on a remote-operated toy truck— as a means for spying on his teenage sister in the "private" interiority of her bedroom, where she dances and lip-synchs to a pop song while trying on different outfits. Critic Lisa Schwarzbaum singled out such clichés of girlhood in her review of the Mandy Moore vehicle *Chasing Liberty* (2004): "Moore's Ana Foster . . . is introduced doing that thing that all teenage girls do in movies that are too lazy to figure out what teenage girls actually do: dancing around her bedroom in innocent imitation of provocative rock-star poses and applying lip gloss."[12] This fantasy of what girls do in their rooms reifies girls as omnivorous consumers of popular culture and fashion, and implies the paradox that girls can best express their individuality through mimicry and eroticized self-display. But boys, apparently, know how to build useful things—a gendered dichotomy that has remained unchanged since Nancy Drew's boyfriend appropriated all forms of technical knowledge in the 1930s film series.

Intercut with scenes of Lizzie's preening and goofing, her brother watches her on the monitor in his room and laughs uproariously at her antics, delighting in the blackmail he will exact when his homemade film is complete. (Implied but not shown, since this is a Disney film, is the fact that he must also be recording Lizzie's nudity as she changes her clothes.) As the framing device for our first sight of Lizzie, this wickedly shrewd and entrepreneurial boy defines the film's ostensible heroine through a mocking, external perspective that seeks to exploit her for profit. The sequence ends when Lizzie, finally having chosen a stylish ensemble of pink and black, undercuts her sartorial suavity by losing her balance and sprawling into the bathtub, pulling the shower curtain down on top of her. Her clumsiness isn't limited to moments of fraternal voyeurism: in the very next scene Lizzie takes another tumble, more publicly and with worse results, at her middle-school graduation exercises. As with *Gidget* on television, and numerous other texts since then, the point is supposedly to "sympathize" with the teen girl while showing her intense humiliation, thus prescribing clumsiness and public embarrassment as normative elements of teen girlhood. Indeed, such klutzy displays seem part of the girl's very definition; we know she is a girl and not a woman because, like an infant giraffe, she hasn't found her balance yet. Similar scenes emerge in movies like *She's All That* (1999), *Confessions of a Teenage Drama Queen* (2004), *What a Girl Wants* (2003), and both of the *Princess Diaries* movies (2001, 2004), in which girl protagonists go skidding, tripping, and thudding their way through certain key scenes, making themselves even more "lovable" by their vulnerability and ineptitude.

Numerous other visual cues also contribute to the construction of teen girls as insufficiently authorized to claim the dignity and respect that accompany personhood. Schwarzbaum reveals this trend in her references to what she calls "lip acting" in girl movies: "Lip acting is what happens when an actress . . . chews her kisser to denote demure hesitation, or sincere thought, or shy romantic interest. Lip acting is the telegraphing and stylizing of intention so that the one doing the lip gnaw can simulate anxiety, sexuality, or anger *without actually owning the grown-up feelings.* (Sometimes this is enhanced by sweater-acting, which involves the tugging of over-long sleeves.)"[13] Schwarzbaum's ruminations underscore a point that has arisen consistently throughout this book: the lip-gnaw and the sleeve-tug (which implies that the "little" girl is drowning in her big, grown-up clothes) diminish the girl performing them. They request the viewer's permission for the girl to express an opinion or a complicated emotion that might otherwise suggest too strong a sense of her own agency. "Please don't take me too seriously," these gestures imply; "I may be saying something, but don't hold that against me. I'm still a girl, still weak enough for you to love."

That message of necessary compensation—of girls' need to give up some power in order to wield any—has attended cultural images of girlhood consistently from the beginning of the twentieth century to the present. Despite all our celebratory talk of "girl power," apologies and compensatory gestures remain compulsory ingredients of girls' images in popular culture. American entertainment has expanded its definitions of girlhood to include some greater degrees of aggression, autonomy, and subjectivity, but none of these developments has wholly erased the imperatives of the girl-image as it was first codified generations ago. Female teens in mass-culture narratives still embody an essence of "lack" that distinguishes them from both grown women and teen boys; they still are required to function first as patriarchy-serving commodities. These mainstream texts continue to tell consumers that girls can successfully advance only by traditionally approved methods (like the perfection of feminized self-display through fashion or musical performance), and that even in those limited venues, their success depends entirely on their not subverting patriarchal hierarchies.

In considering the current state of girls' images, however, it is important to note that mainstream texts do not dominate the cultural marketplace exclusively. Cable television and independent films have often been able to push boundaries and take risks that networks and major studios avoid, and girls' presentations in those narrower media show the most significant departures from stereotypes of adolescence. Since the 1990s, independent films like *Mi Vida Loca* (1994), *Girls' Town*, *Welcome to the Dollhouse*, *Foxfire* (all 1996), *Coming Soon* (1999), and the brilliant *Girlfight* (2000), as well as cable television series like HBO's *Six Feet Under*, have presented characters who frequently do not conform to familiar images of teen femininity—girls who may not be white, or not conventionally "hot" in their attractiveness, who have complex interiority, subjective sexuality, strong same-sex allegiances, and raw, honest anger.

Karyn Kusama's *Girlfight*, for example, centers on Diana (Michelle Rodriguez), a working-class Latina girl whose mother has committed suicide because of her husband's abuse. Growing up with her cold, dictatorial father, who clearly favors his son over her, Diana smolders with a barely suppressed anger that she vents inappropriately at school until she learns to channel it into boxing. The film follows her dogged pursuit of boxing prowess despite discouragements from her family and fellow athletes; along the way, Kusama is not afraid to show us what a girl looks like when sweaty, drably dressed, and illuminated by bare ceiling bulbs. In a stunning moment at the film's climax, Diana unleashes her pent-up rage on its true target: knocking her father to the floor of the dingy kitchen where he has forced her to cook and clean since her mother died, she furiously chokes him nearly to death. Finally a teenage girl gives Daddy exactly what he deserves, without the film's censuring or scolding her in any way. Similarly non-judgmental scenes of girls' lashing out at abusive men and boys appear in *Girls' Town* and *Foxfire*.

But despite the critical acclaim they often receive, independent films or daring made-for-cable series do not have the same cultural impact as major-studio films and network television, for the simple reason that they cannot circulate as widely. Subscription rates make cable television a luxury, and many American towns have no cinemas beyond the ubiquitous multiplexes in malls, which rarely screen anything other than "blockbusters." Independent production companies also have smaller budgets and fewer resources for publicity, so that even the release of such films on video and DVD does not guarantee their widespread notice by consumers. When I discuss independent films in my college courses, the vast majority of students have never even heard of them, let alone seen them. To gauge the most widespread cultural attitudes of girlhood, the ones that have the greatest and most immediate effect on Americans, one must still look at the products of mainstream mass-culture producers. It will likely be a long time before any major studio commits to an image of teen girlhood like the one Kusama fashioned in *Girlfight;* today the dominant venues of the entertainment industries still insist, not only on portraying inept girlhood in original scripts, but on calculatingly diluting the dignity of heroines adapted from children's fiction. As Hollywood eviscerated Nancy Drew in the 1930s, so it eviscerated *Ella Enchanted* in 2004, turning Gail Carson Levine's splendid novel of female agency into a parade of teen-girl stereotypes, including the peculiar insertion of a shopping mall and teen idols into a medieval fairytale context (highlighting girls' roles as consumers) and two mildly risqué dance routines, one of which shows a middle-aged male royal instructing Ella to "shake [her] booty."

Despite the considerable improvements that feminism has brought to American women's lives, the dignity and true agency of teenage girls, when wholly separated from the interests of patriarchy, are just as unthinkable in popular entertainment today as they were seventy years ago. The dominant discourses of American teen narratives have yet to represent a girlhood that truly serves girls: one that deserves and demands a respectful reaction from adults, and demands that girls themselves live as competent, self-determining subjects. Instead, we continue to train girls to accept and even request their own subordination, encouraging them, through a well-established system of rewards, to fashion their identities with signifiers of a romance plot that conflates paternal(ist) interests with sexual commodification. This is the girlhood we call normal, the one that populates the "wholesome" family comedies that comfort and reassure us with their fables of averageness. In the millennium, our most widely available and recycled stories about female youth still trick us with the old bait-and-switch, selling empty slogans of a "girl power" that only means what it meant all along: the power to shop and to excite men; the power to serve capital and patriarchy. If we are to change our culture's construction of girls as non-persons, we must alter the old myths instead of recycling them; we must fundamentally revise the bedtime stories we tell ourselves—and our daughters. They deserve something better to dream about.

Notes

Introduction

1. hooks, *Black Looks*, 170.
2. Austin and Willard, "Angels of History," 2.
3. Said, "Orientalism," 875.
4. "Teen-Age Girls."
5. Girlhood in film is the exclusive focus of Scheiner's *Signifying Female Adolescence* (2000) and Gateward and Pomerance's collection, *Sugar, Spice, and Everything Nice* (2002). Shary's *Generation Multiplex* (2002) includes some feminist-friendly readings of girls' roles in its larger focus on youth films, a welcome departure from earlier youth-film surveys that failed to address gender issues. Collections of essays that highlight girls' interactions with various forms of popular culture include Inness, *Delinquents and Debutantes* (1998); and Mazzarella and Pecora, *Growing Up Girls* (1999).
6. For a few examples, see Alexander, *The Girl Problem*; Formanek-Brunell, *Made to Play House*; Schrum, *Some Wore Bobby Sox*; Odem, *Delinquent Daughters*; Enstad, *Ladies of Labor, Girls of Adventure*; and Kunzel, *Fallen Women, Problem Girls*.
7. One of the cycles explored in chapter 3, the Corliss Archer narratives, offers a slight exception to this general pattern, for she debuted almost simultaneously in three venues at once: magazine fiction, radio, and theater, all in 1943. But several of the Archer tales were produced over the course of the following twelve years, building gradually upon the character's initial success.
8. Writing about similar collections of narratives, Mary Celeste Kearney uses the term "meta-property," meaning "a collection of individual entertainment properties based on a single originary text that was not intentionally produced to generate further adaptations" (Kearney, "Recycling Judy and Corliss," 289 n. 20). Kearney's focus upon the industrial and economic aspects of these texts' production requires a term like "property" to highlight the stories' status as exploited commodities. I use the term "narrative cycle" to serve my focus on the structure and content of the stories themselves.
9. The case of *Junior Miss* is exemplary, and is matched in such examples as *The Aldrich Family*, a highly popular radio series that began as the Broadway comedy *What a Life*. See Stilson, *Ezra Stone*; and Dunning, *On the Air*.
10. In domestic comedies, the genre that most consistently featured teenagers, *The Adventures of Ozzie and Harriet* and *Father Knows Best* are two examples of radio series that made successful transitions to television.

11. One rare exception is the light-skinned African American girl, Peola, in the 1934 film *Imitation of Life* (renamed Sarah Jane in the 1959 version). Peola/Sarah Jane, traumatized by her confinement within racist discourse and obsessed with a desire to "pass," reinforces a suggestion that non-white girlhood is impossible to represent without recourse to the assumed superiority of whiteness. In classic Hollywood texts, as in this character's life, white girlhood is the only imaginable kind.

12. Dyer, "The Colour of Virtue," 2.

13. See, for example, Allison Graham on the film *The Three Faces of Eve*. Analyzing its coding of race and sexuality in the characters of "Eve White" and her alter ego "Eve Black," Graham astutely notes that "Hollywood practices and southern politics may have been closer in spirit than defenders of either would consciously acknowledge" ("'The Loveliest and Purest of God's Creatures,'" 102).

14. Rooney, *Life Is Too Short*, 87–88, my emphasis.

15. Ibid., 88.

16. Shary, *Generation Multiplex*, 17.

17. Schrum, *Some Wore Bobby Sox*, 137.

18. Slotkin, *Gunfighter Nation*, 10, his emphasis.

19. Durham, "Dilemmas of Desire," 386, 369.

20. Rooney, *Life Is Too Short*, 86.

21. Woodward, "Female Foibles," 8.

22. Stilson, *Ezra Stone*, 91–93.

23. Heilbrun, "Nancy Drew: A Moment in Feminist History," 18.

24. Peter Stoneley, *Consumerism and American Girls' Literature, 1860–1940* (Cambridge, U.K.: Cambridge University Press, 2003); and Schrum, *Some Wore Bobby Sox*.

25. Booth Tarkington's adult novel *Seventeen* (1916), about a hapless teenage boy, was a best-seller translated onto stage and screen, but such early examples are uncommon. The popular category of youth in films of the 1920s focused primarily on college students and other young adults, the group that provided Americans with their first images of a distinct youth culture. Georganne Scheiner, focusing specifically on younger teens, notes that between 1921 and 1930 American filmmakers produced "only fifteen feature films about adolescence and only five more about high school," a slim number indeed (*Signifying Female Adolescence*, 30).

26. The knowledge that high school teens had distinct cultural practices came earlier to teens themselves than to the public at large. Paula Fass notes that high schools fostered "peer groups in insulating school environments," which led to a rising youth culture (*The Damned and the Beautiful*, 210). Kelly Schrum, too, argues that peer-group activities centering on popular culture, fashion, and beauty played a large role in forming the subjectivities of high school girls in the 1920s.

27. Kincaid, *Child Loving*, 175.

28. Wood, "Lolita Syndrome," 32.

29. Ibid.

30. Basinger, *Shirley Temple*, 14.

31. Wood, "Lolita Syndrome," 33.

32. Black, *Child Star*, 322. Temple instinctively gave the best possible response: she burst out laughing, whereupon the wounded Freed angrily ordered her out of his office.

33. Dijkstra, *Idols of Perversity*, 50, 58.

34. Ibid., 185.

35. Jordanova, "Natural Facts," 165.

36. For a discussion of the historical tendency to view children's behavior—particularly their sexuality—as "needing" the monitoring gaze of civilized society, see Michel Foucault, *The History of Sexuality*, vol. 1 (New York: Vintage Books, 1990), 27–30, 42.

37. One recent iteration of this apparently timeless theme is the situation comedy *8 Simple Rules for Dating My Teenage Daughter*, which debuted on the ABC television network in the fall of 2002.

38. See Devlin, "Their Fathers' Daughters."

39. Sinclair, *Hollywood Lolitas*, 15.

1. Radical Notions

1. Enstad, *Ladies of Labor, Girls of Adventure*, 201.

2. For further information on the scope and impact of the Stratemeyer properties, see Farah and Nash, *Series Books and the Media;* and Johnson, *Edward Stratemeyer.*

3. Rollins, *Twentieth-Century Teen Culture*, 29–30.

4. For a bibliography and description of nineteenth- and twentieth-century girls' books, see Society of Phantom Friends, *The Girls' Series Companion.*

5. Published under the pseudonym Alice B. Emerson, the series ran from 1913 to 1934 and comprised thirty volumes, a remarkably long lifespan for a series-book character at that time. For an extended analysis of the Ruth Fielding series and its themes, see Billman, *Stratemeyer Syndicate*, 57–77.

6. Because of her changing marital status over the years, this ghostwriter was known first as Mildred Augustine, then as Mildred Wirt, and finally as Mildred Wirt Benson. For the sake of clarity I refer to her consistently in the text as Mildred Wirt, the name she held for the longest period of time during her tenure as a Syndicate author.

7. Martin, "Ghost in the Attic," 17.

8. Ibid. Wirt did not state when or how Edward Stratemeyer expressed these opinions. The Stratemeyer Syndicate Records at the New York Public Library contain letters he wrote to her regarding his opinion of her manuscripts, but these letters do not address the issue of Nancy Drew's characterization.

9. Martin, "Ghost in the Attic," 18.

10. Further changes occurred in Nancy's character in the early 1980s, after Adams's death, when the Syndicate properties were purchased by their publisher, Simon & Schuster. Wanting to reinvent Nancy for a new generation, the publishers initiated a string of spin-off Nancy Drew series which changed her per-

sonality radically, making her, as one sour critic put it, "a professional sex tease for teenyboppers, a 'Dynasty' bimbo wandering through insipid plots" (Holt, "The Updating of Nancy Drew"). Most of those spin-off series had evaporated by the end of the 1990s, but in 2004 Simon & Schuster released a new series: Nancy Drew, Girl Detective. Today, the original full texts of the earliest Nancy Drew books are available in facsimile editions published by Applewood Books.

11. Perhaps the most influential of these was an article whose title sounded even more sensational than the books it criticized: "Blowing Out the Boys' Brains," by Franklin K. Mathiews, appeared in the November 18, 1914, issue of *Outlook* magazine.

12. For this innovation, Stratemeyer became informally known in the publishing industry as "the father of the fifty-center." See Chase, "Rover Boys."

13. "Newarker Who Writes," n.p.

14. "Will of Edward Stratemeyer," *New York Times*, 6 June 1930.

15. Kinloch, "The Menace of the Series Book," 10.

16. The information about books' inscriptions is derived from my own extensive collection of vintage Nancy Drew volumes.

17. Pothier, "Nancy Drew's Back!"

18. Modell, *Into One's Own*, 129.

19. Yost, "The Fifty-Cent Juveniles," 2405.

20. "For It Was Indeed He," 88.

21. Heilbrun, "Nancy Drew: A Moment in Feminist History," 18.

22. Keene, *The Haunted Bridge*, 170–71.

23. Prager, *Rascals at Large*, 80. In a similar vein, Bobbie Ann Mason notes, "Nancy is so accomplished that she can lie bound and gagged in a dank basement or snowed-in cabin for as much as twenty-four hours without freezing to death or wetting her pants" (Mason, *Girl Sleuth*, 52).

24. Chamberlain, "Secrets of Nancy Drew," 5, her emphasis.

25. Ginsburg, "And Then There Is Good Old Nancy Drew."

26. The epigram quoted at the start of this chapter comes from one such article in *Vogue* magazine; see Fitzgerald, "Women, Success, and Nancy Drew," 323.

27. Bumiller, "Squeaky Clean."

28. Tawa, "Nancy Drew's Fans Have a Clue."

29. Kismaric and Heiferman, *Mysterious Case*, 82.

30. Heilbrun, "Nancy Drew: A Moment in Feminist History."

31. Bumiller, "Squeaky Clean."

32. Tawa, "Nancy Drew's Fans Have a Clue."

33. Mason, *Girl Sleuth*, 57.

34. *Congressional Record*, 23 April 1980, 8890.

35. A letter from Edna Stratemeyer to Wirt, regarding 1931's *Secret of Red Gate Farm*, reveals the Syndicate's preference that the criminal women in that volume not show initiative: "The women of this [counterfeiting] band are the wives, who are drawn into unpleasant situations generally through no fault of their own" (box 28, Stratemeyer Syndicate Records, Manuscripts and Archives Division,

The New York Public Library. Astor, Lenox, and Tilden Foundations). Even on the few occasions when criminal women are at fault, they are rarely ringleaders.

36. A good contradictory argument can be found in Gwen Tarbox, *The Club-women's Daughters*. Tarbox reads Nancy's close connection to Bess and George as a strong endorsement of the powers of female community.

37. Zacharias, "Ballbuster," 1037.

38. The first known appearance of this statement is in Wertheimer and Sands, "Nancy Drew Revisited," 1133.

39. Haitch, "At 83, Her Pen Is Far from Dry."

40. Foreman, "Saga of the Mysterious Author."

41. *Storied Life*.

42. Mildred Wirt Benson, interview by the author, August 1998, Toledo, Ohio.

43. Martin, "Ghost in the Attic."

44. McFarlane, *Ghost of the Hardy Boys*, 199.

45. Mildred Wirt Benson, interview by the author.

46. Cornell, *At the Heart of Freedom*, 19.

47. Ibid., 17.

48. Zacharias, "Ballbuster," 1037.

49. Quoted in McNall, "American Children's Literature," 390.

50. Keene, *Nancy's Mysterious Letter*, 32. This volume is one of three ghost-written by Walter Karig in the early 1930s, when Wirt took a brief hiatus from the series. In Karig's hands, these scenes tend to have a more confrontational tone than they do in Wirt's texts. As a middle-aged man, Karig may have found Nancy's awesome authority more fantastical, and hence deserving of dramatic stand-offs. In Wirt's texts, Nancy's powers appear as a just-so fact, taken for granted as normal.

51. Benson, "Ghost of Ladora," 26.

52. Helgeson, "Girlhood Heroine."

53. Cornell, *At the Heart of Freedom*, 10.

54. Ibid.

55. Ibid., 21.

56. A few Hardy titles indicate hidden interiors (*The Secret Panel*, for example), but they are less common than publicly visible images of roads, vehicles, and the exteriors of buildings.

57. Keene, *Old Attic*, 138.

58. Mason, *Girl Sleuth*, 59.

59. Caprio, *Mystery of Nancy Drew*, 31, 33, 34.

60. Sunstein, "'Reading' the Stories of Reading," 104, my emphasis.

61. The first exception to this pattern occurred only in the twenty-sixth volume, *The Clue of the Leaning Chimney* (1949), in which a kindly Chinese man is Nancy's beneficiary. But the Chinese had been insulted much earlier, as a "French-Chinese" villainess appeared in the sixth volume, *The Secret of Red Gate Farm* (1931). Many of those whom Nancy helps are poor, but none has a working-class background; all are "fine" people who have recently fallen upon hard times.

62. "Newarker Who Writes," n.p.

63. Two notable exceptions to this pattern debuted only in 1967, late in the Syndicate's history, and neither of them reflects terribly well on the Syndicate. In the six-volume series Christopher Cool/TEEN Agent (1967–1969), Geronimo, an Apache Native American, serves as the hero's sidekick. But the Syndicate cannot take credit for Geronimo because, in an unusual move, even the plots and characters of this series were devised entirely by their ghostwriter, James Lawrence. Also in 1967, Syndicate partner Andrew Svenson wrote the three-volume Tollivers series, about an African American family. Svenson's construction of black identity consisted of nothing more than putting white characters in blackface. So thoroughly did this brief series omit any ethnic signifiers that, in later years, the Syndicate was able to recycle the texts almost verbatim as volumes in the quintessentially white Bobbsey Twins series.

64. DeWitt, "Hidden Author."

65. Quoted in Zinman, Saturday Afternoon, 418.

66. Offen, "The Real Secret."

67. Lenhart, "Whodunit?" 12.

68. Sunstein, "'Reading' the Stories of Reading," 101, her emphasis.

69. Caprio, Mystery of Nancy Drew, 21, my emphasis.

70. Mary, "Re: racism," e-mail to Girls Series mailing list, post #3317, 6 May 2004, http://groups.yahoo.com/group/Girls_Series. Quoted with Mary's permission.

71. Keene, Old Clock, 141.

72. Keene, Tapping Heels, 78–79.

73. Mason, Girl Sleuth, 68.

74. Keene, Nancy's Mysterious Letter, 12.

75. Keene, Ivory Charm, 22, 23, 39, 76.

76. Siegel, "Nancy Drew as New Girl Wonder," 176.

77. Mason, Girl Sleuth, 58, 72.

78. Keene, Brass-Bound Trunk, 18.

79. As we shall see in the following chapter, the films based on these books participate in a discourse that insists even more vigorously on the exclusion of wage-earning from the construction of approved adolescent femininity.

80. Dyer, White, 122, 125–26.

81. Johnson, Edward Stratemeyer, 150.

82. Ibid., 123.

83. Keene, Missing Map, 5, 49.

84. Fadem, "Mystery of Carolyn Keene."

85. Miller, "Nancy Drew Follows Wellesley Motto."

86. DeWitt, "Hidden Author."

87. When a librarian in Newton, Massachusetts, made news in 1978 by refusing to stock Nancy Drew and Hardy Boys books, dismissing the formulaic tales as "soap opera narratives," the Boston Globe solicited Adams's opinion about the controversy: "She said they may have been badly written when her father, Edward Stratemeyer, started writing them in 1927, but she's changed all that. 'Being a

Wellesley graduate majoring in English, I was able to do that,' she said" (Pave, "Nancy Drew Banned in Newton? Not Quite, But . . ." *Boston Globe*, 14 Sept. 1978).

88. *Storied Life.*
89. Nash, "New Evidence."
90. Martin, "Ghost in the Attic," 15.
91. Fitzgerald, "Women, Success, and Nancy Drew."
92. Keene, *Moss-Covered Mansion*, 25.
93. Ibid., 157, 164.
94. Keene, *Whispering Statue*, 88.
95. Treloar, "'We've *Never* Carried.'"
96. Treloar, "The Artful Ways of Millie."
97. Keene, *Larkspur Lane*, 13.
98. Keene, *Nancy's Mysterious Letter*, 24.
99. Zacharias, "Ballbuster," 1035–36.

2. "Pretty Baby"

1. Schrum, *Some Wore Bobby Sox*, 130; Doherty, *Teenagers and Teenpics*, 49.
2. Farah and Nash, *Series Books and the Media*, 33.
3. Press books were sent by studio publicity departments to media outlets and to local exhibitors. They contained ready-made news items to be placed in newspapers, and also functioned as a catalog from which exhibitors selected posters to decorate the theater and attract viewers to the film. All the press books and other publicity documents from which I quote in this chapter are housed in the USC Warner Bros. Archives, School of Cinema-Television, University of Southern California. These documents are not identified or distinguished individually, but can be found in the "Publicity" folders of each of the Nancy Drew films, which are catalogued by title.
4. As Jowett, Jarvie, and Fuller have argued, however, this book oversimplified the studies' findings and "gave the false impression that the researchers had lent themselves to a moralizing crusade" (*Children and the Movies*, 7).
5. Hayes, *Production Code.*
6. Keene, *Larkspur Lane*, 1–2. Page numbers of subsequent quotations will be cited parenthetically in the text.
7. Interestingly, an early draft of Kenneth Gamet's screenplay for this film—while still placing Nancy constantly in Ted's company—preserved Keene's presentation of Nancy as the primary discoverer and interpreter of the fallen pigeon, as well as Nancy's idea of sending pigeons for help after her capture. The studio's diminution of Nancy seems to have been a deliberate and on-going process. *Nancy Drew — Detective* files, USC Warner Bros. Archives.
8. Beeson, "Translating Nancy Drew," 43.
9. Felando, "Searching," 27.

10. Ibid., 44–76.

11. "Baby Peggy" made nearly fifty comedies between 1921 and 1926—seventeen in 1921 alone, when she was three years old. Jackie Coogan is perhaps best remembered for his touching role with Charlie Chaplin in *The Kid* (1921), when he was seven.

12. Black, *Child Star*, 59. The Depression-era delirium over cute babies—both as symbols of society's redemption and as targets for adults' protective instincts—surpassed the confines of narrative entertainment and spread to the news media, where, for example, the Lindbergh baby's kidnapping (1932) and the birth of the Dionne quintuplets (1934) commanded intense and prolonged national attention.

13. Academy of Motion Picture Arts and Sciences, *Awards Database*, accessed 26 June 2004, http://www.oscars.org/awardsdatabase.

14. Austin and Willard, "Angels of History," 2.

15. Jackson, *Images of Children*, 56.

16. "Just Kids."

17. Doss, "Bonita in Movieland," 13.

18. Modell, *Into One's Own*, 122.

19. Palladino, *Teenagers*, 50.

20. Scheiner, *Signifying Female Adolescence*, 64.

21. *Nancy Drew—Detective* files, USC Warner Bros. Archives.

22. Among the finer points of slang taught by Granville and Thomas to their boss was a reference that Warner Bros. attributed to the influence of the Depression. The "average check" paid by the Works Progress Administration was supposedly $23.80, a sum which had surfaced in youthful slang as "the standard expression used in betting that the speaker's contention is right. It is also used to denote immensity or magnitude." The Nancy Drew films frequently featured either Nancy or Ted saying "I'll bet you twenty-three eighty . . ." Frankie Thomas offered further examples: "When high school kids start something they rally around and get organized. When they talk they 'fan the breeze,' 'disturb the molecules,' or 'knock their jaws together.' A boy no longer speaks of a date. He says, 'I'm going in for some orange peeling tonight.'" Even expressions that sound less arcane to modern ears, such as "get off your high horse" and "chalk one up," are attributed in this publicity item to the innovations of teenagers.

23. The list included Judge Ben Lindsey, a pioneer in establishing the juvenile court system; the heads of the Girl Scouts, the YWCA, and settlement houses such as Hull House and the Greenwich House; editors and writers for popular magazines; F. Scott Fitzgerald (whose stories about the "lost generation" had defined postwar youth in the 1920s); noted educator Angelo Patri; novelist Kathleen Norris; etiquette expert Emily Post; and even Eleanor Roosevelt, whose secretary sent a note of apology saying that Mrs. Roosevelt did not know enough about the topic to offer an expert opinion.

24. *Nancy Drew—Detective* files, USC Warner Bros. Archives.

25. Ibid.

26. "Mowing Down Mendelssohn."

27. Scheiner, *Signifying Female Adolescence*, 117–35.

28. Palladino, *Teenagers*, 51.

29. Erenberg, *Swingin' the Dream*, 35–40.

30. We cannot know whether this claim was true, since Granville's questionnaire has not survived. Either way, the quoted answer served the studio's ideological purposes.

31. Filene, *Him/Her/Self*, 170–71.

32. McComb, "Rate Your Date," 44; Bailey, *From Front Porch to Back Seat*, chapter 2.

33. Kimmel, *Manhood in America*, 199–201.

34. McComb, "Rate Your Date," 44.

35. *Nancy Drew—Detective* files, USC Warner Bros. Archives.

36. *Nancy Drew and the Hidden Staircase* files, USC Warner Bros. Archives.

37. Hillis, "Job Ahead," her emphasis.

38. "Sub-Debs Live in a Jolly World of Their Own."

39. Walkerdine, "Popular Culture," 261.

40. Feminism has apparently had no dampening effect on the popularity of this trope, as it remains common. While driving through a rural Ohio town in 2000, I saw an approaching car with the phrase "I'm a daddy's girl!" emblazoned in large silver letters across the top of the windshield. The driver was a woman at least in her 20s. Moreover, whenever I describe this phenomenon in my college classes, numerous female students acknowledge that they, too, have consciously claimed that identity.

41. Lenhart, "Whodunit?"

42. Minehan, *Boy and Girl Tramps of America*.

43. Devlin, "Female Juvenile Delinquency," 94.

44. Forman-Brunell, "Girls' Rooms," 340.

45. Schuler, "Homeless Girls."

46. Ibid.

47. Sperry-Ripperger, "The Forgotten Woman."

48. "*Life* Goes to a Party"; and "Finishing Schools."

49. Roosevelt, "The Forgotten Man."

50. Scheiner, *Signifying Female Adolescence*, 143, 57–87.

51. Adapted from Frances Hodgson Burnett's Victorian novel, *The Little Princess* tells of a well-to-do little girl sent to a boarding school by her soldier father when he departs for the Boer War. When he is reported missing in action, the little girl is treated like a scullery maid by her evil headmistress, a martyrdom she handles with the grace one expects of a well-bred "princess." In the end, she locates her injured Daddy and returns to a life of happiness. The poverty and humiliation she endures are clearly unjust for a girl of her class; the narrative formula makes it clear that this gross miscarriage of justice will not prevail.

52. *Good Housekeeping* later began another column devoted to teen-girl issues, but it did not have the serious tone or the focus of Hillis's "Terrifying Teens."

53. The archive does not preserve the women's original letters, but offers summaries compiled by studio staffers, with some direct quotations included.

54. *Nancy Drew—Detective* files, USC Warner Bros. Archives.

55. Doss, "Bonita in Movieland."

56. McComb, "Rate Your Date," 56.

57. For reasons not documented, the kissing scene did not make the final cut of the film. It was, however, rehearsed and shot; photographs to this effect are in the Nancy Drew photo files at the USC Warner Bros. Archives.

58. *Nancy Drew — Troubleshooter* files, USC Warner Bros. Archives.

59. Kincaid, *Child Loving*, 175.

60. Kolodny, *The Lay of the Land*.

3. *"Delightfully Dangerous" Girls in the 1940s*

1. League of American Theatres and Producers, *Internet Broadway Database*.

2. Atkinson, "The Play in Review."

3. Black, *Child Star*, 59.

4. The film series spanned the years 1937 to 1946. In the early 1950s, Andy Hardy was the subject of a radio series and a comic book. One final film, *Andy Hardy Comes Home* (1958), attempted to revive the cycle for a new generation, but failed.

5. See the *Internet Broadway Database*; Stilson, *Ezra Stone*, 82–88; Zinman, *Saturday Afternoon*, 386; and Dunning, *On the Air*, 21. There was also a Henry Aldrich comic book contemporaneous with the television series.

6. Mantle, "'Junior Miss' Adds Life."

7. "Episode One," F. Hugh Herbert Collection, American Heritage Center, University of Wyoming.

8. May, "Making the American Consensus," 73.

9. A significant exception to the pattern is the radio and film cycle *A Date with Judy*, in which Judy Foster's father, while still financially secure, has the more mundane position of owning a fish cannery.

10. See the *Internet Movie Database* for this and other examples. Actors Eugene Pallette and Edward Arnold, too, were repeatedly cast as professional men with maddening teenage children.

11. Stilson, *Ezra Stone*, 78–92. Andy and Henry were the most visible of the 1940s' clumsy yet earnest male youth, but others followed suit: *The Adventures of Archie Andrews*, a popular comic book about high school teens, debuted as a radio series in 1943 and ran for a full decade, while *That Brewster Boy* aired from 1940 to 1945. See Dunning, *On the Air*, for these and other examples.

12. Freud's famous line appeared in an undated letter he wrote to a friend; it is quoted in Jones, *The Life and Work of Sigmund Freud*, 2:421.

13. In *Three Smart Girls* (1936) Durbin restores a nuclear family by reuniting her estranged parents; in *100 Men and a Girl* (1937) she finds employment for a group of destitute classical musicians, including her father.

14. Atkinson, "Girls Are People."

15. Crowther, review of *Kiss and Tell*.

16. Ward, "The Bobby Soxers."

17. It is difficult to locate the earliest of the "Junior Miss" stories, for the *Reader's Guide to Periodical Literature* did not index the *New Yorker* until 1940, and the scant biographical sources for Sally Benson do not provide bibliographies of her magazine work. Nor, oddly, did the *New Yorker* itself list the titles of its short fiction in the issues' tables of contents. To find specific stories before 1940, one must examine each issue one page at a time.

18. "Sally Benson."

19. On the development of the teen fashion industry, see Schrum, *Some Wore Bobby Sox*.

20. "Sally Benson."

21. Nilsen and Donelson, *Literature for Today's Young Adults*, 566.

22. "Sally Benson."

23. Ferguson, "Sally Benson."

24. Doherty, *Teenagers and Teenpics*, rev. ed., 74; and Thomas Doherty, *Teenagers and Teenpics* (Boston: Unwin Hyman, 1988), 94.

25. Benson, *Junior Miss*, 186.

26. Chodorov and Fields, *Junior Miss*, 10.

27. Benson, *Junior Miss*, 51.

28. Ibid., 58–59.

29. This same plot would resurface in 1943's *The Youngest Profession* and 1948's *A Date with Judy*.

30. Watts, "Portrait of a Lady."

31. Chodorov and Fields, *Junior Miss*, 90.

32. That line does not appear in the film, however; constricted by the Production Code, the screenplay can only say, "That's some girl you've got there!"

33. Mantle, "'Junior Miss' Adds Life."

34. Watts, "Portrait of a Lady."

35. Griswold, *Fatherhood in America*, 162.

36. Tuttle, *Daddy's Gone to War*; and Griswold, *Fatherhood in America*, 161–84.

37. Palladino, *Teenagers*, 81.

38. Devlin, "Their Fathers' Daughters," 28.

39. "Teenage Girls: They Live in a Wonderful World All Their Own," 93.

40. Quoted in Blum, *V Was for Victory*, 28.

41. Griswold, *Fatherhood in America*, 162.

42. Palladino, *Teenagers*; and Gilbert, *Cycle of Outrage*.

43. Anderson, "'Janie,' New Comedy at the Henry Miller."

44. Scheiner, *Signifying Female Adolescence*, 109.

45. See the introduction, p. 19, for discussion and citation of Kincaid's work.

46. Lake, "Trouble on the Street Corners," my emphasis.

47. Formanek-Brunell, "Truculent and Tractable," 62.

48. Gilbert, *Cycle of Outrage*.

49. Palladino, *Teenagers*, 52.

50. Schrum, *Some Wore Bobby Sox*, chapter 2.

51. Devlin, "Their Fathers' Daughters," 145.

52. "Picture of the Month."

53. Porter, "America's Kid Sister."

54. Time, Inc. was also the publisher of *Time* and *Life* magazines; its newsreels closely mirrored the tone of the articles that appeared in these periodicals.

55. "Jam Session."

56. Lewis, *The Road to Romance and Ruin*. Lewis reads this repeated plot structure as "a thinly veiled search for authority on the part of America's young" (37), though it's likely that such reassertions of social control spoke for adults' fantasies more than youth's.

57. Griswold, *Fatherhood in America*, chapter 5.

58. Downey, "Care and Feeding," 18.

59. Anderson, "'Junior Miss' Opens at Lyceum Theatre"; and Kronenberger, "'Junior Miss' Has a Gay Coming Out."

60. Atkinson, "Girls Are People."

61. One episode from the 1948–1950 series, "The Rainy Day," is housed at the Museum of Television and Radio. Two other episodes, which also appear to post-date the initial 1942 series, occasionally circulate through the informal networks of collectors of old-time radio, but no further episodes are known to be extant.

62. Dunning, *On the Air*, 378; and "Sally Benson." Indeed, Benson crafted a reputation as a writer of youth. Her autobiography, *Meet Me in St. Louis*, became the basis for the renowned Judy Garland film (1944), and Benson wrote or contributed to several screenplays with young heroines, including Hitchcock's *Shadow of a Doubt* (1943). In a neat symmetry, she also penned the book for a 1951 Broadway musical based on *Seventeen* by Booth Tarkington, whose works were so often evoked in critics' responses to *Junior Miss*.

63. *Calling All Girls* folder (series I correspondence: box 33, folder 25), Stratemeyer Syndicate Records.

64. Crowther, review of *Junior Miss*.

65. *Internet Broadway Database*.

66. Dunning, *On the Air*, 191–92, 378.

67. Robert M. Overstreet, *The Overstreet Comic Book Price Guide*, 28th ed. (New York: Avon Books, 1998), 587.

68. Brooks and Marsh, *The Complete Directory*, 667.

69. Herbert, "America's Favorite Bobby-Soxer."

70. In 1944, David O. Selznick sought Herbert's assistance in sculpting "Brig," the younger teen daughter in Selznick's renowned melodrama *Since You Went Away*. Herbert received no screen credit for this project, but Shirley Temple, who played Brig, mentions his contribution in her autobiography, calling Herbert "a demonstrated expert on teenage culture" (Black, *Child Star*, 351). It has also been speculated that Herbert's obsession with teen girls influenced a later, more notorious image of a pedophile: Rachel Devlin persuasively suggests that Vladimir Nabokov named Humbert Humbert, the lecherous stepfather of pubescent Lolita, in a play on the name Hugh Herbert ("Their Fathers' Daughters," 268).

71. Herbert, *I'd Rather Be Kissed*.

72. Herbert, *Kiss and Tell*, 36.

73. Thus did the announcer describe Corliss in the inaugural episode of the radio series (Dunning, *On the Air*, 444).

74. Even a partial catalog of his works proves how thoroughly Herbert's imagination was steeped in these themes. His first novel and subsequent screenplay, *There You Are* (1925), treats a stodgy, middle-aged father who frets over the amorality of his flapper daughter, yet who also feels his own dormant sexuality awakened by her example. Herbert's novel *A Lover Would Be Nice* (1935) begins with its heroine, a sexually capricious fourteen-year-old, flirting with and kissing a man old enough to be her grandfather. In 1938 Herbert co-wrote the film *That Certain Age*, in which teenage Deanna Durbin pursues an older man amused yet irritated by her attentions. The aptly titled film *My Heart Belongs to Daddy* (1942) treats a pregnant burlesque dancer who takes shelter in the home of a professor with whom she falls in love. Herbert's 1946 screenplay for *Margie* centers on a high school girl whose romance with her adult French teacher parallels her yearning for her idolized "papa." In his 1951 Broadway play *The Moon Is Blue*, Herbert highlights frank discussions between an ingénue and an older man about her virginity. (Filmed in 1953 by Otto Preminger, *The Moon Is Blue* became notorious as the first film to violate the Production Code by voicing the word "virgin," thus revivifying Herbert's status as an expert titillator.) And in 1954, in the novel *I'd Rather Be Kissed*, Herbert writes of a fifteen-year-old who plays a dangerous game of sexual teasing with her boyfriend's father. When the teasing leads to a predictable mess—the man calls her bluff, she is terrified, and both feel awful—Herbert carefully blames the girl's machinations, while suggesting that the middle-aged man was simply doing what comes naturally.

75. Whether by accident or plan, Pamela Herbert shared her first name with the destructive sex-tease heroine of her father's novel *A Lover Would Be Nice*.

76. Herbert, *Meet Corliss Archer*, dust jacket blurb.

77. Ibid., 6.

78. Devlin, "Their Fathers' Daughters," 15–16.

79. Herbert, *Kiss and Tell*, 40.

80. *Dictionary of American Family Names*, 368.

81. Herbert, *Meet Corliss Archer*, 136.

82. Ibid., 275, his emphasis.

83. Herbert, "America's Favorite Bobby-Soxer."

84. "Sally Benson."

85. Herbert, *Meet Corliss Archer*, 64–65.

86. Ibid., 149.

87. Ibid., 36.

88. Herbert, "Corliss Archer—Authoress," 24.

89. Herbert, *Meet Corliss Archer*, 139.

90. *Calling All Girls* folder, Stratemeyer Syndicate Records.

91. This is the book which we see a bemused father reading in the *March of Time* newsreel about teenage girls.

92. Grayson, *Do You Know Your Daughter?* 276.

93. Ibid., 278.

94. A photograph of the *Kiss for Corliss* lobby card can be seen in Robert

Windeler's *The Films of Shirley Temple* (Secaucus, N.J.: Citadel Press, 1978), 250. The *Kiss and Tell* lobby cards described here and below are in my own collection of teen-girl film artifacts.

95. Herbert, "Disillusioned," 35.

96. Anderson, "George Abbot"; and Kahn, review of *Kiss and Tell*.

97. Crowther, review of *Kiss and Tell*.

98. Agee, review of *Kiss and Tell*.

99. Sheldon's later creation of *The Patty Duke Show* drew upon his script for *Bachelor*; see chapter 4.

100. Coincidentally, *Dear Wife* was co-written by my own grandfather, playwright and screenwriter N. Richard Nash.

101. On television as on radio, this construction of the family was perhaps best exemplified in *The Adventures of Ozzie and Harriet*.

102. Mona Freeman had also played Lois Graves, the elder and less central sister in *Junior Miss*. Judy Graves had been played by Peggy Ann Garner, who had a more distinguished career. In the same year she made *Junior Miss*, Garner starred in the dramatic film *A Tree Grows in Brooklyn*, for which she won a special juvenile Academy Award.

4. *The Postwar Fall and Rise of Teen Girls*

1. Ehrenreich, *The Hearts of Men*, 42–51.

2. Breines, *Young, White, and Miserable*, 33.

3. May, *Homeward Bound*, 4.

4. Breines, *Young, White, and Miserable*, 50.

5. Ibid., 33.

6. May, *Homeward Bound*, 19.

7. As is often true in the history of formulaic film genres, a certain family resemblance between various portrayals of girlhood can be traced to the fact that the texts in this genre frequently sprang from the same creators. Joe Pasternak produced Durbin's films and the remakes of them, as well as other Jane Powell vehicles, while two of the four writers who contributed to *Nancy Goes to Rio*, Sidney Sheldon and Frederick Kohner, later created *The Patty Duke Show* and *Gidget*, respectively, on television.

8. Spigel, *Make Room for TV*, 60.

9. Palladino, *Teenagers*, 112.

10. Gilbert, *Cycle of Outrage*, 205–207.

11. In the earliest 1950s, the innocent Henry Aldrich was still milking his protracted popularity; he disappeared from both radio and television in 1953, the same year that *The Wild One* was produced.

12. Gilbert, *Cycle of Outrage*, 63–78.

13. Interestingly, none of the gang is a teenager; most of the actors playing these hoodlums were about thirty years old, and looked it. The film manages to

present them as "youth" only by juxtaposing them with "age," the middle-aged and elderly citizens of the small town the gang terrorizes.

14. *Rebel without a Cause* featured an alienated teen girl (Natalie Wood), but her delinquency hardly qualifies for the term, and James Dean's character is clearly the center of the film.

15. Doherty, *Teenagers and Teenpics*, rev. ed. The teen exploitation genre exploded after 1957, but began gradually a bit earlier; Alan Betrock lists several such films made in 1955 and 1956.

16. Betrock, *The I Was a Teenage Juvenile Delinquent Book*, 103.

17. Doherty, *Teenagers and Teenpics*, rev. ed., 159.

18. Unlike most of AIP's exploitation fare, the beach pictures were wholesome, lighthearted, and clean, despite a few suggestive references. Set in "the healthy outdoors," the films also featured casts of actors with clean-scrubbed images, notably Annette Funicello (formerly of *The Mickey Mouse Club*) and teen-idol Frankie Avalon. Featuring prominent roles for girls, these teenpics also had light pop-music soundtracks, combining the exploitation philosophies with some conventions of the musical comedy, a genre traditionally favored by girls.

19. For example, the series *77 Sunset Strip* (1958–1964) centered on a group of young, attractive private detectives in Los Angeles, while *Hawaiian Eye* (1959–63) did the same in Hawaii. *My Favorite Martian* (1963–66), *My Mother the Car* (1965–66), and *The Jetsons* (1962–63) addressed youth through science-fiction/fantasy gimmickry. This was also the period when comedies about teenage girls began to proliferate, including *Margie* (1961–62), *Karen* (1962–63), *Tammy* (1965–66), *The Patty Duke Show* (1963–66), and *Gidget* (1965–66).

20. Brooks and Marsh, *The Complete Directory*, 40.

21. In April 2002, Dick Clark told *TV Guide* that *Bandstand's* audience in its heyday (the late 1950s and early 1960s) far outstripped that of modern-day music television shows: "MTV's *Total Request Live* has an audience of about 800,000. *Bandstand* would pull seven and eight million people a day.... Everybody knew what it was, no matter your age." Holland, "Keep on Dancin'."

22. Zinsser, "The Tyranny of the Teens."

23. Hechinger and Hechinger, *Teenage Tyranny*, x.

24. Roddy, "The Networks Turn to Teen-Agers."

25. Luckett, "Girl Watchers," 97.

26. Hatch, "Fille Fatale," 164.

27. Douglas, *Where the Girls Are*, 83–98.

28. Ibid., 65.

29. For example, the 14 Aug. 1962 issue of *Look* magazine published Virgil Damon's "My Daughter Is in Trouble," about teen pregnancy. The next year, a few weeks before the premiere of *The Patty Duke Show*, the same magazine ran "The Tense Generation," in which Samuel Grafton asked, "Why do teen-agers from 'good' homes steal, take dope and shock their parents with their sexual delinquency?"

30. "President Kennedy Talks to Teens."

31. Douglas, *Where the Girls Are*, 22.

32. "Teen-Age Opinions."

33. Edwards, "Teen-Age Career Girls," 437.

34. Quoted in Kimmel, *Manhood in America*, 268.

35. Sheldon recalls, "When I began writing for 'Patty Duke,' it was in the days when there were 39 shows per year, so it was unheard of that just one person would write all the scripts for a specific show. The network hired a backup staff of three writers just in case I got stuck or couldn't come up with a script. In all the time I wrote for that show, they were never used" ("Television Credits," *The Sidney Sheldon Website*, 2004, accessed 13 Dec. 2004, http://www.twbook mark.com/features/sidneysheldon/television.html).

36. Douglas, *Where the Girls Are*, 108.

37. Ibid.

38. Hamamoto, *Nervous Laughter*, 80–81.

39. Douglas, *Where the Girls Are*, 110.

40. McRobbie, *Feminism and Youth Culture*, 87.

41. Raddatz, "Sally Field's a Lot Like Gidget."

42. For an overview of television schedules, see Brooks and Marsh, *The Complete Directory*.

43. *Gidget* files, box 14, folder 11, Harry Ackerman Collection, American Heritage Center, University of Wyoming.

44. Morley, *Family Television*, 148, 150.

45. Stillman, introduction to *Gidget*, by Frederick Kohner, xv, xvii. Some of Stillman's comparison is more accurate than she realizes, for a stylistic analysis of *Gidget* reveals that Kohner studied Salinger's *Catcher in the Rye* extremely closely— not only do both novels use the device of the first-person teen narrator, but Kohner also borrowed multiple turns of phrase directly from Salinger. For example, Salinger's narrator complains about high school girls who wear "those damn falsies that point all over the place" (3), and Kohner's narrator complains of high school classmates who wear "those damn falsies that stick out all over the place" (10).

46. "Goodbye, Gidget."

47. Douglas, *Where the Girls Are*, 4.

48. *Gidget* files, box 14, folder 8, Harry Ackerman Collection. Although adults of both sexes gave the show a positive response, women were likelier than men to enjoy the program, and the highest rankings of all came from young girls.

49. Unlike the Kohners, however, the "Hofers" were not Jewish. As did many Jewish artists in the film industry, Kohner jettisoned his ethnicity from his professional work.

50. Kohner, *Affairs of Gidget*, 2.

51. Kohner, *Gidget in Love*, 106.

52. Bresler, review of *Gidget*.

53. "Gidget Makes the Grade."

54. Zuckerman, foreword to *Gidget*, by Frederick Kohner, ix.

55. McParland, *Cowabunga!*, 2.

56. Kohner, *Gidget*, 1.

57. Quoted on the back cover of the 1958 Bantam paperback edition of *Gidget*.

58. Kohner, *Affairs of Gidget*, front cover.

59. Kohner, *Gidget,* 50.
60. Kohner, *Affairs of Gidget,* 13.
61. Herbert, *I'd Rather Be Kissed,* 6.
62. Whitney, "Gidget Goes Hysterical," 69.

Epilogue

1. Scheiner, *Signifying Female Adolescence,* 139.
2. Devlin, "Their Fathers' Daughters," 273.
3. Shary, *Generation Multiplex,* 6.
4. Thanks to my colleague Gwen Tarbox for sharing this observation with me.
5. Clover, "Her Body, Himself."
6. The series granted increasing wisdom and emotional strength to Buffy after the third season, when she and her cohort graduated from high school. The final season in particular carried a strong message of female competence and dignity. But throughout its run, *Buffy the Vampire Slayer* burdened many of its specifically high-school-aged girls with familiar, oppressive stereotypes of teen femininity—most cartoonishly in the character of Dawn, Buffy's younger sister, who joined the cast in the fifth season.
7. Anderman, "Lolitas with a Beat."
8. Binelli, "Confessions of a Teenage Drama Queen," 60.
9. Ibid.
10. "2004 Must List."
11. Binelli, "Confessions of a Teenage Drama Queen," 60.
12. Schwarzbaum, "Mandy-capped." This same scenario opens the Britney Spears film *Crossroads* (2002).
13. Ibid., my emphasis.

Bibliography

"2004 Must List: Lindsay Lohan." *Entertainment Weekly*, 25 June–2 July 2004, 66.

Agee, James. Review of *Kiss and Tell*, directed by Richard Wallace. *Nation*, 27 Oct. 1945, 44.

Alexander, Ruth. *The Girl Problem: Female Sexual Delinquency in New York, 1900–1930*. Ithaca: Cornell University Press, 1995.

Anderman, Joan. "Lolitas with a Beat." *Boston Globe*, 23 Jan. 2000, D1.

Anderson, John. "George Abbot Presents Gay Comedy Based on the Archer Family Sketches." *New York Journal-American*, 18 March 1943. Cited in *New York Theatre Critics' Reviews* (hereafter *NYTCR*) 4, no. 25 (1943): 356.

———. "'Janie,' New Comedy at the Henry Miller." *New York Journal-American*, 11 Sept. 1942. Cited in *NYTCR* 2, no. 33 (1942): 245.

———. "'Junior Miss' Opens at Lyceum Theatre." *New York Journal-American*, 19 Nov. 1941. Cited in *NYTCR* 2, no. 24 (1941): 211.

Atkinson, Brooks. "Girls Are People." *New York Times*, 30 Nov. 1941, sec. 9, p. 1.

———. "The Play in Review: 'Junior Miss.'" *New York Times*, 19 Nov. 1941, 28.

Austin, Joe, and Michael Nevin Willard. "Angels of History, Demons of Culture." In *Generations of Youth*, ed. Joe Austin and Michael Nevin Willard, 1–20. New York: New York University Press, 1998.

Aylesworth, Thomas G. *Hollywood Kids: Child Stars of the Silver Screen from 1903 to the Present*. New York: E. P. Dutton, 1987.

Bailey, Beth. *From Front Porch to Back Seat: Courtship in Twentieth-Century America*. Baltimore: Johns Hopkins University Press, 1988.

Basinger, Jeanine. *Shirley Temple*. New York: Pyramid Publications, 1975.

Beeson, Diana. "Translating Nancy Drew from Fiction to Film." *Lion and the Unicorn* 18, no. 1 (1994): 37–47.

Benson, Mildred Wirt. "The Ghost of Ladora." *Books at Iowa* (Friends of the University of Iowa Libraries) 19, no. 20 (Nov. 1973): 24–29.

Benson, Sally. *Junior Miss*. New York: Random House, 1941.

Bentham, Josephine, and Herschel Williams. *Janie: A Comedy in Three Acts*. New York: Samuel French, 1944.

Betrock, Alan. *The I Was a Teenage Juvenile Delinquent Rock 'n' Roll Horror Beach Party Movie Book: A Complete Guide to the Teen Exploitation Film, 1954–1969*. New York: St. Martin's Press, 1986.

Billman, Carol. *The Secret of the Stratemeyer Syndicate: Nancy Drew, the Hardy Boys, and the Million Dollar Fiction Factory*. New York: Ungar Publishing Company, 1986.

Binelli, Mark. "Confessions of a Teenage Drama Queen." *Rolling Stone*, 19 Aug. 2004, 60–64.

Black, Shirley Temple. *Child Star*. New York: Warner Books, 1988.

Blum, John Morton. *V Was for Victory: Politics and American Culture during World War II*. New York: Harcourt Brace Jovanovich, 1975.

Boose, Lynda E., and Betty S. Flowers, eds. *Daughters and Fathers*. Baltimore: Johns Hopkins University Press, 1989.

Breines, Wini. *Young, White, and Miserable: Growing Up Female in the Fifties*. Boston: Beacon Press, 1992.

Bresler, Riva T. Review of *Gidget*, by Frederick Kohner. *Library Journal* 82 (1957): 1906.

Brooke, Henrietta B. "Father—Meet Your Daughter!" *Rotarian*, Dec. 1938, 18–21.

Brooks, Tim, and Earle Marsh. *The Complete Directory to Prime Time Network and Cable TV Shows*. New York: Ballantine Books, 1995.

Brown, John Mason. "*Junior Miss* Transports Stories of Sally Benson to the Stage." *New York World-Telegram*, 19 Nov. 1941. Cited in *NYTCR* 2, no. 24 (1941): 214.

Bumiller, Elizabeth. "Squeaky Clean and Still Eighteen: Nancy Drew, Detective, Marks Half a Century." *Washington Post*, 17 April 1980.

Caprio, Betsy. *The Mystery of Nancy Drew: Girl Sleuth on the Couch*. Trabuco Canyon, Calif.: Source Books, 1992.

Chamberlain, Kathleen. "The Secrets of Nancy Drew: Having Their Cake and Eating It Too." *Lion and the Unicorn* 18 (1994): 1–12.

Chase, Frederick. "He Invented the Rover Boys." *Christian Science Monitor*, 5 Dec. 1942, magazine section.

Chodorov, Jerome, and Joseph Fields. *Junior Miss: A Comedy in Three Acts*. 1942. Reprint, New York: Dramatists Play Service, 1944.

Clover, Carol J. "Her Body, Himself: Gender in the Slasher Film." 1989. Reprinted in *Feminist Film Theory: A Reader*, ed. Sue Thornham, 234–50. New York: New York University Press, 1999.

Congressional Record, 23 April 1980: 8890–91.

Considine, David. *The Cinema of Adolescence*. Jefferson, N.C.: McFarland, 1985.

Cornell, Drucilla. *At the Heart of Freedom: Feminism, Sex, and Equality*. Princeton, N.J.: Princeton University Press, 1998.

Crowther, Bosley. Review of *Junior Miss*, directed by George Seaton. *New York Times*, 25 June 1945, 15.

———. Review of *Kiss and Tell*, directed by Richard Wallace. *New York Times*, 26 Oct. 1945, 16.

Damon, Virgil G. "My Daughter Is in Trouble." *Look*, 14 Aug. 1962, 26–35.

Devlin, Rachel. "Female Juvenile Delinquency and the Problem of Sexual Authority in America, 1945–1965." In *Delinquents and Debutantes: Twentieth-Century Girls' Cultures*, ed. Sherrie A. Inness, 83–106. New York: New York University Press, 1998.

———. "Their Fathers' Daughters: Adolescence and the Problem of Sexual Authority in America, 1941–1965." Ph.D. dissertation, Yale University, 1998.

DeWitt, Karen. "The Case of the Hidden Author." *Newsday*, 8 Aug. 1977, A4ff.

Dictionary of American Family Names, vol. 1. Ed. Patrick Hanks. New York: Oxford University Press, 2003.

Dijkstra, Bram. *Idols of Perversity: Fantasies of Feminine Evil in Fin-de-Siècle Culture.* Oxford: Oxford University Press, 1986.

Doherty, Thomas. *Teenagers and Teenpics: The Juvenilization of American Movies in the 1950s.* Rev. ed. Philadelphia: Temple University Press, 2002.

Doss, Helen Grigsby. "Bonita in Movieland." *American Girl*, July 1939, 11–13, 49–50.

Douglas, Susan J. *Where the Girls Are: Growing Up Female with the Mass Media.* New York: Random House, 1994.

Downey, Fairfax. "The Care and Feeding of Fathers." *American Girl*, Jan. 1940, 18–19, 50.

Dunning, John. *On the Air: The Encyclopedia of Old-Time Radio.* New York: Oxford University Press, 1998.

Durham, Meenakshi Gigi. "Dilemmas of Desire: Representations of Adolescent Sexuality in Two Teen Magazines." *Youth and Society* 29 (1998): 369–89.

Dyer, Richard. "The Colour of Virtue: Lillian Gish, Whiteness, and Femininity." In *Women and Film: A Sight and Sound Reader*, ed. Pam Cook and Philip Dodd, 1–9. Philadelphia: Temple University Press, 1993.

———. *White.* London: Routledge, 1997.

Edwards, Anne. "Teen-Age Career Girls." *English Journal* 42 (1953): 437–42.

Ehrenreich, Barbara. *The Hearts of Men: American Dreams and the Flight from Commitment.* Garden City, N.Y.: Anchor Press/Doubleday, 1983.

Enstad, Nan. *Ladies of Labor, Girls of Adventure: Working Women, Popular Culture, and Labor Politics at the Turn of the Twentieth Century.* New York: Columbia University Press, 1999.

Erenberg, Lewis A. *Swingin' the Dream: Big Band Jazz and the Rebirth of American Culture.* Chicago: University of Chicago Press, 1988.

Fadem, Susan Sherman. "The Mystery of Carolyn Keene." *St. Louis Globe-Democrat*, 21 Dec. 1974, C3.

Farah, David, and Ilana Nash. *Series Books and the Media: An Annotated Bibliography of Secondary Sources.* Rheem Valley, Calif.: SynSine Press, 1996.

Fass, Paula S. *The Damned and the Beautiful: American Youth in the 1920's.* Oxford: Oxford University Press, 1977.

Felando, Cynthia Lee. "Searching for the Fountain of Youth: Popular American Cinema in the 1920s." Ph.D. dissertation, UCLA, 1996.

Ferguson, Mary Anne. "Sally Benson." *American Women Writers*, vol. 1. 2nd ed. Detroit: St. James Press, 2000.

Filene, Peter Gabriel. *Him/Her/Self: Sex Roles in Modern America.* New York: Harcourt Brace Jovanovich, 1974.

"Finishing Schools." *Time*, 8 Nov. 1937, 15–16.

Fitzgerald, Frances. "Women, Success, and Nancy Drew." *Vogue*, May 1980, 323–24.

"For It Was Indeed He." *Fortune*, April 1934, 86–89, 193–94, 204, 206, 208–209.

Foreman, Judy. "The Saga of the Mysterious Author." *Boston Globe*, 3 July 1980.

Forman-Brunell, Miriam. "Girls' Rooms." In *Girlhood in America: An Encyclopedia*, ed. Miriam Forman-Brunell, 1:338–42. Santa Barbara, Calif.: ABC-Clio, 2001.

———. "Maternity, Murder, and Monsters: Legends of Babysitter Horror." In *Sugar, Spice, and Everything Nice: Cinemas of Girlhood*, ed. Frances Gateward and Murray Pomerance, 253–67. Detroit: Wayne State University Press, 2002.

Formanek-Brunell, Miriam. *Made to Play House: Dolls and the Commercialization of American Girlhood, 1830–1930*. New Haven, Conn.: Yale University Press, 1993.

———. "Truculent and Tractable: The Gendering of Babysitting in Postwar America." In *Delinquents and Debutantes: Twentieth-Century American Girls' Cultures*, ed. Sherrie A. Innes, 61–82. New York: New York University Press, 1998.

"From You to Us." *Calling All Girls*, Dec. 1948, 6–7.

"Gidget Makes the Grade." *Life*, 28 Oct. 1957, 111.

Gilbert, James. *A Cycle of Outrage: America's Reaction to the Juvenile Delinquent in the 1950s*. New York: Oxford University Press, 1986.

Gilmore, Cecile. "Want to Help 'Type' the Sixteen-Year-Old Girl?" *New York Evening Post*, 19 Aug. 1939.

Ginsburg, Jane. "And Then There Is Good Old Nancy Drew." *Ms.*, Jan. 1974, 93–94.

Goldsmith, Clifford. *What a Life: A Comedy in Three Acts*. New York: Dramatists Play Service, 1939.

"Goodbye, Gidget." Narrated by Anne Taylor Fleming. *Newshour*. PBS, 8 June 2001.

Grafton, Samuel. "The Tense Generation." *Look*, 27 Aug. 1963, 17–23.

Graham, Allison. "'The Loveliest and Purest of God's Creatures': *The Three Faces of Eve* and the Crisis of Southern Womanhood." In *Classic Hollywood, Classic Whiteness*, ed. Daniel Bernardi, 95–110. Minneapolis: University of Minnesota Press, 2001.

Grayson, Alice Barr. *Do You Know Your Daughter?* New York: D. Appleton-Century, 1944.

Griswold, Robert. *Fatherhood in America: A History*. New York: Basic Books, 1993.

Haitch, Richard. "At 83, Her Pen Is Far from Dry." *New York Times*, 27 March 1977, sec. 11, p. 19.

Hall, G. Stanley. *Adolescence: Its Psychology and Its Relations to Anthropology, Sociology, Sex, Crime, Religion, and Education*. New York: D. Appleton and Co., 1904.

Hamamoto, Darrell Y. *Nervous Laughter: Television Situation Comedy and Liberal Democratic Ideology*. New York: Praeger, 1989.

Haskell, Molly. *From Reverence to Rape: The Treatment of Women in the Movies*. New York: Holt, Rinehart and Winston, 1974.

Hatch, Kristen. "Fille Fatale: Regulating Images of Adolescent Girls, 1962–1996." In *Sugar, Spice, and Everything Nice: Cinemas of Girlhood*, ed. Frances

Gateward and Murray Pomerance, 163–81. Detroit: Wayne State University Press, 2002.

Hayes, David P. *The Production Code of the Motion Picture Industry (1930–1968).* 2000. Accessed 8 Dec. 2004. http://prodcode.davidhayes.net/.

Hechinger, Grace, and Fred M. Hechinger. *Teenage Tyranny.* New York: William Morrow and Co., 1963.

Heilbrun, Carolyn. "Nancy Drew: A Moment in Feminist History." In *Rediscovering Nancy Drew,* ed. Carolyn Stewart Dyer and Nancy Tillman Romalov, 11–21. Iowa City: University of Iowa Press, 1995.

Helgeson, Sally. "Who Was Your Girlhood Heroine?" *Glamour,* Oct. 1977, 64–66.

Herbert, F. Hugh. "America's Favorite Bobby-Soxer." Magazine advertisement for *A Kiss for Corliss,* 1949.

———. "Corliss Archer—Authoress." Radio script for *Meet Corliss Archer,* 28 Sept. 1944. F. Hugh Herbert Collection, American Heritage Center, University of Wyoming.

———. "Disillusioned." *Good Housekeeping,* May 1943, 34ff.

———. *I'd Rather Be Kissed.* New York: Random House, 1954.

———. *Kiss and Tell: A Comedy in Three Acts.* New York: Dramatists Play Service, 1945.

———. *Meet Corliss Archer.* New York: Sun Dial Press, 1944.

Hillis, Marjorie. "Dream It and Do It!" *Good Housekeeping,* April 1939, 91.

———. "Job Ahead." *Good Housekeeping,* Nov. 1938, 13.

———. "Your Own Money." *Good Housekeeping,* Jan. 1939, 58.

Holland, Ty. "Keep on Dancin'." *TV Guide,* 27 April 2002, 7.

"Hollywood Thinks You're a Jerk!" *Varsity,* Nov. 1950, 10.

Holt, Patricia. "The Updating of Nancy Drew." *San Francisco Chronicle,* 19 Oct. 1986.

hooks, bell. *Black Looks: Race and Representation.* Boston: South End Press, 1992.

"I Giggle." *Newsweek,* 8 June 1959, 104–105.

Internet Movie Database, Inc. *Internet Movie Database.* Accessed 31 Oct. 2004. http://www.imdb.com.

Jackson, Kathy Merlock. *Images of Children in American Film: A Socio-Cultural Analysis.* Metuchen, N.J.: Scarecrow Press, 1986.

"Jam Session." *Scholastic,* 29 Oct. 1945, 30.

Jessup, Margaret E. "New Careers For Girls." *Calling All Girls,* March 1943, 59.

Johnson, Deidre. *Edward Stratemeyer and the Stratemeyer Syndicate.* New York: Twayne, 1993.

———. *Stratemeyer Pseudonyms and Series Books.* Westport, Conn.: Greenwood Press, 1982.

Jones, Ernest. *The Life and Work of Sigmund Freud.* Vol. 2. New York: Basic Books, 1955.

Jordanova, Ludmilla. "Natural Facts: A Historical Perspective on Science and Sexuality." In *Feminist Theory and the Body,* ed. Janet Price and Margrit Shildrick, 157–68. New York and London: Routledge, 1999.

Jowett, Garth S., Ian C. Jarvie, and Kathryn H. Fuller. *Children and the Movies: Media Influence and the Payne Fund Controversy*. Cambridge: Cambridge University Press, 1996.

"The Juniors Take Over." *Commonweal*, 29 June 1945, 263.

"Just Kids." In *Screen Album for 1937*, 33–34. New York: Dell Publishing Company, 1937.

Kahn. Review of *Kiss and Tell*, directed by Richard Wallace. *Variety*, 2 Sept. 1945.

Kearney, Mary Celeste. "Girls, Girls, Girls: Gender and Generation in Contemporary Discourses of Female Adolescence and Youth Culture." Ph.D. dissertation, University of Southern California, 1998.

———. "Recycling Judy and Corliss: Transmedia Exploitation and the First Teen-Girl Production Trend." *Feminist Media Studies* 4, no. 3 (2004). 265–95.

Keene, Carolyn. *The Clue of the Leaning Chimney*. New York: Grosset & Dunlap, 1949.

———. *The Clue of the Tapping Heels*. New York: Grosset & Dunlap, 1939.

———. *The Haunted Bridge*. New York: Grosset & Dunlap, 1937.

———. *The Mystery at the Moss-Covered Mansion*. New York: Grosset & Dunlap, 1941.

———. *The Mystery of the Brass-Bound Trunk*. New York: Grosset & Dunlap, 1940.

———. *The Mystery of the Ivory Charm*. New York: Grosset & Dunlap, 1936.

———. *Nancy's Mysterious Letter*. New York: Grosset & Dunlap, 1932.

———. *The Password to Larkspur Lane*. New York: Grosset & Dunlap, 1933.

———. *The Quest of the Missing Map*. New York: Grosset & Dunlap, 1942.

———. *The Secret in the Old Attic*. New York: Grosset & Dunlap, 1944.

———. *The Secret of Red Gate Farm*. New York: Grosset & Dunlap, 1931.

———. *The Secret of the Old Clock*. New York: Grosset & Dunlap, 1930.

———. *The Sign of the Twisted Candles*. New York: Grosset & Dunlap, 1933.

———. *The Whispering Statue*. New York: Grosset & Dunlap, 1937.

Kimmel, Michael. *Manhood in America: A Cultural History*. New York: The Free Press, 1996.

Kincaid, James. *Child Loving: The Erotic Child and Victorian Culture*. New York: Routledge, 1992.

Kinloch, Lucy M. "The Menace of the Series Book." *Elementary English Review* 12, no. 1 (1935): 9–11.

Kismaric, Carole, and Marvin Heiferman. *The Mysterious Case of Nancy Drew and the Hardy Boys*. New York: Simon & Schuster, 1998.

Kohner, Frederick. *The Affairs of Gidget*. New York: Bantam, 1963.

———. *Gidget*. New York: G. P. Putnam's Sons, 1957.

———. *Gidget in Love*. New York: Dell, 1965.

Kolodny, Annette. *The Lay of the Land: Metaphor as Experience and History in American Life and Letters*. Chapel Hill: University of North Carolina Press, 1975.

Kronenberger, Louis. "'Junior Miss' Has a Gay Coming Out." *New York Newspaper "PM,"* 19 Nov. 1941. Cited in *NYTCR* 2, no. 24 (1941): 213.

Kunzel, Regina. *Fallen Women, Problem Girls: Unmarried Mothers and the Profes-*

sionalization of Benevolence, 1890–1945. New Haven, Conn.: Yale University Press, 1993.

Lackman, Ron. *The Encyclopedia of American Radio*. Rev. ed. New York: Checkmark Books, 2000.

Lake, Eleanor. "Trouble on the Street Corners." *Reader's Digest*, May 1943, 43–46.

"A Last Word." *Esquire*, July 1965, 100.

League of American Theatres and Producers. *Internet Broadway Database*. Accessed 31 Oct. 2004. http://www.ibdb.com.

Lenhart, Maria. "Whodunit, Nancy Drew?" *Christian Science Monitor*, 11 May 1979, 12.

Lewis, Jon. *The Road to Romance & Ruin: Teen Films and Youth Culture*. New York: Routledge, 1992.

"*Life* Goes to a Party at an Honor Farm." *Life*, 13 Sept. 1937, 108–109.

Luckett, Moya. "Girl Watchers: Patty Duke and Teen TV." In *The Revolution Wasn't Televised: Sixties Television and Social Conflict*, ed. Lynn Spigel and Michael Curtin, 95–118. New York and London: Routledge, 1997.

Mantle, Burns. "'Junior Miss' Adds Life and Color to Adolescent Season." *New York Daily News*, 19 Nov. 1941. Cited in *NYTCR* 2, no. 24 (1941): 212.

Martin, Linnea. "Ghost in the Attic." *Hiram Magazine* (Hiram College), summer 1988: 14–18.

Mason, Bobbie Ann. *The Girl Sleuth*. Rev. ed. Athens: University of Georgia Press, 1995.

May, Elaine Tyler. *Homeward Bound: American Families in the Cold War Era*. New York: Basic Books, 1988.

May, Kirse Granat. *Golden State, Golden Youth: The California Image in Popular Culture, 1955–1966*. Chapel Hill: University of North Carolina Press, 2002.

May, Lary. "Making the American Consensus." In *The War in American Culture: Society and Consciousness during World War II*, ed. Lewis Erenberg and Susan Hirsch, 71–102. Chicago: University of Chicago Press, 1996.

Mazzarella, Sharon R., and Norma Odom Pecora, eds. *Growing Up Girls: Popular Culture and the Construction of Identity*. New York: Peter Lang, 1999.

McComb, Mary. "Rate Your Date: Young Women and the Commodification of Depression-Era Courtship." In *Delinquents and Debutantes: Twentieth-Century American Girls' Cultures*, ed. Sherrie Inness, 40–60. New York: New York University Press, 1998.

McFarlane, Leslie. *Ghost of the Hardy Boys*. Toronto: Methuen, 1976.

McNall, Sally. "American Children's Literature, 1880–Present." In *American Childhood*, ed. Joseph M. Hawes and N. Ray Hiner, 377–414. Westport, Conn.: Greenwood Press, 1985.

McNeil, Alex. *Total Television: The Comprehensive Guide to Programming from 1948 to the Present*. New York: Penguin Books, 1996.

McParland, Stephen J. *Cowabunga! Gidget Goes Encyclopedic*. North Strathfield, N.S.W.: CMusic Publications, 2001.

McRobbie, Angela. *Feminism and Youth Culture: From* Jackie *to* Just Seventeen. Boston: Unwin Hyman, 1991.

McRobbie, Angela, and Jenny Garber. "Girls and Subcultures." In *The Subcultures Reader*, ed. Ken Gelder and Sarah Thornton, 112–20. New York: Routledge, 1997.

"Meet TV's Newest Darling: Gidget!" *TV Picture Life*, Dec. 1965, 29ff.

Meyerowitz, Joanne. "Beyond the Feminine Mystique." In *Not June Cleaver: Women and Gender in Postwar America, 1945–1960*, ed. Joanne Meyerowitz, 229–62. Philadelphia: Temple University Press, 1994.

———. *Women Adrift: Independent Wage Earners in Chicago, 1880–1930*. Chicago: University of Chicago Press, 1988.

Miller, Margo. "Nancy Drew Follows Wellesley Motto." *Boston Globe*, 4 March 1978, 8.

Minehan, Thomas. *Boy and Girl Tramps of America*. New York: Farrar and Rinehart, 1934.

Modell, John. *Into One's Own: From Youth to Adulthood in the United States, 1920–1975*. Berkeley: University of California Press, 1989.

Moore, Dick. *Twinkle, Twinkle, Little Star (But Don't Have Sex or Take the Car)*. New York: Harper and Row, 1984.

Morley, David. *Family Television: Cultural Power and Domestic Leisure*. London: Comedia Publishing Group, 1986.

"Mowing Down Mendelssohn: Swing Invades the Sacrosanct to Get Rugcutter Tunes." *Newsweek*, 18 Sept. 1939, 39.

Mulvey, Laura. "Visual Pleasure and Narrative Cinema." 1975. Reprinted in *Feminist Film Theory: A Reader*, ed. Sue Thornham, 58–69. New York: New York University Press, 1999.

Nabokov, Vladimir. *Lolita*. New York: G. P. Putnam's Sons, 1955.

Nash, Ilana. "New Evidence in the Authorship of Nancy Drew." *Dime Novel Round-Up* 70, no. 2 (2001): 57–63.

"Newarker Who Writes for Most Critical of All Readers Has Far Exceeded Standard of Success His Mother Set." *Newark Evening News*, 4 June 1927.

Nilsen, Alleen Pace, and Kenneth L. Donelson. *Literature for Today's Young Adults*. 4th ed. New York: HarperCollins College Publishers, 1993.

Odem, Mary. *Delinquent Daughters: Protecting and Policing Adolescent Female Sexuality in the United States, 1885–1920*. Chapel Hill: University of North Carolina Press, 1995.

Offen, Carol. "The Real Secret of the Hardy Boys, Nancy Drew, the Bobbsey Twins, and Tom Swift Jr." *New York Sunday News Magazine*, 8 April 1979, 8ff.

Palladino, Grace. *Teenagers: An American History*. New York: Basic Books, 1996.

Peiss, Kathy. *Cheap Amusements: Working Women and Leisure in Turn-of-the-Century New York*. Philadelphia: Temple University Press, 1986.

"Picture of the Month." Review of *The Youngest Profession*, directed by Edward Buzzell. *Good Housekeeping*, June 1943.

Porter, Amy. "America's Kid Sister." *Collier's*, 27 Oct. 1945, 17.

Pothier, Dick. "Nancy Drew's Back!" *Detroit Free Press*, 10 Oct. 1975, 1C.

Prager, Arthur. *Rascals at Large; or, The Clue in the Old Nostalgia*. Garden City, N.Y.: Doubleday and Co., 1971.

"President Kennedy Talks to Teens." *Teenagers Ingenue*, July 1964, 19, 76.

Raddatz, Leslie. "Sally Field's a Lot Like Gidget." *TV Guide*, 28 May 1966, 15–17.

Roddy, Joseph. "The Networks Turn to Teen-Agers." *Look*, 5 Oct. 1965, 34ff.

Rollins, Lucy. *Twentieth-Century Teen Culture by the Decades*. Westport, Conn.: Greenwood Press, 1999.

Rooney, Mickey. *Life Is Too Short*. New York: Villard Books, 1991.

Roosevelt, Franklin D. "The Forgotten Man." Speech delivered 7 April 1932. *The New Deal Network*. Accessed 23 Nov. 2004. http://newdeal.feri.org/speeches/1932c.htm. Text from *The Public Papers and Addresses of Franklin D. Roosevelt, Vol. 1 (1928–32)* (New York: Random House, 1938), 624.

Rosen, Marjorie. *Popcorn Venus: Women, Movies, and the American Dream*. New York: Coward, McCann & Geoghegan, 1973.

Rouverol, Aurania. *Skidding: A Comedy in Three Acts*. New York: Samuel French, 1929.

Said, Edward. "Orientalism." In *Literary Theory: An Anthology*, ed. Julie Rivkin and Michael Ryan, 873–86. Oxford: Blackwell Publishers, 1998.

Salinger, J. D. *The Catcher in the Rye*. Boston: Little, Brown and Co., 1951.

"Sally Benson." In *Current Biography 1941*, 69–70. New York: H. Wilson Co., 1941.

Scheiner, Georganne. *Signifying Female Adolescence: Film Representations and Fans, 1920–1950*. Westport, Conn.: Praeger, 2000.

Schrum, Kelly. *Some Wore Bobby Sox: The Emergence of Teenage Girls' Culture, 1920–1945*. New York: Palgrave Macmillan, 2004.

———. "'Teena Means Business': Teenage Girls' Culture and *Seventeen* Magazine, 1944–1950." In *Delinquents & Debutantes: Twentieth-Century American Girls' Cultures*, ed. Sherrie A. Inness, 134–63. New York: New York University Press, 1998.

Schuler, Loring A. "Homeless Girls." *Ladies' Home Journal*, July 1933, 20.

Schwarzbaum, Lisa. "Mandy-capped." *Entertainment Weekly*, 16 Jan. 2004, 47–48.

Shary, Timothy. *Generation Multiplex: The Image of Youth in Contemporary American Cinema*. Austin: University of Texas Press, 2002.

Siegel, Deborah. "Nancy Drew as New Girl Wonder: Solving It All for the 1930s." In *Nancy Drew and Company: Culture, Gender, and Girls' Series*, ed. Sherrie A. Inness, 159–82. Bowling Green, Ohio: Bowling Green State University Popular Press, 1997.

Sinclair, Marianne. *Hollywood Lolitas: The Nymphet Syndrome in the Movies*. New York: Henry Holt and Company, 1988.

Slotkin, Richard. *Gunfighter Nation: The Myth of the Frontier in Twentieth-Century America*. New York: Atheneum, 1992.

Society of Phantom Friends. *The Girls' Series Companion*. Rheem Valley, Calif.: SynSine Press, 1997.

Sperry-Ripperger, Henrietta. "The Forgotten Woman." *Ladies' Home Journal*, Aug. 1933, 24.

Spigel, Lynn. *Make Room for TV: Television and the Family Ideal in Postwar America*. Chicago: University of Chicago Press, 1992.

Stillman, Deanne. Introduction to *Gidget*, by Frederick Kohner, xi–xviii. New York: Berkley Books, 2001.

Stilson, Kenneth L. *Ezra Stone: A Theatrical Biography*. Jefferson, N.C.: McFarland, 1995.

The Storied Life of Millie Benson. Produced by Gregory Tye. PBS. WGTE, Toledo, Ohio. 11 Sept. 2001.

"Sub-Debs Live in a Jolly World of Their Own." *Life*, 27 Jan. 1941, 77–79.

"Summer Job Information for High School Girls." *Calling All Girls*, May 1948, 22–23.

Sumner, Cid Ricketts. *Tammy out of Time*. Indianapolis: Bobbs-Merrill Co., 1948.

Sunstein, Bonnie. "'Reading' the Stories of Reading: Nancy Drew Testimonials." In *Rediscovering Nancy Drew*, ed. Carolyn Stewart Dyer and Nancy Tillman Romalov, 95–112. Iowa City: University of Iowa Press, 1995.

"Susan Says." *Calling All Girls*, Sept. 1941.

"Susan Says." *Calling All Girls*, Dec. 1941.

Tarbox, Gwen Athene. *The Clubwomen's Daughters: Collectivist Impulses in Progressive-Era Girl's Fiction, 1890–1940*. New York: Garland, 2000.

Tarkington, Booth. *Seventeen*. 1916. Reprint, New York: Bantam Books, 1963.

Tawa, Renee. "Nancy Drew's Fans Have a Clue." *Los Angeles Times*, 25 March 1996, E1.

"Teen-Age Bill of Rights." *New York Times Magazine*, 7 Jan. 1945, 16ff.

"Teen-Age Girls." *The March of Time* 11, no. 11. Time, Inc., 1945.

"Teenage Girls: They Live in a Wonderful World All Their Own." *Life*, 11 Dec. 1944, 91–99.

"Teen-Age Opinions." *Dig*, July 1964, 37.

"Teen-Age Trials." *Dig*, Nov. 1955, 34.

Treloar, James A. "The Artful Ways of Millie: Nancy Drew Was Her Brainchild." *Detroit News Magazine*, 13 Aug. 1971.

———. "'We've *Never* Carried Any of That Trash!' Rasped the Librarian Hoarsely." *Detroit Free Press*, 1 May 1966, magazine section.

Tuttle, William. *Daddy's Gone to War: The Second World War in the Lives of America's Children*. New York: Oxford University Press, 1993.

Walkerdine, Valerie. "Popular Culture and the Eroticization of Little Girls." In *The Children's Culture Reader*, ed. Henry Jenkins, 254–64. New York: New York University Press, 1998.

Ward, L. E. "The Bobby Soxers." *Classic Images*, 174 (Dec. 1989): 30, 32, 57.

Watts, Richard, Jr. "Portrait of a Lady." Review of *Junior Miss. New York Herald Tribune*, 19 Nov. 1941. Cited in *NYTCR* 2, no. 24 (1941): 213.

"We 'Took It' in Hawaii." *Calling All Girls*, April 1942, 9–11.

Wertheimer, Barbara S., and Carol Sands. "Nancy Drew Revisited." *Language Arts* 52 (1975): 1131–34, 1161.

Whitney, Allison. "Gidget Goes Hysterical." In *Sugar, Spice, and Everything Nice: Cinemas of Girlhood*, ed. Frances Gateward and Murray Pomerance, 55–71. Detroit: Wayne State University Press, 2002.

Wood, Bret. "Lolita Syndrome." *Sight and Sound* 4, no. 6 (1994): 32–34.

Woodward, Elizabeth. "Female Foibles." *Ladies' Home Journal*, Jan. 1945, 8.

Yost, Edna. "The Fifty-Cent Juveniles." *Publishers Weekly*, 18 June 1932, 2405–2408.

Zacharias, Lee. "Nancy Drew, Ballbuster." *Journal of Popular Culture* 9, no. 4 (1976): 1027–38.

Zinman, David. *Saturday Afternoon at the Bijou*. N.p.: Castle Books, 1973.

Zinsser, William K. "The Tyranny of the Teens." *Horizon*, Jan. 1959, 137–39.

Zuckerman, Kathy Kohner. Foreword to *Gidget*, by Frederick Kohner, vii–x. New York: Berkley Books, 2001.

Index

Ilana Nash is Assistant Professor of English at Western Michigan University, where she teaches and researches the intersecting histories of youth, gender, literature, and popular culture.